Algernon Sydney Sullivan

Algernon S. Sullivan.

Algernon Sydney Sullivan

By

ANNE MIDDLETON HOLMES

Illustrated

Published by
THE NEW YORK SOUTHERN SOCIETY
1929

Copyright, 1929
by
Anne Middleton Holmes

RUMFORD PRESS
CONCORD

THE realization of the ideal life is the great design of God and the great work of man. The advancement and elevation of humanity is most surely promoted by whatever best and permanently develops the individual man. It is by the enlightened and disinterested service to his fellow beings that he most surely strengthens and idealizes his own nature.

ALGERNON SYDNEY SULLIVAN.

PREFACE

In publishing the biography of Algernon Sydney Sullivan, the Committee desires to recall incidents inseparable in the minds of the original members from the establishing of New York Southern Society. The Society was founded in 1886 to fill the need for and to encourage fraternal intimacy among the multitude of Southerners in New York.

For many years previous, before the time was ripe or conditions warranted this formal gathering together, scores of these young men had found in the heart and home of Mr. Sullivan a warmth of welcome which descended upon them as manna in the wilderness, assuaging that poignant home-hunger which never fails at some time to overtake the stranger in a great city. To these men the memory of early years of struggle was coincident with recollections of the hospitable home of Mr. Sullivan, whose never-flagging interest and zeal on their behalf brought to many the opportunities which otherwise they might have sought in vain.

It was Mr. John Marshall of Virginia, together with Messrs. Walter McCorkle and Howard Bayne of the same State, Mr. Percy Mallett of Louisiana, and Mr. Charles Deshon of Alabama, who took the initial step towards establishing the New York Southern Society. This self-constituted committee, enlarged at once by some forty additional and equally enthusiastic members, promptly adopted a constitution and by-laws, and selected "that distinguished lawyer and golden-hearted gentleman, Algernon Sydney Sullivan," for their first President. Mr. Sullivan served in that capacity until his death, giving to the Society the stamp of his aristocratic personality, his time and energy in the promotion of its aims; and leaving it the honored heritage of his enthusiastic interest and approval.

After the sudden and untimely death of Mr. Sullivan, a Citizens' Memorial Committee composed of seventy-seven of New York's most prominent men, and upon which the Southern Society had ample representation, functioned for many years in perpetuating the influence of one so widely considered to have reflected in his life the highest type of manhood. Each of the several memorials erected by this committee served to hold contemporary and personal recollection of Algernon Sydney Sullivan as one greatly beloved, highly honored, worthy of emulation. And contemplation of such a character, set apart from other men by a great nobility of purpose, can but induce the beautiful thoughts of spiritual uplift. In order, however, to complete the full design of the committee to perpetuate the influence of such a life, more is needed than monuments or similar representations of honor and admiration.

In selecting an effectual means of encouragement for the cultivation of like characteristics in this, and in future generations, it was obviously impossible for the Memorial Committee to ignore the necessarily transitory nature of any relatively small group of individuals, or the impracticability of such a group proving adequate in the management of a permanent foundation. Hence, in 1925, the committee, considering this fact in relation to its objective, invited the New York Southern Society to act jointly with it in establishing in the George Peabody College for Teachers at Nashville, Tennessee, an Award for excellence of character and service to humanity. The success of this effort was shortly followed by the disbanding of the committee, which delegated to the Society, as its sole successor, its entire authority and responsibility for carrying out its proposed plan to establish the Award in other institutions, and for the disposition of the fund provided for that purpose.

The Award consists of a copper medallion, an engraved certificate, and this volume. Recipients are chosen yearly from the graduating class of each university and college, which also has the privilege of honoring one other person conspicuously helpful to and associated with the institution in its effort to encourage and preserve a high standard of morals.

The New York Southern Society's Committee in charge of the Algernon Sydney Sullivan Award feels honored by the trust imposed in it and it takes pride in reporting that the Award is established in fifteen institutions of higher learning.

The Committee welcomes the opportunity to publish the life of one who "perhaps more than any other man of his generation possessed so many qualities of enduring usefulness to his community," and it

is gratified beyond measure that the value of this
Award in promoting the application of those high
ideals so frequently considered impractical in the
intimacies of daily contact, is already demonstrated
in the enthusiasm and interest of the thousands of
students concerned, and the splendid letters of appreciation from the faculty committees in immediate
charge of presentations.

The Committee {
WALTER L. McCORKLE
JOHN P. EAST
T. FOSTER GAINES

CONTENTS

LIST OF ILLUSTRATIONS

FOREWORD

SIGNIFICANT of the impression made by Algernon Sydney Sullivan is the fact that some forty years after his death there is in the hearts of those who knew, or who knew of, him an affectionate desire to still further extend and make permanent the influence of those ideals to which Mr. Sullivan aspired and which were typified by his life.

The interest thus manifest is of still greater significance when one considers that in Mr. Sullivan's life there is to be found no spectacular achievement culminating in high office or conspicuous honors. Mr. Sullivan sought neither the one nor the other, and for a man so keenly appreciative of the duties of citizenship and so active in the interests of civic reform, he was singularly indifferent to his own personal advancement.

He was a profound scholar, a great lawyer, a brilliant orator, a man of artistic taste. His dignity was impressive; his magnetism and charm were appealing, and socially he was prominent. To an unusual degree he inspired in others that sincerity of affection which he himself desired to feel towards every man, and it is largely because of this quality in his character that his memory is yet fragrant, that the value of his influence is still perceptible. For though men admired Algernon Sullivan and honored him for his integrity and his nobility, above all they loved him—loved him for his gentle kindliness, his great sympathy, his limitless generosity. And those who knew him best like best to thus recall his image.

The incentive for this book lies not in any wish to perpetuate the name Algernon Sydney Sullivan, but to make enduring the beneficent influence of a life which exemplifies the highest type of manhood. In the effort to encourage in others the cultivation of such wholly admirable qualities, it is not the desire, far less the duty, of Mr. Sullivan's biographer to bring to this delicate task a litany of compliments nor to surfeit the reader with paragraphs of fulsome praise. It is, rather, to follow with sympathetic intimacy the development of an unusually fine character brought to maturity without the aid of great wealth or the weight of influence, and despite more than the ordinary temptations of life.

Hence, facts and incidents even of lesser import have been included; testimonials and eulogies, seemingly redundant, have been allowed to appear as confirmatory and in the hope that they will abundantly diffuse the inspiration and encouragement which is the gift of a man who in his life time "reached out both hands in constant helpfulness to his fellow-men."

A. M. H.

Algernon Sydney Sullivan

Coat Armorial of the Sullivan Family

ARMS—Per fesse—the base per pale, in chief or, a dexter hand couped (cut) at the wrist grasping a sword erect, pomel and hilt gules, the blade entwined with a serpent (ppr) (natural color) between two lions rampant respecting each other, of the second, the dexter base vert, charged with a buck trippant or, on the sinister base, per pale argent and sable a boar passant counterchanged.

CREST—On a ducal coronet or, a robin in the beak a sprig of laurel ppr. (natural color.)

MOTTO—Lamb foisdine ach an uachtar.
What we gain by conquest we secure by clemency.

ALGERNON SYDNEY SULLIVAN

T HE ancient and honorable family of Sullivan traces its lineage in an unbroken line as far back as 950 A. D. and numbers the Kings of Munster amongst its progenitors. As nearly as the Irish word can be written in English letters it was *Suilleabhain*, and its nearest English sound Sullivan, or O'Sullivan. The prefix *O*, being merely a contraction of *Hua* meaning *the decendants of*, was dropped or retained at the whim of the bearer, and the name is found in both forms throughout the history of the two original lines, whose chieftains were respectively O'Sullivan-Mor and O'Sullivan-Beare. The latter, and younger, took his title from his castle of Bearra, now known as Bearhaven, in County Cork. From this branch was descended Algernon Sydney Sullivan, as was a collateral line represented in America by Major-General John Sullivan, the Revolutionary officer and friend of General Washington.

The Sullivan domain in their native Ireland stretched over the mountainous counties of Kerry and of Cork, but many members of the sept bore arms with distinction under foreign banners and frequently sought domicile in countries ruled by less stringent laws than their own. One of these was Thomas Lyttleton Sullivan, the son of a prominent barrister of

Charleville, County Cork.   The elder Sullivan held
office under the crown, but lost it through the order
forbidding the investiture of Roman Catholics.   In
1784 the son, Thomas, fled these arbitrary laws and
sought freedom in America where he settled in
Augusta County, Virginia.   There in 1791 he married
Margaret, daughter of James Irwin of Scotch descent
but lately come from the neighborhood of Chambers-
burg, Pennsylvania.

Margaret Irwin was a woman of strong character
and practical ideals; she was a Methodist and of a
deeply religious nature.   Her husband was a devout
Roman Catholic, but the bigotry and intolerance
through which he had suffered in his own country were
not allowed to prevent his marriage or to make of it a
failure on the score of religious controversy.   Though
neither husband nor wife ever attempted one to con-
vert the other and each remained throughout life a
firm adherent of their respective faiths, it is said that
in moments of particular fervour Margaret Irwin felt
constrained to "expound" on the merits of Method-
ism to her husband.   But Thomas Sullivan was not to
be led into discussion or argument.   A quiet and patient listener, he invariably embraced the first pause
to remark, "Maggie dear, I think I'll take a little
walk."   And let it be said of his wife, there was
neither reproach nor bitterness in her greeting upon
his return.   So these two excellent people, the grandparents of Algernon Sydney Sullivan, lived a tranquil
and useful life leaving upon their descendants the
well-marked imprint of their own splendid natures.

THE EARL OF BEAR AND BANTRY

Two children were born of this union, both in Harrisonburg, Rockingham County, Virginia. The first was a daughter named for her mother; she lived but a few weeks. The second, Jeremiah, was born on July 21, 1794, and lived to become an eminent and important member of the judiciary of another State.

Although destined for the priesthood by his father, Jeremiah early showed a disinclination to follow that life. His practical nature was nevertheless highly colored with spiritual leanings, obviously his natural heritage and the logical result of his rearing in an atmosphere of devout and simple faith. Both care and thought were expended by his parents upon the education of this idolized son who made good use of his long hours with the village schoolmaster in preparing to enter the College of William and Mary. He graduated from that college with honors, though we learn from old correspondence that his studies there had been interrupted by a "wayward fancy" to go a-soldiering. He enlisted in the War of 1812 against Great Britain and brought back from his several engagements a commission as "Captain in the United States Army, for Bravery and Good Conduct." The army might well have held the young officer had he not been willing to harken to the wishes of his parents whose hopes for their only son lay in other channels. Therefore he resumed his studies at Williamsburg and upon their completion returned to Harrisonburg to read law under the direction of Mr. George Harrison. In 1816 he received from the Commonwealth of Virginia a license to practice and was offered a partnership with his late instructor whose friend and confidential assistant he had become. But the enterprising youth preferred to adventure. With two friends he set out on horseback, his face to the West and in his mind some vague thought of Louisville or Cincinnati as a destination. Arriving at the latter he heard little talked of but the wondrous opportunities in the new State down the Ohio River, for in 1816 Indiana was closing the territorial chapter of her history and taking her place in the Union.

In this vast wilderness neither roads nor canals had yet been made, the diminutive towns were accessible only by Indian trails, and the most primitive of conditions were not bettered by constant danger of attack by hostile tribes. But these facts did not prevent the young man from feeling its allure. Quite likely the frontier life and fortune-seeking in the midst of its hazards strongly appealed to him as a substitute for the Army career which had been so tempting. In the light of future events they were no obstacles to his success. Others had gone before him—sturdy pioneers of this age of buckskin and homespun, unpretentious men of common sense, of dogged determination, of undaunted courage. Jeremiah Sullivan, blessed with bodily strength to support the ambition and enthusiasm of youth, was well qualified to join their brotherhood and wise to trust his vision of the future.

Some ninety miles below Cincinnati was the little settlement called Madison. Spread out on flat land running down to the Ohio, its water front offered excellent landing facilities for river craft. No magic mirror envisioned for chance voyagers the rapidity with which this little hamlet was to grow into importance; nor could they descry the shadow of a cogwheel railroad, the first of its kind in America, laboring to the heights of that precipitous bluff which then in unmolested peace brooded protectingly in the background.

The wild beauty of the country no less than the evident practical value of the site appealed strongly to the young Virginian who, having heard in Cincinnati that a man of his profession was needed in the new community, decided to end his journey there. So definitely attracted was he that he forthwith purchased land and engaged for the immediate raising of a house in the simple architecture of the period. Staking his all upon a mighty determination to succeed and a strong faith in the future of the new State, Jeremiah at once set out upon the return journey to Virginia to fetch his parents, pausing at Pittsburgh but long enough to arrange for the construction of a flatboat which was to be ready against his return. This audacious youth seems to have set at naught the weariness of so many weeks of travel and its accompanying dangers. The wayfarer of 1817, traveling westward, was indeed an adventurer, for he must make his way through dense forests and over almost pathless mountains. Beyond the established cities of that part of the new country already looked upon as old, habitations were scattered far apart and loneliness was not the least of the perils likely to be encountered along the way.

In Virginia the young man tarried only to secure the cumbersome wagons which were to transport his family and their possessions, and then again he turned his face toward the land which was henceforth to be home. There is no record of aught save eager willingness on the part of Thomas and Margaret Sullivan to leave Harrisonburg and fare forth to a new land of promise. Pioneering was an urge not unfamiliar in their day and generation and neither of them had yet reached the age when opportunity ceased to beckon. Perhaps it was that voice to which they hearkened; or perhaps the parents of Jeremiah Sullivan felt the strength of their son's shrewd determination and in their deep affection for him their own wishes weighed lightly, if at all, against the idea of a permanent separation. In any case they seem to have joyfully undertaken the long trek to a new home.

From the vantage point of this era in which science and mechanical genius are combined in a surpassing efficiency, the vicissitudes of travel in the early nineteenth century become colorful and romantic in their picturesque detail. The reality presented a darker canvas with harsher lines; journeys into the vast unknown were trials of courage and strength, and the survivor, whether man or woman, emerged as tested metal. However vividly the skilful brush of history preserves the panorama of wagon train or solitary prairie schooner round which many a romance has been woven, the result must lose something of that valiant determination which spurred the wayfarer onward.

The Sullivans traveled alone; they were but a tiny link in the great migratory chain which stretched from old world to new and across it to the ever advancing frontier. Their circuitous way led them at length to Pittsburgh where the heavy wagons were sold as soon as their contents had been transferred to the flat-boat. The balance of the journey, on the bosom of the winding Ohio, was made in comparative comfort though with scarcely greater safety, for marauding bands of savages infested the shore, and the treacherous and shifting river bottom was a constant menace. The watchful Jeremiah, still on horseback, made his way along the bank, keeping in sight the tent-like deck shelter of the boat and the men at the sweeps who guided the craft as it rose and swayed to the current. At evening the horseman chose a camp site and with mighty effort the boat was poled shoreward. Who can say that this leisurely approach to their destination had not merit? Certainly it fed not upon monotony.

In so radically departing from the easy-going, restful, exquisitely self-poised Virginia life, it might appear that Jeremiah Sullivan had made his decisions hurriedly and without due deliberation; but despite his youth, his mental processes functioned with great clarity and he was a man of action. The better part of a year had been consumed in his journeyings to and from Virginia, and when the flat-boat was moored to the shore at Madison he found his dwelling ready as he had planned, so that little time was lost in settling the new home and taking up the business of life into which this energetic youth plunged with vigor and enthusiasm.

In July of 1818 Jeremiah married, at Madison, Charlotte Rudesel Cutler of Richmond, Virginia, acquiring in his wife a helpmeet of exceptional qualities. She was a descendant of the Rudesel and Cutler families, both prominent in Virginia, and her education was that accorded to all women of gentle breeding, which in those days was little enough in an intellectual sense. She was, however, a woman of judgment, of well-defined religious beliefs but broad-minded and tolerant. Her disposition was happy and unselfish, and her wit and vivacity radiated a brightness which brought great joy into the lives of her family and her friends. In that age when house-wifery was no less a prideful occupation because of its necessity, Mrs. Sullivan soon became famed; and by temperament and ability she was eminently fitted to cope with the exigencies of frontier living. For though lawyers were perhaps the most important members of a community in those early days of Indiana's statehood, settlers' wives in common had that to contend with which needed a strong con-stitution, a valiant spirit, adaptability and a serene mind. To these pioneer women the mede of praise is apt to be all too slight; for how, in the dimness of a light obscured by so many years, can the sting of their deprivations be felt, or the bitterness of the struggle which must have been the routine of their daily lives, be tasted?

In the sparsely settled land which the Sullivans had chosen for their home they found themselves entirely without the conventional forms of religious worship. In this almost-wilderness, meeting houses were often open spaces roofed by the spreading branches of great trees and the congregation kneeled upon the earth. Those who sought the comfort of regular pastoral exhortation or religious discourse must mount a horse and follow the course of a circuit rider. Jeremiah Sullivan, growing into a serious student of religion, used this method, he himself frequently substituting for a delayed parson. Of an orderly and systematic mind, he discerned the urgent need of some central religious interest in Madison. Realizing that in the newness of the community the many beliefs might easily become "harmoniously confused," he familiarized himself with the inclinations of his near neighbors, and on his days of leisure he rode on horseback far out among the remote settlers to discuss this important question with them. Becoming convinced that Presbyterianism held for the majority that sustaining power which is the cornerstone of true religion, he adopted that faith himself in order that he might lead others in the path which they wished to tread. In his own home, despite the wide difference of religious opinion, he found exemplified a great respect and deference for the beliefs of others; therefore it is not strange to find this eminently practical young man concentrating upon the fundamentals of Christianity and ordering his life in the practice of a doctrine which seemed to him to offer the broadest spiritual opportunities, rather than following unquestioningly the faith professed by one or the other of his parents.

As a Presbyterian, then, Jeremiah Sullivan labored in the early settlement of Madison. As the town grew into a city his activities increased and eventually he became a Ruling Elder of the church he attended and President of the Bible Society of the State of Indiana.

With equal rapidity in his profession, as a man of ability and unblemished integrity, he was early marked for positions of prominence. A member of the Whig party, he became upon its dissolution a Republican, but his political ambitions were not such as to urge him to seek office. He was, however, sent to the Indiana State Legislature in 1820, then meeting at Corydon, and in an official letter among Governor Baker's correspondence in the archives of the State of Indiana, we find that it was Mr. Sullivan who, as a member of the committee appointed to choose the name for the new capital, suggested Indianapolis. He was also at this time designated by the Governor as a special commissioner to adjust various matters which required the greatest finesse and which were of vast importance to the State. From 1837 to 1846 Jeremiah Sullivan sat upon the Bench of the Supreme Court; in 1869, just before his death, he was appointed Judge of the newly established Criminal Court of the State. It was, however, as Judge of the Supreme Court that he earned his fame. A contemporary writes:

He was a deep thinker, and his appreciation of equity in jurisprudence was such that his decisions possessed unusual weight and authority.   His honorable position in the Commonwealth and in his profession was considered by him to be of importance and value only so far as he could through them advance the cause of religion and morality, and bring comfort and encouragement to his fellowmen.

Much of a similar nature has been written by associates of the Judge, whose long public career fulfilled the promise of his early manhood.

None the less conspicuous was the tranquillity and beauty of life in his own home—that home so impulsively built by the youthful adventurer, so joyfully approached through weariness, so happily used in the light and shadows of speeding years.   Its serenity, more than anything else, impressed those who were privileged to pass its portals.   In its peaceful safety Thomas and Margaret Sullivan spent their declining years; there, in the fullness of their love, lived and died Jeremiah Sullivan and his wife Charlotte Cutler; and there were born their eleven children, of whom the second son was Algernon Sydney, named in honor of the famous Englishman and liberal politician so greatly admired by the child's father.

❖

Algernon Sydney Sullivan was born on the fifth of April, 1826. He was a delicate child, mentally precocious. His devotion to books was encouraged under the careful supervision of his father whose scholarly tastes were reflected in the boy's early love for the classics. At the age of nine he was being drilled in true Rugby fashion in Latin and English by Mr. Roswell Elms, an Englishman of uncommon attainments, to whom Algernon owed his thorough mastery of expression in both languages, an accomplishment which in later years added greatly to the forcefulness of the speeches through which he acquired no little fame as an orator. Between the frail but studious child and his able father there was a tender intimacy strengthened by a similarity of natures, and in this close association the boy acquired habits of direct and logical thinking, a love for the best in art and literature, and a fine sense of values in human relationships.

The town of Madison during Algernon Sullivan's childhood was an inviting gateway to those vast unsettled regions which, reaching out to the Pacific Ocean, were some day to become states. The Ohio River brought to its doors much of that steady stream of adventurous folk who joyfully sought fortune in the great wilderness beyond. From the old world and from the new, resolute homesteaders toiled westward, and Madison bid them God-speed. Some found but disappointment and retraced their steps in weariness and destitution; and these, worthy or unworthy, Madison must succor in their need.

As the meeting place of these cross currents of travel, the town presented an ever-changing and conflicting scene of intense interest to an observant boy who, through the prominence of his father, was brought into close touch with the exigencies of life under these almost frontier conditions. Thus the youthful Algernon became familiar with the frailties and the needs of men, so many of whom sought the aid of Judge Sullivan; and the sympathies of this boy were awakened not by tales and preachments, but by the tragedies lived before his eyes. He saw discouragement turned into hope by wise words of advice, he saw the bitterness of defeat absorbed by renewed confidence at the touch of a friendly hand, and he dwelt in an atmosphere of constructive endeavor of which the concrete expression was part and parcel of the daily routine of those around him. It would be a mistake to say that he was taught or trained in that great love of humanity which so dominated his later life; the boy lived quite naturally according to the code of his parents. His impressionable mind unavoidably became a storehouse of vivid memories, and instinctively he developed a thoroughly altruistic nature.

At the age of seventeen he was admitted to Hanover College, in the town of the same name, some twenty miles below Madison on the Ohio River. In common with other river towns Hanover shared the beauty of that section of Indiana which, by native Hoosiers, is frequently referred to as the Switzerland of Indiana. In these lovely environs, and under the care of his father's friend, Dr. McMasters, Algernon pursued his studies diligently, too diligently indeed for his health's sake. Frequent letters from his family warned him to consider his physical welfare lest a breakdown definitely conclude his career as a student. But the boy took the matter lightly. With the lack of judgment due to youth he was foolhardy in his determination to show his appreciation of the advantages provided at no little effort by his father. All thought of injury to his health was dismissed, and his affectionate nature spent itself in an absorbing devotion to the father whose approval he sought with passionate concentration, and whose letters were treasures read and reread. In a moment of real fear that he might fail in his duty toward this loved parent, the boy wrote upon one of these letters: "A father once wrote on the back of his son's portrait, 'He never caused me to sigh except when he left home. May God bless him.' I would give a right eye if the same could be said of me. My constant endeavor shall be, henceforth, to live worthy of such a father as my own, by practicing obedience to what I know to be duty, and particularly by exercising a prudent and cautious self-control and avoiding all disingenuousness."

This youthful grandiloquence was none the less sincere and enduring. Many years later, when he was prominent in the affairs of a great city whose government was notoriously corrupt, he was sitting in a meeting of an important committee. His conception of a point or policy under discussion seemed to his associates to be ultra conservative and unnecessarily over-conscientious. However, since they had for him

Drawing by W. E. Mears

A FLAT-BOAT ON THE OHIO RIVER

Typical of the one used in 1817 by Jeremiah Sullivan and his family in their journey from Virginia to Indiana

a great respect and real liking, they paused to consider his suggestion and advice. During this pause one of them turned to him and said, "Sullivan, have you never been tempted to do anything which you thought was wrong?" There was a silence for a few seconds while everyone turned their eyes upon him. Then he quietly replied, "Yes, frequently, but I always thought of my dear old father and then I could not do it."

Despite the constitutional weakness which unceasingly hampered him in his studies, Algernon Sullivan compressed into one year at Hanover the work of two, and did so creditably. He was much attached to Dr. McMasters and followed him to Miami University when he became president of that institution at Oxford, Ohio. Distressing periods of illness interrupted the following two years, but did not deprive the young man of his degree in 1845. At the University he had established a reputation as a brilliant and precise student, uncommonly gifted in those arts which foreshadowed his success of later years as an orator. He was a useful and enthusiastic member of the Alpha Delta Phi Fraternity, strongly entrenched in the affection of his associates by his generous and loyal friendship. Paradoxically, therein lay the weakness of his character, for beyond all reason his belief in the good intentions of others was complete, and in his intense desire to be of service, he was, in relation to his own welfare, far more idealistic than practical. Frequently he invited imposition that grew in later years in proportion to his prominence and influence, continuing, in fact, to the end of his life.

Entirely under the influence of his father's sincerely religious views, Algernon Sullivan's conception of his spiritual duties was somewhat arbitrary, though for that period it was in no way narrow; nor did the conscientious observance of these principles in his youth make of him a bigot. On the contrary, this training was the foundation upon which rested the structure of his wholly admirable life. As he matured he realized that following the precepts of these early years was thoroughly compatible with the enjoyment of the wholesome pleasures of life, where social contacts furnished opportunities for expanding, rather than obliterating, the spiritual outlook which was so utterly characteristic of his nature.

The city of Madison to which the young man returned from college in 1845 was at that time the largest and most important in Indiana. Having become a busy river port, its flourishing activities were rapidly carrying it toward a period of being the richest. The rows of great shade trees which lined its streets preserved in a measure some of the forest's grandeur. Substantial brick or stone houses, porticoed in front in the fashion of Virginia, and set off with lawns and gardens of great beauty, vied with the white paint of New England in lending dignity and charm to this fast growing city. The finest blood of the South and East, united in its early settlers, had produced a society which, despite the encroaching commercialism, yet adhered in large measure to the stately and formal customs of the Colonial period. Piety and chivalry dictated the punctilious manner, the reserved personal demeanor. The language of the day was elaborate, the pleasures extremely simple. Hospitality was unbounded, and an unharassed existence was reflected in general light-heartedness and gaiety; for the States were not yet feeling the faint stirrings of that social unrest which was nevertheless so surely hovering over them.

Jeremiah Sullivan, though his position and reputation were enviable, had not acquired wealth. The reason is revealed in the yellowing sheets found in his letter files. Though able and diligent, he was ever at the call of relatives and friends who seem never to have spared him in their demands. His home had not been altered to follow changing styles, but had remained the simple and beautiful brick house erected for him while he was journeying over the mountains to and from Virginia some thirty years before. Enlarged merely to meet the growing needs of his family, its dignity had not been disturbed. Streets laid out by the city of Madison had fashioned the ample grounds into a corner lot. Long porches on one side of the house, screened with rambler roses and honeysuckle, invited the eye of any visitor who might turn into the flower-bordered walk leading from a side gate into the garden. Though it was in every sense a simple home, it was also a place pointed out to city visitors.

Within, the large rooms were colorful with growing plants on broad windowsills; deep fireplaces were flanked by winged chairs in some two of which the gentle grandparents, now rapidly approaching their allotted span, were usually to be found. The library, lined with heavy laden shelves of much-used books, held frequent gatherings of the most cultured and finest minds of that vast new country—and Indiana's contribution to the list of her country's great men is imposing. Here young Algernon was to read law under his father's guidance, with the added privilege of hearing many of the scholarly discussions between Judge Sullivan and his associate Judges of the Supreme Bench, Justices Blackford and Dewey, a trio justly famed for their erudition and notable throughout the country.

Thus intimately associated with men of exceptional ability and high-mindedness, Algernon Sullivan absorbed with his legal training a sound philosophy, an intellectual independence, and a strong sense of the obligations of manhood. These advantages might easily have been nullified by the casual acceptance which is so common an attitude of youth toward opportunity. Happily they were highly valued by the discerning young man whose attentive ear missed nothing, and whose hungry mind reached out for knowledge.

It was during this period of Algernon Sullivan's legal studies in Madison that the question of establishing free schools in Indiana was having a spirited revival, and ways and means of providing for their maintenance were under discussion throughout the State. Ever since 1833, when Caleb Mills, Dartmouth graduate and tireless apostle of education, left his professorship at Wabash College and inaugurated

his struggle for free public schools in Indiana by addressing the Legislature in behalf of universal education, his proposals were argued intermittently and
with varying degrees of interest.   Illiteracy was prevalent; the township schools were without guaranteed
means of support; and while free schooling was advocated in all communities, eagerness to submit to the
necessary taxation was noticeably lacking.

Algernon Sullivan was keenly anxious to acquire
knowledge himself, and his appreciation of its advantages constantly increased in his association with the
learned and intellectual circle of friends who made his
father's house the centre of their gatherings.   He
became greatly interested in the agitation for enact-
ments which would secure to the people of Indiana the
advantages of a public school system built upon the
basis of gratuitous instruction.   Having also a strong
desire to try his wings in a field which attracted him,
the young man determined to interrupt his studies and
tour the doubtful counties of his State as a stump
speaker in favor of taxation for the support of free
schools.

When the elections approached, the youth of twenty
set out on horseback.   As he journeyed he lodged with
the farmers, shared their board and spent his evenings
at their firesides, inviting their confidence which he
met with sympathetic interest.   Thus he familiarized
himself with the objector's point of view wherever it
existed.   On the next day, with a speech couched in
simple, straight-forward language, he explained away
the objections and set up the merits of the cause he

pled. He was exceedingly attractive in his youthful
dignity, and appealing in his sincerity and earnestness; so eloquently and convincingly did he argue that
he was called *The Young Demosthenes.*

The success of this, his first venture, was reassuring,
and Algernon Sullivan returned with renewed enthusiasm to his law studies which, with but one other
interruption, an enforced rest of a few weeks in Virginia, proceeded to their conclusion in 1849. Then,
equipped with his license to practice, a vast determination to succeed and the supreme confidence of
youth, he betook himself to Cincinnati.

There he followed the custom, then common among
novices, of combining office and living quarters in one
large room in whose front windows appeared his
"shingle" painted by himself. Behind a half-partition
a tiny bed chamber looked out from the sunny side
of the house on to a patch of flower-planted back yard.
It was a combination much better than most.

But making a place for himself was no sinecure. A
congenial partnership with Mr. Scott, a man of ability
who had been a fellow law student and a college acquaintance, was soon interrupted by the marriage of
the latter and his removal from Cincinnati. With
such men as Salmon P. Chase, Timothy Walker,
Bellamy Storer, William S. Groesbeck, Charles Anderson, George H. Pendleton, and other brilliant lawyers in full practice in the city, the outlook for rapid
advancement for the newcomer might have been dis-
couraging. It was soon apparent, however, that
Algernon Sullivan was making an impression. He

had no influential backing save the reputation of his
father; nor did he come with a sheaf of letters which
might have guaranteed him a welcome and easy
access to the inner circles of his profession. Un-
deniably he was a handsome youth, not easily over-
looked in any gathering, but his finely cut features,
his white skin so sensitive to the flush of emotion,
his clear and steady black eyes gave an impression of
spiritual rather than bodily beauty. Prone to ideal-
ize his enthusiasms, he was nevertheless far from
being a dreamer. His erect figure carried with easy
grace, a frankness of manner not always an asset
because of his impulsiveness, and an unfailing attitude of courteous attention marked him a high-bred
gentleman. In the heritage from his Irish forebears
a sense of humor was not lacking; and it required
but slight acquaintance with him to discover the
quality of his integrity, inborn but also nurtured
with unceasing care in his rearing.

Fresh from the environment of the past three
years spent so closely associated with his father and
in intimate contact with minds of rare quality,
Algernon Sullivan's tastes quite naturally led him to
seek circles of culture, and his attainments fitted him
for the companionship he craved. He was invited
to join the Literary Club of Cincinnati, organized
in October 1849 by men many of whom later attained great prominence—Rutherford B. Hayes,
A. R. Spafford, Thomas Ewing, J. D. Buchanan,
William Ferguson, M. Hazen White, and others.
Mr. Sullivan's name appears among those of the

first year of the membership, which was limited to one hundred. Logically, too, Mr. Sullivan found himself drawn into civic affairs, and as he grew into thoughtful manhood his youthful enthusiasms became definite ambitions. Even in those taxing first years of his professional struggle he made time for what he considered his civic duties, fraternizing with his fellows, using in every worthy common cause his great and exceptional gift as a speaker, and indulging his passionate desire to be of service. Almost at once he became a working member of the School Board; then, a member of the Common Council, one of the board of directors of the House of Refuge, a corporate member of the Historical Society, and an active associate of his pastor, Dr. Fisher, of the Second Presbyterian Church. It was thus he began a career which, when critically considered at its close many years later by his prominent contemporaries, yielded the universal judgment, "He reached out both hands in constant helpfulness to his fellow men."

Algernon Sullivan was, nevertheless, neither a pedagogue nor a paragon of virtue; nor was it among his ambitions to become a pattern of rectitude. The processes of his character building proceeded in logical sequence and as a result of consistent personal effort. Contrary to the usual human being who sees his life in retrospect, he was thoroughly conscious of his shortcomings and the weaknesses which beset him along the way. "I see," said he, in an address made not long before he died, "no fault committed that I could not have myself committed at some time in my life."

Yet there was about him no suggestion of the anchorite. In striving to attain his ideals it was far from his desire to remove temptation by cutting himself off from worldly enjoyment and all associations save those of a spiritual nature. He loved life and beauty; society attracted him and he readily responded to its appeal. The handsome and brilliant young barrister making so rapidly an enviable name for himself in Cincinnati's courtrooms, became an equally popular and noticeable figure in drawing-rooms. How insidious might have been the destroying talons of the adulation he received!

At this time the letters of Judge Sullivan to his son show concern. It was natural but unnecessary. The young man keenly appreciated his advantages in the new environment; he welcomed his opportunities and found interest in the new ways of the more progressive city, but by nature and training he was not apt to have his head turned or lose his sense of values.

"Conclude all your business transactions with honor," wrote his father. "Let not *success* or *amusement* turn your thoughts away from God." The theatre was an amusement utterly frowned upon by Judge Sullivan, and he experienced the keenest anxiety upon learning that his son chose it as one of his diversions. For the Judge it was a deep inhibition inherited from his Methodist mother, and he never reconciled himself to the acceptance of any form of theatrical entertainment as a harmless recreation.

"Curb your *excitability* and your *impulsiveness*," he

urged in another letter. And there indeed his counsel was pertinent. Outward calm was acquired by Algernon Sullivan at great effort; impulsiveness he never entirely overcame.

❖

On January 2, 1851, Algernon Sydney Sullivan was married to Mary Slocum Groesbeck. His happiness in the companionship of this charming girl, who was known both for her beauty and for her sweetness of character, was but short-lived. Her sudden death the following September left him crushed and bewildered, and in his struggle for readjustment he devoted himself with even greater earnestness to his professional and other duties, and to study. He was not given to morbid introspection; intellectual interests were of basic importance in his life, and at no time was study a drudgery. It was, rather, a luxurious relaxation craved by an active and brilliant mind, and one in which he was not always at liberty to indulge. In his scheme of life personal gratifications were not allowed precedence, and now, more than ever, most of his energy and time was absorbed in promoting matters of public interest.

It was just at this time that Louis Kossuth, the Hungarian patriot, was about to visit the United

States to solicit for his oppressed country, in its struggles for freedom, the support of a great Republic. In 1851 visits of foreign celebrities to this country were sufficiently uncommon to arouse a nation-wide desire to participate in the attendant festivities, and Kossuth was a visitor of special interest who was invested with an aura of romance by his recent release from an unjust imprisonment. The whole country was inspired towards some exceptional effort of hospitality; a great welcome was held in New York, whither other large cities sent their delegates. The city of Cincinnati, recognizing Mr. Sullivan's zeal and ability, chose him as its representative. It was before a mighty throng at New York's City Hall that he so eloquently made the address offering to the visitor the congratulations of Cincinnati's citizens, and their invitation to visit the Queen City. His speech aroused special comment in the *New York Times* of December 19, 1851:

> At the close of Kossuth's reply to Mr. Sullivan's eloquent address, the Governor * received Mr. Sullivan with greater cordiality than we have seen him exhibit toward any other delegate.

A sentence from what reviewers termed "his exquisite address" fairly illustrates Mr. Sullivan's lofty conception of his theme, and demonstrates the purity of diction which characterized its presentation.

> The Government that intermeddles to assist one nation to oppress another is as much the enemy of liberty and happiness as the pirate on the high seas. Every man's hand should

* Kossuth.

be against her and there should be no sanctuary of precedent or policy whither she could fly for safety.

Over seventy years passed between this visit of Louis Kossuth and the unveiling of a statue in his memory in New York City in March of 1928. For the ceremony "a great delegation made a long pilgrimage from Hungary," says M'Cready Sykes in his article 'The Obverse Side' in the *Journal of Commerce and Finance.** And harking back he continues,

> The older among the editors recalled traditions heard in boyhood of the tremendous welcome given to Kossuth when he visited this country in 1851. We suppose almost no one now living remembers it, but the old files were taken down and the scene recalled. Lafayette, Kossuth, Dewey, Lindbergh— these and but a few others make up the list of the really tremendous receptions that have roused the country to an intense and universal enthusiasm. . . . In truth, the present monument to the Hungarian patriot seems belated recognition of the fame of one whose name has fired the hearts of the American people as the names of few have done throughout our history. Kossuth represents the tradition of the struggle for liberty in continental Europe. He personified that spirit of nationality which became one of the dominant forces of the nineteenth century, one whose profound and far reaching outgrowths have not yet revealed their ultimate results.

Though identified with politics so continuously, Mr. Sullivan was not in every sense a politician. His interest in public affairs developed from environment and training. In his father's house, as a small boy and later as a student, he grew to feel his responsibil-

* March 21, 1928.

ity as a citizen as he grew in his love for his fellow men. The desire to be of service led him to seek opportunities for usefulness from the beginning to the end of his career, but his methods were characterized by an independence which did not secure for him any great political preferment. His ability was never underestimated; his power would have been far greater had he not, in the years of his prime, been of the minority group of his party and irrevocably bound and hampered by principles which led him to consider self-advancement of less than secondary importance.

Reared by his father in the fold of the Whig party, he remained, with him, its active supporter until in its consolidation with various political factions it was reorganized into what became known as the Republican party. Then, considering its aims and doctrines as sectional and therefore pernicious to the good of the country, he allied himself with the Democrats, whose principles he believed to be fundamentally sound and applicable to the needs of the entire nation. Thus establishing his political code, he entered the field in 1855 as a campaign speaker against the Republican party, which, however, elected Salmon P. Chase, its first gubernatorial candidate in the State of Ohio.

In the spring of that year Mr. Sullivan became engaged to Mary Mildred Hammond, who was the daughter of a prominent Virginian, George Washington Hammond, and who, with her father, was a visitor in the Cincinnati home of her great-uncle, Mr. Griffin Taylor. The young people were a perfect complement one to the other in characteristics, yet sufficiently similar in tastes to presage the happiness which endured throughout their long years of companionship.

Miss Hammond was the eldest of six children left motherless in 1846 when she was but ten years old. Though the little family was adopted by their great-aunt, Mrs. Bushrod Taylor, "our eldest," as Mary Mildred was affectionately known, was encouraged to share responsibility with her great-aunt. Mrs. Taylor, a woman of strong personality and wide experience as mistress of a large plantation, spared neither care nor her ample means in procuring for her niece every advantage. The young lady's popularity was not acquired through the beauty of her sparkling black eyes alone; she possessed an exceedingly agile mind, and its activites had been well directed in the building of a strong and forceful character which lent wisdom beyond her years to a kindly nature. The wedding took place at Aspen Hill, the Taylor homestead in Winchester, Virginia, the following December, 1856.

Throughout the year before his marriage Mr. Sullivan had followed a full program of campaign speaking in addition to carrying on his law practice and other activities. Overwork brought a return of those physical disabilities which were the bugbear of his student days. Periods of enforced but not altogether unhappy rest took him several times to the Virginia Springs not far from the Hammond home. Opportunity was thus offered for intimacy with his future wife's relatives, and in this congenial association was developed an affectionate admiration, reciprocal and lasting.

The return of the newly-wedded pair to Cincinnati after a brief wedding journey was closely followed by misfortune in the shape of serious financial losses to Mr. Sullivan. The present system of banking, with its conveniences, its unifications, its safeguards, was not then even in its infancy. Banking was chiefly conducted by private individuals, and their credit was always a matter of daily and anxious inquiry.

Financial transactions between individuals were almost entirely carried on by means of personal drafts and personal notes which were generally required to be endorsed by one or more parties. This endorsement was usually a courtesy accorded without compensation or security, and was regarded as a matter of course between friends. The result was the creation of a vast net-work of mutual endorsements, and the encouragement of speculation, which, in the Western States, was largely concerned with real estate ventures in the territory under development farther west.

No name on a man's note was more readily accepted than that of Algernon Sullivan; and no one was more eager to oblige a friend by thus placing his signature. His implicit confidence in others was childlike; his instinctive unwillingness to lose the smallest opportunity for service made refusal almost an impossibility. There was no wisdom in his generosity, and the penalty he paid was heavy.

The inevitable crash which brought financial disaster to the whole West in 1857, sparing neither persons of large nor of small property, caught Mr. Sullivan in the ruins.   What at first seemed to be but an unhappy involving of his affairs in certain failures of his friends quickly developed into the catastrophe of his personal financial ruin.   His small fortune was swept away in an effort to meet the obligations thus thrust upon him, and which, even after the sale of his fine and highly prized library and other effects, remained unsatisfied.   In fact, a large portion of his life was spent in wiping out these debts.   To add to his difficulties, the business depression growing out of the uncertain political situation was especially severe in the cities of the Northwestern States where his investments were at the moment greatly depreciated, and the necessity for realizing upon them immediately was no small part of his misfortune.

Overwhelmed as he contemplated the collapse of nearly ten years of hard work, Mr. Sullivan determined to choose a new environment in which to make the unavoidable fresh start.   He was extremely sensitive to the position he must occupy in Cincinnati as a bankrupt, and he shrank from daily contact with creditors he could not pay.   He felt that away from the constant reminders of his burden of debt, he could more readily concentrate upon acquiring the means of lifting it, and materially expedite the process.   It was the obvious recoil of a highly developed moral sensibility.

The broader opportunities to be found in New York City were an attraction, and thither he removed in May 1857.   Though he had introductory letters to

ALGERNON SYDNEY SULLIVAN AT THE AGE OF TWENTY-THREE

Mr. Daniel Lord, one of the leaders of the New York
Bar, and other prominent people, this removal was
none the less a radical change; it required courage.
To flee the scene of failure and misfortune is an
inclination mothered by the pleasing prospect of new
and perhaps greater activities. Interest in the
unknown spurred by the splendid self-confidence of
youth lightens the burden of accepted difficulties
and sacrifices. But Algernon Sullivan was no longer
a youth; his activity was hampered by a frail body,
and his nature was far too sensitive and gentle to
serve him adequately in such a struggle. Despite
the drawback of the daily reminders of his failure
and indebtedness, he would have been wiser had he
remained in Cincinnati where he had good friends
who urged him to do so; or to have gone to some
place smaller than New York and more sympathetic,
where competition would have been less keen and
not so ruthless.

However, he was from first to last an optimist, often
unwarrantably so; his confidence in the ultimate success of work undertaken with a sincerity of purpose
was not impaired; and this supported him in the
course which he elected to pursue. This course, dictated partially by the prevailing custom and partially
by a personal pride in rehabilitating his fortunes
upon his own merits, led him to again "hang out his
shingle," in a small room in William Street near
Wall, rather than accept employment with an
already established firm, where, though his progress
might be more rapid, he could scarcely expect to

have entire freedom of decision or action in his practice. And he would not be bound by any save his own conscience. Algernon Sullivan was prepared to give of his best and was prodigal of effort. Equally in error, he underestimated the price he must pay and the inexorable nature of the competition he must meet.

His preference was endorsed by his wife who shared his anxieties but understood and sympathized with his motive. Able and intellectual, Mrs. Sullivan soon gathered round them a circle of charming friends in their new home. Her courage seemed never to ebb, and their life in the pleasant boarding house on West Fourteenth Street was immeasureably brightened by her cheerful loyalty.

At best these were difficult times. Illness in Mrs. Sullivan's family and the death of her father augmented their trouble, to which was also added anxiety for the health of Judge Sullivan. At that time he was greatly harassed by the vagaries of one of his sons and the unsatisfactory financial condition of another, whose inherent ability was nullified by extreme optimism and poor judgment. As the result of these, or of other influences, both young men were constantly in need of their father's assistance, and were a severe tax upon his peace of mind. As in all questions of great moment to the aging Judge, he sought comfort and counsel from his son Algernon, who, though actually in no position to give monetary assistance, never failed to make his father's anxieties his own and treat them as such at a personal sacrifice

which even the most exacting conception of filial
duty might term unjustified.

The acquisition of wealth merely as a possession
never intrigued Algernon Sullivan; had it done so, his
ability could have brought him great fortune. It
must not be supposed, however, that he was insensible
to the advantages of possessing money. He did not
underestimate his powers, nor was he without ambition to achieve, acquire, and live in accord with
his endowments. Very properly, and normally, he
sought recognition; he desired the stimulation he
found in social activity; and he looked forward with
pleasant anticipation to the repose and ease of later
life as the fulfilment of his exertions.

But withal, the significance of acquisition dwindled
in the inevitable comparison of values which con-
fronted a man of his calling and position. Thoroughly disliking ostentation, money, beyond that necessary to properly provide for his family—and he often
lost sight of their needs and his own in his compassion
for others—was a detail to which he gave far too little
consideration, and the want of it seriously embarrassed him not only in his own affairs but when he
found himself powerless to relieve the need of others—
needs which, however legitimate, his sensitive and
sympathetic nature took much too seriously.

On a blustering day not long after he came to New
York, he stood talking with two friends in City Hall
Park, when a mutual acquaintance approached them
for a loan. As one of them tells the story, he, himself, was obliged to refuse, but Mr. Sullivan auto-

matically felt in his pockets, finding there only some
small change.   A glance at the man's flimsy overcoat
halted the refusal he was about to explain.   Instead, "I have no money," he said, "but you can get
some with this."   And he pressed his watch into the
hand of the astonished applicant who, to his credit,
refused to accept it.

However crushing was the blow of his recent losses,
bitterness had not taken possession of Algernon Sullivan, nor had his sweet and instinctively generous nature suffered blight.   Far better had these benevolent
impulses been dulled by experience, but that was
never to be.   His sympathy for the need or suffering
of another so completely mastered him that for the
time being he forgot all else.

✢

Mr. Sullivan was admitted to the New York Bar on
the motion of Mr. Daniel Lord.   As the representative of certain Western and Southern interests he
rapidly made friends and clients among those coteries
in the city; the transacting of their business matters
became for him important channels in the building up
of his practice.   In his association with several
prominent Virginians he attended a convention of
the Sons of the Old Dominion, during the course of
which was developed the proposal to transfer the

remains of James Monroe, fifth President of the
United States, from the old Second Street Cemetery
in New York City to his native soil of Virginia.
The suggestion particularly appealed to Mr. Sullivan,
who knew of the friendship which had existed between
his father and the late President, and the satisfaction
it would be to the Judge could such a removal be
accomplished. His interest at once became active.
He accepted the position of secretary to the committee appointed to advance the proposal, and fostered
the idea by persistently calling regular meetings until
the removal became an accomplished fact attended
by a great civic and military demonstration in both
States, with the Seventh Regiment, Colonel William
R. Peyton commanding, as Guard of Honor. The ex-
humation occurred on July 2, 1858, the centennial year
of Monroe's birth, and on July 5, in Richmond, Virginia, the body of the man whose administration has
been called "The Augustan Age of the American
Union," was laid in its fitting and final resting place.

From this time forward Algernon Sullivan was
identified with countless enterprises of public interest
and concern to the city. The same qualities of mind
and character which made for him a place in Cincinnati were to bring him prominence in New York, but
not so speedily. He had arrived in that city unknown and broken in fortune, and upon the heels
of that sudden and almost wholly unlooked for commercial panic of 1857. Although his connections
were highly desirable, they were few. But his fine
appearance, his noble bearing, his courteous demeanor

were impressive. Even on slight acquaintance his erudition and keen perception were apparent, and from the purity of his diction and the power and lucidity of his public speeches, he quickly became known as "the silver-tongued orator from Ohio," and recognized as a valuable member of the legal profession. His progress was consistent but not spectacular, as it might have been in less turbulent times. Nationally, the political situation was, to say the least, unsettled, the struggle in Kansas already becoming a topic of general and heated conversation, with sectionalism breeding disorganization as it developed.

And it developed apace.

The presidential aspirations of Douglas led him a merry dance to the tune of Lincoln's fiddle, a dance which, under the "rail-splitter's" bow, assumed the appearance of acrobatics ending in catastrophe for the "little giant." For Douglas defied his party, despite the warnings of the weary and discouraged President Buchanan, and chose to support a free Kansas; the consequent split in the Democratic forces was largely responsible for the victory of the Black Republicans in 1860.

Meanwhile, the argument in Congress was descending to the undignified level of a free-for-all fight, and in the South was developing a sectionalism matching in intenseness that of the most rabid Northern abolitionists. It was fathered by such men as William Yancey, Jefferson Davis, Robert Rett—all men of action and devotees of the cause of a free and independent South either in or out of the Union—men vio-

lently determined to oppose any encroachment by the
North upon what they conceived to be the rights of
the Southern States.

In the midst of this turmoil, which was rapidly approaching a crisis, Algernon Sullivan found himself in
a position of embarrassing complexity.   As always, he
considered his personal anxieties as of secondary importance to his public responsibilities, governing his
actions accordingly.   In the events which threatened,
the two were so closely bound together there was little
chance to separate them or to lighten either.

At the birth of their son in 1859 Mr. and Mrs. Sullivan were still living at Mrs. Howland's boarding
house in West Fourteenth Street.   The peace and
happiness which should have been theirs was soon disturbed by the atmosphere of dread and premonition
which was general.   Mrs. Sullivan, heavy-hearted,
watched the war clouds gathering and faced the realization that the war, if it came, would be carried on in
the land which was her home, where still her family
lived and owned property.   Financially, Mr. Sullivan
was largely dependent upon his affiliations with the
Southern interests of which he was the legal representative in the North; politically, he was a Democrat.
His personal attitude was one of impeccable patriotism, and his standards were arrived at through his
decisions which he based upon legal knowledge and
impartial judgment.   While slavery had ever been
abhorrent to him, and its ultimate abolishment a
cause to be supported, the thought of bloodshed sick-
ened him.   Conflicting emotions overwhelmed him.

In the following, written some years ago by a member of his family, an interesting light is thrown upon this state of mental confusion in which Mr. Sullivan and a large number of others also found themselves.

Mr. Sullivan was born and reared in Indiana, among its first settlers—pioneers who valued their own freedom and their right to local self-government (States Rights) and enjoyed the practice of it. They also opposed the holding of others in bondage.

Mr. Sullivan was opposed to slavery on principle, but he recognized the undeveloped condition of the negro race, and believed the welfare of that race and of the Nation would best be served by gradual emancipation in association with their development by education. . . .

As to the Union, Mr. Sullivan believed that the permanent union of the States was of fundamental importance, as providing for them strength for protection from external attack, as well as opportunity for the development of broad national ideas and the advantages of sympathetic exchange of thought and experience between the varied parts of a great nation. He also supported the Union as being an almost conclusive prevention to a breaking up of the Continent into separate, independent nations.

On the other hand, he felt that the union of the States should be voluntary; and that the semi-independence of each State and its right to that independence, was the only, and the needed, protection of liberty from internal aggression. To put it another way I may say that from his rearing under the influences of the sturdy pioneers, and from his study of history, he believed thoroughly that the maintenance of the independent rights of each separate State was the one strong assurance against a drift back to Monarchy and the establishment of a ruling class.

Therefore, when the Southern States seceded, he had conflicting feelings. He felt that their act was exceedingly unwise;

but when the Northern States determined to coerce them by armed invasion, into remaining in the Union, he felt the corner-stone of Liberty was being assailed. And feeling that way he expressed his opinion openly and publicly.

The Northern Government, however, had assumed a stupendous task. It felt impelled, at any cost, to prevent the breaking up of the Continent into many smaller countries; and its own condition was critical—so critical that it dare not per-mit public expression of disapproval.

Mr. Sullivan's outspoken criticism was fearless and honest, but it was not wise. There were any number of trouble-makers in the city only too ready to grasp any excuse which opened the way for them to shine in the light of patriotic endeavor. Some of these were fellow-guests at Mrs. Howland's, and life there became none too pleasant for Mr. Sullivan or for his family. However, he maintained an attitude of absolute neutrality in the conduct of his affairs, swerving neither to right nor to left in the performance of his duty as he saw it, and though his heart was heavy, he lost neither his courage nor his trust in the Almighty.

Soon after the outbreak of the war, in May 1861, the Confederate schooner *Savannah* of Charleston, having been fitted out as a privateer, captured the sugar-laden and Federal-owned brig, *Joseph*, and was in turn taken by the United States Brig-o'War, *Perry*, in command of Captain Parrott. Captain Parrott brought his prisoners to New York, where they were treated as pirates rather than privateers, and imprisoned for "robbery on the high seas and nine other counts."

The Confederate Government immediately assumed responsibility for their defense, engaging the
firm of Laroque and Barlow as counsel. Associated
with them were many prominent lawyers such as
James T. Brady, Daniel Lord, Joseph Dukes, Algernon Sullivan, and others. Mr. Sullivan's selection
was due, undoubtedly, to the reputation he had made
in the South among its business men. At first
brought to their notice through his activities connected with the transferring of the remains of President Monroe to Virginia, and as administrator of the
Hammond estate, which was a large one for that day
and involved important properties belonging to the
Washington family, he had become well known in
Baltimore, Richmond, and Winchester as a man of
unbiased prejudices and meticulously honorable
standards. Mr. Sullivan's acceptance of the case,
however, was vehemently opposed by his family and
friends, as it was clearly a position of great personal
danger for a man of his fearlessly pronounced utterances. But, though his private worries—his wife's
anxieties and his little boy's ill-health—were weighing
heavily upon him at this time, he could not be per-
suaded to refuse or to change his conception of his
duty toward the trust placed in him.

For some time disagreeable, perhaps jealous, en-
thusiasts had made use of the facts of Mr. Sullivan's
Southern connections to look askance at his position
of neutrality. His wife was known to be a Virginian
whose relatives were actively engaged in the Confederate ranks. Thinly veiled threats and vicious re-

marks were a constant source of embarrassment, often terrifying to the young wife despite her own intrepid nature and the courageous calm of her husband.

The case of the privateersmen, prosecuted by the Attorney-General of the Federal Government, came up in the United States Circuit Court before Judges Nelson and Shipman on July 17, 1861. Because of the illness of Judge Nelson, the case was postponed until October, but Mr. Sullivan's appearance at the July session seemed to be the signal for instant activity amongst his enemies. Hectoring him with frequent and unsigned insults, and warnings to "leave New York by order of the Vigilance Committee," some malicious person went a step further and denounced him falsely to the Federal Government at Washington, admittedly signing a fictitious name.

As in ancient Venice the *Lion's Mouth* snapped off many an innocent head, this scurrilous missive evoked a telegram from Secretary of State Seward ordering the instant arrest of Algernon Sullivan, and on September 7, without warning or given cause, he was unceremoniously thrown into prison at Fort Lafayette in New York harbor. Though charged with aiding, abetting, and communicating with the enemy by means of surreptitious correspondence, no documentary evidence was ever produced to sustain or justify the accusation. A correspondence with Confederates in the interests of his client, Captain Baker, Commander of the *Savannah*, under trial for his life, had necessarily been carried on by Mr. Sullivan in an official capacity and openly through ordinary channels possible in time of war. No code or cypher had been used, nor could Mr. Sullivan have been said to have overstepped his legal rights in these communications, or otherwise transgressed, unless it were in the use of two or three phrases which most unwisely indicated his intense disapproval of one group of States endeavoring to coerce another by force of arms. These few casual phrases which today, in reading the records, seem so harmless, were seized upon by the Federal Government as a technical reason for arrest and a means both to silence Mr. Sullivan and to deprive the *Savannah* crew of one of its able legal defenders.

The arrest was speedily proclaimed an outrage secured with malicious intent. Judges throughout the country rose to Mr. Sullivan's support, and, joined by the foremost legal talent of the North, declared their belief in his fundamental loyalty and their opinion that no military or political purpose could be served by his imprisonment on such a flimsy basis of cause.

In this connection it is interesting to note that accusations similar to those lodged against Algernon Sullivan were later made against the well-known lawyer Daniel Lord, also of counsel for the defence in the case of the *Savannah* privateers; and against Stewart L. Woodford, no less prominent and in the service of the Federal Government. It was Mr. Woodford, who afterwards became a general in the United States army, and later, Ambassador to Spain, who was sent by the authorities at the time of Mr.

Sullivan's incarceration, to call upon Mrs. Sullivan to gather as much information as possible. When Mr. Woodford himself was threatened with arrest, he was fortunate enough to receive a warning a few hours in advance and promptly hurried to Washington where he was able to dispose of the charges, which were proved to have been made in retaliation for a personal grudge.

On October 21, 1861, Mr. Sullivan was released fully vindicated, though, curiously enough, hardly had he left the fort when a telegram was received from Secretary Seward revoking the release. No attempt was made to enforce the order, nor was it ever explained, but it evoked another open letter expressing the disapproval of some zealous busy-body who harbored a personal dislike for Mr. Sullivan.

In the diary of Lawrence Sangston, who was at the same time a prisoner in the fort together with other members of the Maryland Legislature, is found this entry:

> Oct. 22d: Three discharges yesterday . . . Messrs. Sullivan, . . . The former is a New York lawyer . . . of counsel defending the privateers . . . An hour after his release an order came revoking it, but he had gone and they let him alone.

This episode in Mr. Sullivan's career, almost fatal because of the extremely unsanitary conditions in the fort, left upon him a never-fading impression of pitiless injustice, all the more poignant because of the constantly recurring reminders, obstacles which automatically opposed and hindered his progress, despite his willingness to ignore them. Some twenty years later, when he had risen to power and influence in the community, in his profession and in politics, he was asked why he had never consulted the Government archives in Washington to ascertain who had been his enemies. He replied, "I did not do it because I did not wish to feel toward any person as I would feel toward them, had I known their identity."

On October 23, two days after his release from Fort Lafayette, Mr. Sullivan appeared in court when his client's case was called, and he did it despite the warnings of his friends that a band of young fanatics had sworn that if Sullivan appeared "in behalf of the pirate," he would never "leave the courtroom alive." That Mr. Sullivan's doom might equally be sealed by some over-zealousness in his pleading to which the Government might take exception was also cause for concern in the minds of his friends. But to Mr. Sullivan himself neither possibility had sufficient weight to deter him. To him his duty was clearly defined and it was not in his nature to evade it. He proceeded to his place in court and there to sum up the case in a final address of startling power and simplicity.

The case was closed; the jury disagreed. The prisoners were later relieved of the onus of piracy and exchanged as prisoners of war. Considering the bitter persecution which Mr. Sullivan had endured during his incarceration, and his lack of time for preparation, this summing-up for the defence was a remarkable address. One who was present has written:

Drawing by W. E. Mears

FORT LAFAYETTE IN 1861

Let those who have access to the records, read—How absolutely fearless was his lucid voicing of the delicate principles involved; which other counsel clothed in a little more of the obscurity dictated by caution; and yet how conciliatory the whole argument, how persuasive, how entirely imbued with the spirit of peace and gentleness, how absolutely devoid of every trace of bitterness which his painful experiences must necessarily have engendered in any other breast!

It is no wonder that Judge Nelson, stirred by the magnificent soul of this man, rose and came down from the Bench to take his hand in public recognition of a superb and courageous loyalty to his client and to his State. Thus did he confirm the opinion of his learned associates throughout the country, that "Algernon Sullivan was incapable of any collusion with the enemy or with unprincipled people; and in all his undertakings he was actuated and possessed by humanitarian motives of the first order."

❖

A time of serious illness followed upon Mr. Sullivan's release from prison. In fact, a chronic ailment resulted from the dangerous attacks of dysentery which he suffered there, and for the balance of his life the days when he was utterly incapacitated were frequent. He fared no worse in the old fort, however, than did his fellow-guests of the Federal Government. Many of these were members of the Maryland

Legislature—nearly one half of that distinguished body—who, having been suspected of being about to pass a vote of secession, were, together with the Mayor and the Police Commissioner of Baltimore, summarily despatched to Fort Lafayette and detained there until the elections were over. Diaries kept by certain of these gentlemen were later published, and they agree as to the cause of the distressing illness which victimized nearly all of them.

> The Fort had not been garrisoned (before the Civil War). For over twenty years the cistern (for drinking water) had not been cleaned. When the supply was low, fully twenty tadpoles one-quarter to five-eighths inches developed, could be counted in one glass of water.*

Ignoring this added handicap, Mr. Sullivan refused to retire from his usual activities. Idleness offended his sense of human obligation, and he considered his own endurance last of all. As a natural consequence of his arrest under suspicion, his practice melted away; it was reclaimed slowly and at a great disadvantage. Though the charge was proven false, the stigma remained to hamper him; only a man of his compelling individuality could have maintained a position of dignity, despite his sensitiveness to the inevitable petty slights and cruel criticisms, and become, as he did eventually, a prominent and distinguished figure in the professional, political, and social life of New York. Only a man of intrepid courage and sublime unselfishness would have risked

* *The Bastiles of the North* by a member of the Maryland Legislature, Lawrence Sangston.

calling to himself at this time, the attention of the Governor of New York State in the following letter:

To Honorable Horatio Seymour:

At the recent election in this State the people invested you with a power greater than that which will attach to your office merely. The moral power which belongs to public opinion is centered in you. The people have said of you, "Behold the exponent of our views"; and said to you, "Our motto is Lex Rex." I appeal therefore, to you on behalf of the political prisoners in the United States who have been the subjects of arbitrary arrests and imprisonment, and to whom hitherto a trial has been denied. More particularly do I urge upon your attention the prisoners at present in Fort Warren and Fort Lafayette.

When I left some of them in Fort Lafayette, a year ago, they again and again demanded a trial, according to the constitution and the laws of the land, and on each weary day since, until now, have they renewed that reasonable demand.

But the ears of the Chief Magistrate have been deaf. The people of the country, however, have responded that the prisoners should be released or tried at once, and if not found guilty shall have honorable remuneration for their wrongs. To hasten that consummation is a part of your mission. It is the public expectation that you will accomplish it. I venture, therefore, to request that you and the other democrats and conservatives who have recently been elected to Congress will unite in a petition to the President and that he will forthwith open the doors of the military prison, or else at once cause the inmates who are political prisoners to be fairly tried according to law, if indeed there be any charges made against them. Their weight of character as citizens, your representative character from the people, and the intrinsic rightfulness of the demand, will now render the acquiescence of the President certain.

I am led to urge this application through you, first, because no other third party can make such an application, as you will perceive by the following extract, which was read to the prisoners in Fort Lafayette, by Lieutenant Wood, the commandant of the post. The letter was written by a commissioner who came from the State Department about one year ago:—

To the Political Prisoners in Fort Lafayette:

I am instructed by the Secretary of State to inform you that the Department of State of the United States will not recognize any one as an attorney for political prisoners, and will look with distrust upon all applications for release through such channels, and that such applications will be regarded as additional reasons for declining to release the prisoners.

Secondly, because an agent of the government, while endeavoring to persuade the prisoners to take certain proposed forms of oaths, stated that "It were best to take them, for the government would not give them a trial; no, not if they stayed there twenty years."

And, thirdly, because it is idle to talk in general terms about preserving any law or liberty in this country so long as this violation of both is tolerated before our eyes. No surer evidence of the decay of public virtue can be given than popular indifference to such wrongs upon individual citizens.

When a community are not sensitive to injuries perpetuated upon their humblest member, by an abuse of power, they are but one step from ignominy and ruin.

I will surely be pardoned for urging you to action in this matter. There are citizens of various States now in the fort who have been imprisoned there for sixteen months. No habeas corpus can reach them. Perhaps they are forgotten by those who consigned them to the casements. Such cases occurred in the French Bastile, and why not here?

Prisoners grown old therein, when their mouldy cells were opened at last by the fiat of the people, walked forth with an enfeebled memory, which could scarcely recall when they were entombed; and there was no man living in France who remembered anything about it. Again, I pray you, do what you can to let daylight and justice into your Bastile.

Respectfully,

ALGERNON SYDNEY SULLIVAN.

New York, November 8, 1862.

Once more during the course of the war Mr. Sullivan was drawn into what might have been a situation having for him serious personal consequences, and it was due to his rare faculty of impressing great masses of people that destruction of property and bloodshed were averted.

During the Draft Riots of 1863—those fanatical and violent disturbances precipitated by conscription—large groups of malcontents, often incited by alcohol, paraded the streets of the city bent upon depredation. Reprisals for what they considered a discriminatory law were directed mainly towards those whose wealth enabled them to evade the military service thrust upon the less fortunate.

The palatial home of Dr. Thomas Ward stood at Fifth Avenue and Forty-seventh Street. Dr. Ward, who had not the slightest connection with things military, was one of the city's social leaders, and possessed a library and an art collection of rare treasures. One day when he was alone in his house with the ladies of his family and a domestic staff which included no man, he realized with alarm that a mob was beginning to assemble before his doors. He sent a messenger from a rear entrance for help to Mr. Sullivan who, fortunately, was at his new home nearby in Forty-fifth Street.

Mr. Sullivan ran at once to the assistance of his elderly friend—hatless and unarmed. Pushing his way through the yelling crowd of hoodlums who were already forcing from their sockets iron palings to be used as weapons, he was finally able to mount the coping of the stone steps. As soon as it became evident that he was not a member of the attacking party, jeers and curses and missiles of all descriptions were hurled at him. Mr. Sullivan, showing an utter disregard for danger, finally succeeded in raising his voice above the din; in catching the attention of someone to whom the courage of this man, entirely at their mercy, appealed.

They listened.

And Mr. Sullivan spoke to that angry, reckless, vicious crowd, subdued to almost total silence, for more than fifteen minutes. His voice was not raised in anger nor invective; nor in persuasive pleading. He spoke simply, translating what to them had been but curt and drastic orders from an autocratic military, into practical measures of necessity to the preservation of the Union—measures taken by their Government in good faith. With uncanny directness the speaker touched their manhood. The tall spare figure, erect and magnificently poised, forceful and emphatic despite his gentleness, had caught the spirit of the Great Master.

The crowd dispersed.

❖

New York City, having escaped the ravages of war, braced herself to withstand the widely predicted wave of viciousness which was almost certain to break out among her discharged soldiery, men inured to the brutalities of conflict and ripe for the excesses of the inevitable after-war period of moral relaxation. These, however, to the confusion of the prophets, returned readily enough to their peaceful avocations and left the city to solve other and greater problems, and to contend with conditions far more threatening to her welfare.

The facilities for resuming the rapid development written into the history of the last ten years of the city's progress were not impaired, but there was a financial depression—a commercial stagnation—widespread and affecting all trades and professions. There were great fortunes and big men to meet these conditions, but unfortunately the municipal government was in the hands of the corruptionists whose efforts to obtain control, spread over a number of years, were unhappily about to be crowned with success.

Scarcely had the business lethargy which followed the war begun to show signs of breaking up in a normal manner, when the city was swept by a sudden wave of excessive speculation encouraged, perhaps started, by the fraudulent schemes of the notorious Tweed Ring, and eventually developing into the frenzied manipulations which precipitated that great financial panic of 1873.

By 1869 the Ring was at the height of its power.

Municipal improvements throughout the city, engineered by dishonest officials to fatten their own purses, had sent realty values soaring. Business was buoyant, but under the protection of infamous politicians great corporations descended to bribery to attain their ends, and stock-jobbing and swindling were carried on openly and without interference.

That colossal rogue, William M. Tweed, product of Cherry Hill, whilom fireman and erstwhile member of the Common Council of 1852 commonly known as *The Forty Thieves*, had the city in his grip. Having contrived his election as Grand Sachem of the Tammany Society, he proceeded to use its members, and its great mass of supporters, largely drawn from the ignorant hordes of immigrants, to establish the supremacy of his party whenever the city went to the polls. Conceit and impudence were the chief characteristics of this man whose aldermanic career had closed with his arrest, though he not only escaped punishment but secured influence which sent him to congress. His term there had not been profitable, however, and he had returned to New York to become a member of the Board of Supervisors, serving four times as President. It was there he built up his iniquitous system of public plundering, enlisting the aid of Peter B. Sweeney, commonly known as the brains of the Ring, and "Slippery" Dick Connolly, whose sobriquet adequately explains his selection. Other and less important members of this infamous group managed to escape the onus of supreme guilt which rested upon these three, so notorious in this shameful period of the city's history.

These years in New York following the Civil War presented conditions obviously trying to a man of Algernon Sullivan's temperament and characteristics. His ability was hampered by sensitiveness, his generosity and altruism invited imposition, and his code of morals, generally considered far too idealistic, admitted of no discrimination in favor of his own advancement. His natural inclination toward political activity hindered rather than helped him personally, for though he was a Democrat, he was a member of the minority group of that party, openly independent and in favor of reform.

The powerful element, corrupt, and completely in control of the city government, had been so successful in hoodwinking the people that it had been able to extend its influence to all branches of the legislature. Great national issues were occupying the energies of those respectable citizens of sufficient influence to block these nefarious operations, and those whose suspicions were aroused to the point of dissatisfaction were confused by the wheels within wheels so cannily contrived by these plunderers of the city treasury, and overwhelmed by the apparent hopelessness of combating a situation so involved and a machine so insidiously powerful.

Sporadic attempts of the reform Democrats, known as The Young Democracy, to force an investigation and thereby dislodge the thieves masquerading as municipal officers, repeatedly met defeat. By degrees, however, the public distrust increased and the meetings of the "opposition" held in Appollo Hall* were more largely attended. The candidates put up by this group for office in the city government could naturally not survive the election frauds maneuvered by the Ring, but occasionally they secured, in spite of the power of their opponents, an appointment to some minor post—wedges eventually to be driven home by the impelling force of such men as Samuel J. Tilden, Joseph H. Choate, and William H. Havemeyer.

Algernon Sullivan was one of these. In 1870, when the Young Democracy was struggling for recognition as the party organization at the Rochester Convention, Mr. Sullivan was appointed an Assistant District Attorney of the City of New York. He served for three years under partisans of the Ring and in the midst of indiscriminate mud-slinging. When reputations were falling all around him, incredible as it may seem, he emerged from office without the least stain upon his character. It was not the modesty of his office which saved him from becoming a tool of unscrupulousness; he sought no personal gain, yet he was able, forceful and conspicuous in even the routine of his duties; a commanding figure impressive in his sincerity, loyal to his ideals.

The realization of the ideal life is the great design of God and the great work of man. The advancement and elevation of humanity is most surely promoted by whatever best and

*The Ring, supported by the Metropolitan Police, retained possession of Tammany Hall.

permanently develops the individual man. It is by the enlightened and disinterested service to his fellow-beings that he most surely strengthens and idealizes his own nature.

The life of any man whose aim is to be of service rather than to be personally great is not likely to include the stimulation of a meteoric rise to fame or fortune. Algernon Sullivan, in reality, and notwithstanding his taste for the life, as had been said before, was not in the accepted sense a politician. His own (the Reform) group recognized his value to the Commonwealth and made a determined effort to place him upon the Supreme Court Bench, but Mr. Sullivan learned that one of his personal friends, though aware of this, had accepted the advances of Tammany Hall toward nomination for the same office, and he withdrew his name. He was really physically unfit for any struggle which seemed to him might grow into a bitter personal quarrel. He was, with justification, incensed at what he considered his friend's disloyalty, but primarily he shrank from being drawn into any controversy in which his own advancement might seem to be the chief or only motive, and which might embarrass his supporters and friends.

Also Algernon Sullivan had a great antipathy to arguments likely to engender and to be carried on on a basis of purely personal enmity. His extreme sensitiveness to the reaction of discouragement which frequently follows upon failure or affront, and which so often spells ruin to men of certain characteristics, led him to avoid all controversies unless the issue rested upon a morally sound principle. His insight directed his consideration for others; but in questions of purely self-interest his defences were greatly weakened by it, and as it was so distinctly anomalous to his firmness and persistency in fighting the cause of justice, that it created comment. His associates, who honored his knowledge and admired his courage, were, in their friendliness, puzzled and sometimes irritated by this inconsistency, until, at a meeting with other lawyers in a discussion which included both a matter of business and one of legal ethics, Mr. Sullivan briefly stated his self-imposed rule:

> In a matter presenting a question of right or wrong the decision, if it rests with me, must be for the right as I see it and my energies must be directed toward upholding it.
>
> When another man's interests and mine conflict, and the decision rests with me, if I am in doubt, I decide against myself.

The intentional elimination of his personal interests in consideration for the advancement of a worthy public cause reacted in no small measure upon Mr. Sullivan's progress. Such eliminations were frequently unnecessary; often they were errors of judgment which cost him considerable effort, and, in certain quarters, prestige.

In a similar manner he allowed his intense sensitiveness to any personal enmity or unfriendliness to be a distinct drawback to the full exercise of his great powers; and through it he was exposed to many an injustice. To the end of his life he suffered severely from any reminder of his arrest and of the resulting years of coolness from men who later sought his friendship. When some of these, a group of lawyers, formed the Association of the Bar of the City of New York to combat the malevolent influences of the corruptionists among the judiciary, and to elevate the standards of the profession, they did not invite him to coöperate with the organizers. Mr. Sullivan believed that they were influenced by prejudices engendered by the Civil War and that it was a personal matter. Later, when asked to join, though he cordially approved of the general purpose of the Association, he had not yet outlived that feeling, and fearing the possibility of future embarrassment, he declined.

No matter how complete is the vindication of one falsely accused, it is the accusation which remains in the minds of men, and Mr. Sullivan so keenly felt this attitude of unjust suspicion, he so resented its unfairness, that he could not welcome associations where the influence of that prejudice might be kept alive and become an obstruction to his efficiency.

Knowing himself to be the equal at the Bar of the men who organized the Association, it is natural to attribute to him a feeling of hurt pride at being excluded by them when the organization was formed. As he became older and grew more and more in self-control and in the knowledge of men, his broader comprehension, his clearer perception and the poise and vigor of his moral traits allowed him to sit in judgment upon himself, and he regretted his action.

It was from these contradictions in his intensely human nature that Algernon Sullivan evolved an indisputable quality of greatness.

❖

The year 1871 found opposition to the Tweed Ring and its flagrant corruption assuming proportions which reflected the rapidly rising tide of general indignation, but the reckless and confident Tweed refused to heed the warnings of his downfall. The *New York Times*, aided by disgruntled and jealous underlings of the Ring, was able to print authenticated records of their nefarious transactions. The cartoons of Thomas Nast in *Harper's Weekly*, persistently published drawings and famous thorns-in-the-side of the wiley Boss of Tammany, who admitted that his people had eyes though they could not read, were thoroughly substantiated by the records. The public, convinced at last, held a tremendous mass-meeting and forthwith plunged into the task of unmasking the scoundrels. By 1873, Tweed had been arrested on some two hundred counts, and though he managed to evade wearing the convict's stripes until the following year, the Ring was broken.

And then New York, in the turmoil of municipal reorganization, found herself struggling against the demoralization of great financial panic, the logical

ALGERNON SYDNEY SULLIVAN IN 1855
At the time of his marriage to Miss Hammond

outcome of that treachery within her gates from
which she had suffered disaster far more injurious to
her progress than any brought upon her by the late
war; and her need for fearless and able leaders was far
greater. She found them in Tilden, Havemeyer,
O'Conor, Ottendorfer, and scores of others whose
names appear less conspicuously in the records of her
rehabilitation, and so History credits them.

> Yet even as the brightest feature of a great war . . . is the
> heroism and the sacrifice which attend it, so too, in the suc-
> ceeding struggle with the corruption and fraud, the efforts of
> those who successfully opposed it, winning the victory when
> victory seemed most improbable, and when the plunderers
> seemed most strongly intrenched, shine out all the more
> brightly for the sordidness and public apathy that surrounded
> them. There was no waving of plumes, no blare of martial
> music about their triumph, yet their struggles in the dusty
> law-courts and in the devious paths of municipal diplomacy
> were just as real as those of the heroes of 1861–65 on bloody
> battlefields, and they saved the city of New York just as truly
> as those others saved the Union.*

No ostentation surrounded the part played by Algernon Sullivan in the readjustments of the city's
political conditions. He was constantly active to,
and beyond, the limit of his strength; particularly
as a speaker, or, as chairman of various committees,
he was invaluable to his party. Upon the collapse
of the Tweed administration, Mr. Sullivan was
proposed as the Democratic candidate for Mayor.
Frequently recurring periods of ill-health and the
need for developing his law practice, prevented him
from considering the nomination, but it is interesting

*Memorial History of the City of New York, James Grant Wilson.

to read what the contemporary press had to say upon the subject.

From the *Evening Telegram:*

Under the reorganization there is talk among the progressives and reform Tammany Democrats of running Assistant District Attorney Sullivan for Mayor. Although a prominent Tammanyite and an office holder under the old regime, the name of Mr. Sullivan gathered lustre from the contacts that darken the record of his old associates, the Chiefs of Tammany. When almost every office-holder was charged with dishonesty or prosecuted for malfeasance and peculation, Mr. Sullivan stood so far above suspicion that even insinuation never whispered aught against him. He is one of the few Democratic politicians who would adorn the place.

From the *Tribune:**

The name of Assistant District Attorney Sullivan was mentioned as a probable and popular candidate under the Tammany nominations. Mr. Sullivan held office under the old corrupt Tammany organization but was one of the few connected with it who escaped calumny and stood always above reproach.

We concur very cordially with the above in the estimate of Mr. Sullivan's fitness for the office of Mayor. Mr. Sullivan's legal and scholarly attainments are of a high character; his principles and personal bearing are those of a gentleman; the *sauviter in modo* with the *fortiter in re*, which eminently characterize him, are qualities peculiarly suitable to the office of Mayor of this great city.

In the discharge of his duties as District Attorney, while faithful to his duties, he has studiously excluded all partisan spirit. With a very general popularity among the Democrats, he is, perhaps, as little exceptionable to the Republicans as any genuine member of the Democratic party.

* The Republican organ.

It has been said that it would be difficult to find one who possessed more qualities of enduring usefulness to his community than did Algernon Sullivan. He commanded the respect and confidence of his fellows by quietly pursuing his way along the paths of right living which were clearly marked by his own deep convictions. His gentleness and generosity and his joyous acceptance of life's contrasts endeared him to friends and acquaintances alike. He allowed himself no foibles of character; his infirmities he met squarely. There were discords in his life from which he courageously evolved harmony, and his misfortunes and disappointments were not allowed to make him sombre.

So buoyant and hopeful was his disposition . . . so contagious and inspiring was his courage . . . I met him but once, and then he spoke to me but a few words, but such was the influence of his encouraging and assuring smile that ever afterwards in periods of despondency his face came back to me and he was my inspiration to self improvement.

From the time of Mr. Sullivan's arrival in New York in 1857, conditions had never been propitious for his success; he progressed in spite of them. Never free from real financial distress, and with the added burden of physical disability, he might well have acquired a bitter and misanthropic outlook, but never would he allow any faltering of the spirit to unfit him for the day's problems. Frequently he rose at dawn after a night of wakefulness and worry, refreshing his worn body with several hours' ride on a ferry boat before appearing at his office to conduct the day's business.

After serving for three years as an Assistant District Attorney, Mr. Sullivan resigned and turned his attention to private practice as the senior member of the firm of Sullivan, Kobbe and Fowler.* Five years later, in 1878, this partnership was dissolved and in 1879 he established the firm of Sullivan and Cromwell, still existing and known internationally.

Mr. Sullivan now rapidly became prominent in his profession but he never became wealthy. The low fees he charged were often absurdly out of proportion to the amount of labor involved as well as to the client's income. His attention to the affairs of the poor was gratis. Incredible as it is, many who were well able to pay for his services, knowing of his generous openheartedness, managed with poor luck tales to evade settling even his modest charges; or, by the use of bad checks or worthless securities, succeeded in defrauding him. His business associates condemned him for his leniency and exaggerated concern for the reputations of others which was, financially, nothing short of suicidal; but he could never bring himself to prosecute people with whom he had once enjoyed the intimate relations of counsel and client, even though they stooped to such chicanery. It is not difficult to understand why he died a poor man, but curiously enough this amazing attitude which was the cause, was confined to his own personal affairs. In direct reversal, when conducting the affairs of others he was firm and adamant, impervious to persuasion, resentful of imposition, quick to discern any contemplated encroachment upon the

* Mr. Fowler later attained distinction as the Surrogate of New York City

MARY MILDRED HAMMOND
From a portrait painted in 1855

rights and privileges of a client, and indefatigable in his effort to secure for him a full meed of justice.

> Mr. Sullivan's distinguished professional character is exceedingly unique: the services of one of the most able lawyers New York City has ever known, not only were not uniformly employed in suits of celebrity but are largely buried with the unwritten history of the lower courts in the humble litigations of the unfortunate.

Though Mr. Sullivan never sought to make laws, but only to apply them, and was not nationally important, he was nevertheless an important and unique figure in New York. His refusal to undertake any case in the justness of which he did not believe cost him many a large and tempting retainer. As a speaker he had few peers at the Bar.

> He was recognized as one of the strongest, readiest and most successful jury lawyers in the city of New York. An opponent to be feared . . . yet respected and loved, revered by Bench and Bar. His kindness, candor and fairness, even during the heat of trial was always the subject of remark in the courtroom.

The Hon. Henry W. Bookstaver of the Court of Common Pleas, said:

> He was always welcomed by the Court in any case in which he appeared because it was felt that his learning, ability and absolute truthfulness would assist the Court in the trial of any question of law and fact with which it had to deal.

Algernon Sullivan was noted for seeking out young and impecunious lawyers struggling in the great city far from home and friends, and finding opportunities for them to secure a foothold. It was he who, in the

General Term of the Supreme Court, on May 10, 1880, made the motion to admit to the Bar the first colored lawyer, John F. Quarles, not only a negro, but born a slave.*

The *New York Sentinel* of April 3, 1880, under the heading "Men about Town," prints the following:

SULLIVAN. A ripe scholar, an accomplished gentleman, a graceful and fluent speaker, and a person of magnetic influence is Algernon S. Sullivan, whose attainments, natural gifts, and manly attributes, fit him for a most exalted station. A lawyer by instinct and education, he is one of the most brilliant pleaders of the New York Bar. He entertains the highest ideas of the counsel's relations to a client, and never adopts any of the tricks of the profession. His convictions of duty prevent him from assuming the defence of those whom he believes to be unworthy of assistance, and deserving of severe punishment. Yet, he is not vindictive nor bitter. When Assistant District Attorney he attracted attention on account of his fine appearance, noble bearing, erudition, keen perception, graceful oratory, courteous demeanor, and skill in presenting cases to the jury. He was logical, earnest, fair, effective. He made no attempt at noisy declamation, nor vituperation. Much of his influence with a jury was due to his quiet, undemonstrative manner of talking directly to the point of a case, and avoiding all tergiversation or variance from the direct issue. He did not depend upon superficial accessories of loud intonation, violent gesticulation or extravagant expressions to fortify his position. His simplicity, clearness, perspicuity, and keen logic did the work. Mr. Sullivan was obviously fitted for a higher position. He is a man of fine literary attainments, and some of his contributions in prose and poetry to the pages of magazines such as *The Atlantic Monthly* and *The North American Review*, show him to be one of the first litterateurs in the land. He possesses a higher order of talents than those usually found in the local

*See page 152.

politician; and he has statesmanlike qualities. He is broad and liberal in his views, regards the innermost workings of matters, is a deep thinker, and is given to research and exhaustive investigation. He is not misled by the superficial consideration of questions natural to the average legislator; but whenever he speaks upon a topic of public interest, throws some new and clear light upon it. He lacks the characteristics which are unhappily frequently needed to secure political preferment, being unwilling to condescend to the tricks and devices deemed indispensable to secure nominations and elections. He despises the arts of the demagogue, and the wiles of the professional politician, and will take no part in the bargains and agreements which so frequently enter into the candidacy for places. Such men of real ability, fine attainments, and moral courage are rare in the community, deserving much more recognition than they receive.

In 1875 Mr. Sullivan was appointed Public Administrator for the City of New York, and held office for ten years. He instituted many reforms, reduced the charges upon the estates he administered, and, in the face of great pressure, retained his able assistants irrespective of their political affiliations. In announcing the appointment a contemporary newspaper declares:

The duties require a man of tact and sympathy, an able lawyer and an honest man. Large amounts of money are intrusted to him . . . the duties are varied, honorous, romantic, and it (the office) has its relief by escaping the drudgery of routine. For a wonder in our politics, the man is fitted to the office and the office to the man.

"ARIEL."

Of interest is the old *Report of an examination of the office of Public Administration:*

To the Honorable W. R. Grace (Mayor):

NEW YORK, October 5, 1882.

The books are clearly and accurately kept. The accounts are in perfect order and the balance deposited. . . . The expenses of the Public Administrator we find amount to rather less than 2 and ⅔ per cent upon the value of the estates so that we think we are justified in saying that the business has been economically administered.

Commissioners of Accounts { W. P. SHEARMAN
J. W. BARRON

When he accepted the office of Public Administrator it was apparent that Mr. Sullivan's physical condition was improving. As it did so, it was consistent with his nature to find him adding recklessly to his activities. From that time forward to the year of his death, no great movement in New York for public welfare, the alleviation of suffering, or the encouragement of scientific or artistic effort was without his warm support, his strong sympathy, and his efficient aid.

He was President of the New York College of Music, a secretary of the Presbyterian Hospital, a life member of the American Numismatic Society, and a member of the Metropolitan Museum of Art. For the Saratoga Monument Association he was a member of the Committee on Design and a trustee of its funds. This Association, formed by Hamilton Fish, Horatio Seymour, and others, proposed to erect a shaft at Saratoga in commemoration of the closing event of the most important chapter of the American Revolution—the surrender, on October 17, 1777, of

General Burgoyne and the finest army ever sent out from England.

After many years of concerted effort on the part of a large and energetic committee, the monument was raised, but Mr. Sullivan was not well enough to attend its dedication, which occurred on September 15, 1887, a few months before his death.

In working for the success of the proposed and ill-fated world's fair of 1883, Algernon Sullivan expended untold energy and strength. This movement of national importance, sponsored by ex-President Grant as president of a committee composed of New York's most prominent citizens and men of foremost consideration throughout the country, was to have been known as The United States International Exhibition, and held at Inwood-on-the-Hudson in celebration of the one hundredth anniversary of the Treaty of Peace and the recognition of American Independence. Despite the strenuous exertions of those most actively interested—and among them was Mr. Sullivan—the commercial value of the enterprise seemed to make little impression upon the public, and eventually the proposal was abandoned.

But Algernon Sullivan's interest and effort did not depend upon the stimulation of success. He exerted himself without stint in behalf of every worthy cause brought to his notice, and into the last ten or twelve years of his life was crowded an unbelievable amount of work, professional, religious, philanthropic, educational, and social.

With what seems to have been an almost uncanny

conviction that his newly acquired vigor, so longed for
during his younger days, could not last, he withheld
himself from no call upon his sympathies, time,
strength, or the contents of his very slender purse.   It
was in a measure the fulfilment of his deep desire to be
of service which in his first years in New York necessarily had to be curbed.

❖

To return to those first years: it was not long after
his arrival in New York that he attached himself to
the Five Points Mission, that hotbed of strife just east
of Chatham Square where the city's most degraded
and lawless elements elbowed each other in vice, infamy and viciousness.   The ring-leaders were divided
into gangs historically famous, and fighting among
themselves alternated with their depredatory excur-
sions into other localities.   The police force, either because of collusion with them or fear of their brutal
retaliation for interference, never seemed to gain
control of the situation.
    Mr. Sullivan was one of those who visited the mis-
sion and regularly addressed the indiscriminate
gatherings, whether they were interested and docile or
curious and actively antagonistic.   The charm of his
personality, the simplicity of his manner, the fellowship and understanding that his words brought to

them were curiously effective. There was little heckling when he spoke, and in contrast to the common experiences of others, he was never molested in his frequent passage through the neighborhood.

In 1860 Mr. Sullivan became, and was for ten years following, Superintendent of the Sunday School at the Brick Presbyterian Church, where his devoted service made him conspicuous. When he moved to his home in West Eleventh Street, in 1870, he became a member of the First Presbyterian Church which he attended, and in the affairs of which he was active, until his death. His portrait, under which is written "as a reminder of a life worthy of emulation in every way," hangs in the present Sunday School room, and a memorial window in the church is dedicated to his memory. Both were gifts of the Young People's Association which had made him its leader.

The Arcadian Club, a coterie of New York's struggling young lawyers, newspaper men, artists, and writers was slowly dying of stagnation, when in 1872 Mr. Sullivan was urged to become its president. This he could not do, but he accepted the vice-presidency and energetically assumed the obligation of injecting new life into the organization which meant so much to its impecunious members. Under the stimulus of his leadership monthly receptions to people of note were inaugurated. The first of these was in honor of Isaac Hays, the Arctic explorer. Emily Faithful, when that devoted advocate of remunerative employment for women, which at that time in England was considered an impossibility, made her first lecture tour in the United States, was also thus honored.   Charlotte Cushman, the actress, and the venerable philanthropist, Peter Cooper, upon the occasion of his eighty-fourth birthday anniversary, were among the many others.

It was Mr. Sullivan whose enthusiasm, whose speeches of warm welcome, made these functions a success.   In the midst of a busy life and many cares he could so subordinate his personal problems that he could create for others an atmosphere of light-hearted conviviality which frequently found no echo in his own breast, save in the pleasure he took in witnessing the joy of others, and in securing the interest of persons of influence for their less fortunate brothers.

This by no means indicated that Mr. Sullivan had lost his fondness for society.   On the contrary, he enjoyed mixing with his fellows in no small degree, and though essentially a man's man, was popular with New York's most exacting hostesses.   Rarely was he absent from any important social gathering.   Frequently the prime mover in affairs of public interest, he was nearly always the speaker of the day, or on a program with Mr. Chauncey Depew, the Hon. William M. Evarts, or Frederick Coudert, Joseph H. Choate, Robert Ingersoll, Henry Ward Beecher and men of similar prominence.   He appeared conspicuously in the laying of the corner stone and in the opening of the Produce Exchange, in the ceremonies attendant upon the placing of the Obelisk in Central Park near the Metropolitan Museum of Art, at the

Memorial Service conducted by the Grand Army of
the Republic for the murdered President of the United
States, James A. Garfield, and upon countless other
occasions of equal importance to the city of New
York.   Mr. Sullivan's speeches, many of them hastily
written, are of value in that they reveal the man who
wrote them to such an extent, and are so indicative of
his practical applications of the high ideals for which he
stood, that it would be a definite loss to exclude them.
Though far too numerous to appear in their entirety,
selections have been made to be included in this
volume.

> There is sterling substance in every word. He spoke
> quietly and distinctly, yet he could fill the great Academy of
> Music from parquet to dome, and hold his audience spellbound
> for an hour or more.

Mr. Sullivan was an astute analyst; his extensive
reading taught him new principles of interpretation,
and in Cicero, Homer, Plato, Demosthenes, in their
own tongues, he found inspiration and serenity.   As
often perhaps he turned to Montaigne or Mme.
De Staël, or Carlyle, or Ruskin, or his dearly-loved
Emerson; for his shelves were heavy with treasures
for which he had far too little leisure.

Upon Mr. Sullivan's retirement from the office of
Public Administrator in 1885, he thereafter refused
office of any sort.   Throughout these years of greater
physical strength, and until he began to realize the
terrific strain under which he had been living, he had
been an active member of the Democratic party,
speaking frequently in behalf of a wiser and purer

political code.   He was chairman of the great mass-
meeting held in Tammany Hall on November 2, 1876
for the National, State, County, and City Democratic
tickets, and he is said to have averted a riot by his
calm determination and impressive control of heated
arguments.

In 1883, in an address before the Harlem Democratic
Club, Mr. Sullivan voiced strongly his hope that "the
ideal party shall become the strong party."

A press clipping of February 17th replied:

THE AMERICAN CHESTERFIELD

It is not surprising that Mr. Algernon Sydney Sullivan, who
is our American Chesterfield, should feel dissatisfied with
existing political parties and should desire to raise politics and
politicians to a higher plane.   The Hall * in which restraint is
placed on the opinions of independent thinkers and where
ignorance out-votes intelligence; the primaries with their
packed ballots and coarse brutality; the conventions with their
prearranged programmes and their shouting crowds, are offen-
sive to a man of pure and cultivated mind and refined nature,
who feels it to be a citizen's duty to interest himself in politics.

Mr. Sullivan's hope that the ideal party will be the strong
party may be disappointed.   He may not find a sufficient
number of men with the will and the courage to follow him in
selecting tickets for the best nominations to raise the movement to the dignity of a party.   Yet his advice and his efforts
may do much good in making more imposing organizations
careful in the character of their nominations . . . choosing
those who could differ as gentlemen and conduct discussions
with fairness and courtesy.   Any party founded by Mr.
Sullivan would be of such a character and would work a
desirable revolution in our present corner-grocery political
system.

* Tammany.

Periodically during these years Mr. Sullivan's name had been advanced for election to Congress and other posts of political responsibility, even for that of President of the United States.   In the latter instance, as he was at the time Vice-President of the Ohio Society, and a prominent figure in both Indiana and Virginia, it is interesting to read what was printed in *Echoes from the People* on November 9, 1883:

The current of political events, past as well as present, makes it a necessity, in order to insure success, for the Democratic Party to nominate for the President a candidate who can carry New York.   Indiana and Ohio are also important factors, and citizens of each of these States have been prominently mentioned in connection with the office.   But the most important battleground is this State.   In order to carry New York the candidate must be one acceptable to all factions of the party in New York City.

The person who can accomplish this will be a desirable nominee.   There is one gentleman who can be counted upon to do this, and who in addition has elements of strength in Indiana and Ohio.   That gentleman is Hon. Algernon Sydney Sullivan.   He is probably the most popular Democrat in this city; he has not been identified with the local factional disputes, and he is esteemed and honored all over the State, and has also a national reputation. . . . His career has been distinguished for its purity and integrity of purpose as well as for the ability which has placed him among the foremost in his profession.   His nomination would result in a responsive echo in the hearts of the public.

As a citizen he has been outspoken and fearless, being governed entirely by the force of his convictions.   It is a curious but interesting fact that it was he who moved for the admission to the Bar of the first colored lawyer in New York. *Who will second this nomination?*

But Mr. Sullivan would not encourage these suggestions. Even had he felt inclined toward a life of political prominence, he realized his inability to cope with anything so strenuous as a campaign. He felt too definitely the strain of these crowded years during which his business had grown tremendously, and the youth and endurance of his partners had set a standard of accomplishment which taxed his strength to the utmost. He had little left for things outside, nor was he wealthy, and so able to ignore the demands of his profession for other issues. Yet it is no exaggeration to say that no day passed when he did not happily and voluntarily assume the burdens of other men in an effort to clear away the complexities of a less happy life, or strengthen the character of some weaker brother.

It must not be supposed that Algernon Sullivan, in coming to New York, had lost touch with his family in the West. Nor had the affectionate intercourse established with his wife's relatives in the South been interrupted. In the large number of letters from Judge Sullivan to his son, are to be found the intimate details of family matters transmitted with great regularity. Interest in the affairs of the younger man, solicitude for his welfare, wise council and offers of assistance fill the pages of the earlier missives. Later, as the good Judge added to his years and felt their weight and the cares of his long life, he turned with affectionate reliance to the sympathy and understanding of a son who had never failed him. In fact, meagre though his resources were, and heavy as were his own burdens,

Algernon Sullivan was the mainstay of his whole family in every emergency. Thoughtless or unfortunate relatives forced assistance from him with little ceremony. Again and again he was called upon to face embarrassment or loss on their behalf, to protect his aging parents, to save his sisters heartbreak and discouragement. Amply repaid by the devotion of some, he could afford to ignore the indifference, the lack of appreciation, of others.

In his own home he found a very real and satisfying companionship. The deep affection which bound the little family together was their fortification in trial and trouble—their security of a "measureless content." The profound admiration Mr. Sullivan felt for his wife was expressed with a tender deference and courtesy tinged with the romanticism of his poetic nature and the chivalry of an old-school training.

But ten days before his death Mr. Sullivan was an honored guest at a dinner given by Mr. H. L. Bateman for a prominent English visitor. As the evening neared its close, Mr. Sullivan suggested that the very beautiful flowers which adorned the table be sent to Mrs. Bateman. Upon the menu he inscribed a greeting to accompany the elaborate bouquet, and amidst the applause which greeted his suggestion he rose to say:

The flowers that have just left our table have gone to the Annie Laurie of our host—the Annie Laurie of the evening—but I am doing no injustice to Mrs. Bateman, nor an unkindness to our host in stating that such beautiful flowers as have just left our table always remind me, and must remind every other gentleman present, of the Annie Laurie that each of us has left at home. What would our lives be without the love and affection which *our* Annie Laurie gives to each of us? What would our lives be without those tender hands and sympathy, when in sickness or in trouble?

All the best part of my nature, all the success that has come to me in this life, has come from the helping hand of *my* Annie Laurie; and I cannot separate from my host, and his friends, tonight without asking that each of us drink the health of the particular Annie Laurie of his heart.

This was Mr. Sullivan's last appearance in public. He was gravely ill at the time, yet he let no hint of this escape to mar the pleasure of the occasion for others; nor did his thoughts turn in lugubrious fashion upon himself. They were concerned, rather, with his companions of the moment, and with the dear ones at home.

The toast to his wife was no empty compliment. Mrs. Sullivan combined in an unusual degree a womanly gentleness with extraordinary strength of character. None more gracious, charming, tactful, than she; progressive beyond her day, able and active, she was, as she had been in her youth, a definite factor in the lives of those around her, and a dominant influence in the various philanthropies to which she gave freely of her seemingly unlimited endurance. For over thirty years she organized, conducted and led the Charity Ball, New York's most successful social effort of the period, revived, built up and carried on by her indomitable determination, for the benefit of the Nursery and Child's Hospital, where for sixty years she was active, and for forty of those held high office. It was a stupendous task, and it is recognized and referred to as such upon each recurrent anniversary of the ball in the messages sent to her now that she, well over ninety years old, must relinquish the activities so dear to her energetic spirit. Mrs. Sullivan's identification with the Nursery and Child's Hospital followed upon her arduous labors in forming and carrying to phenomenal success the New York Southern Relief Association for the aid of the stricken inhabitants of the South directly following the Civil War. This, and countless other charities, Mrs. Sullivan sponsored despite her personal anxieties, not the least of which was constant concern for the health of her son.

The little boy had inherited his father's delicate constitution, and was obliged to spend many months of the year in Virginia with his mother's relatives, in order to escape the northern climate and to secure the freedom of outdoor life on the plantations. His health was thus greatly improved, and occasionally he was indulged in the longing every city boy has to go barefooted with the farm children, a privilege of which he was especially proud, and which, upon one occasion, he insisted should be demonstrated to his absent father by means of a tin-type. This fading bit of metal was never far from Mr. Sullivan's hand.

In spite of a determined search for a beneficial climate, the child never became robust. Though his life was to be one of continued activity, he was to depend upon nervous energy and determination, rather than health or strength to carry him through.

The Sullivans were a family of exceedingly close ties; their daily life was marked by affectionate consideration and unselfish devotion which, however, was neither narrow nor self-centered. Mr. Sullivan never fully revealed himself emotionally to any save those closest to him, but his home radiated the hospitality both he and Mrs. Sullivan loved to bestow.

For many years Mrs. Bushrod Taylor, Mrs. Sullivan's great-aunt and adopted mother, and Mrs. Sullivan's two younger sisters were permanent members of the household. In their companionship Mr. Sullivan took a real and constant pleasure; no matter how trying his day's work might have been he was never too weary for the evening's half hour of conversation, or reading aloud from his Latin Bible, to which the elderly Aunt Bet looked forward with keen impatience. And rarely did he return from his office unaccompanied by some lonely youth hungering for the atmosphere of the home which was perhaps many miles away. On Sunday nights the Sullivans kept open house, first in their home on Twenty-first Street, just after the Civil War, and later in Eleventh Street. High tea was served; informal discussions reached out into the fields of art, literature, politics; and for a short space the drawing-room echoed to favorite and well-known hymns led melodiously by the host, who was always the center of the group gathered round the piano. It was an atmosphere of warmth and congeniality irresistible in its appeal, especially to those young Southerners who sought, in

GEORGE HAMMOND SULLIVAN AT THE AGE OF NINE
From a tintype taken when the boy was recuperating from an
illness on a Virginia plantation

the strange and not too friendly city, business opportunities not to be found during that period of reconstruction, in the States below Mason and Dixon's line.
In Mrs. Sullivan, with her wide acquaintance throughout the South, they found a strong bond of common
interest, of mutual ties, and a sympathetic friend.

When the New York Southern Society was organized in November 1886, Mr. Sullivan was asked to
become its first President.   He lived but little over a
year in which to contribute to its development, but
his work for the Southern Society had been done in
the twenty years which preceded its formation.   The
idea was complete, and there were those who were
interested and able to carry it out.

An old and intimate friend describes him in the last
year of his life as pitiful—a noble, loving soul whose
mental vigor and passionate desire to be of service to
God and man inspired him to struggle valiantly under
the crushing weight of bodily deficiencies.

Mr. Sullivan's last public effort was the organization of a citizen's committee to forward a three-day
jubilee as a centennial celebration of the inauguration
of General Washington in New York.   It was to be an
impressive memorial to be held on April 29, 30, and
May 1, 1888; the circulars, written by Mr. Sullivan,
were sent out on November 5, just one month before
his death.   Late in the same month he contracted a
severe cold which was rapidly followed by a typhoid-
pneumonia complication, and on December 4, at the
age of sixty-one, he passed peacefully to his eternal rest.

The suddenness of his death was a shock to the entire community. The flags of this great city, curiously shaken from its impersonal attitude, were at half-mast; many of the courts adjourned,* and society interrupted its gaieties to pay tribute, not to a man of wealth whose possessions aided in their pursuit of pleasure, but to one of their members respected, admired and loved—above all, loved. Peculiarly significant is the following which appeared on December 8, 1887, in *Town Topics*, a paper which lent itself seldom to expressions of this character:

> I pause for a moment—cast off the mood of raillery; discard the masque of humor; lay down the lance—and with simple tenderness and admiration place a leaf of homage upon the memory of a man Society could ill afford to lose. The death of Algernon Sydney Sullivan takes out of the high social sphere one of its prominent and graceful figures. Of refined instincts, he sought the ennobling influences of the arts, and although not a collector, he was a visitor at all of the exhibitions, and was apace of the best minds in his fancies. His interest in music is shown by his presidency—a purely honorary position —of a musical college. In charities he was conspicuous and for many years had been a leading spirit in the organization of the Charity Ball. As a lawyer, watchful and jealous of every vantage for his client, he was ever the courteous opponent. In society punctilious, yet gracious; the old school courtliness blended with ripe geniality, made his presence always welcome, and the mention of his coming a gladsome sound. The announcement of the death of Algernon S. Sullivan caused many a *grande dame*, even on the threshold of a season of unusual festivities, to stop and give utterance to words of deep regret.

* This was the last time such an adjournment was taken in New York City as a mark of public mourning for the death of a private citizen.

From all parts of the country condolences poured in upon Mr. Sullivan's family; the press of every State carried obituaries. One editor referred to him as "of a kindness of heart not to be measured." Another quoted a hotel waiter as saying "He was a man great enough to be able to treat those below him with respect." Another, "He was a politician really pure."

"I never knew," says an associate of Algernon Sullivan, "an unkind, uncharitable or vulgar remark to pass his lips."

"For more than fifteen years," says one yet closer, "I have been looking daily into his heart, and during all those years and under thousands of temptations of a busy life, professional, social and political, I never found the remotest approach to sin—not an unkind or hard word to any human being; not a falsehood, not a bitter thing; not a profane or indelicate thought ever passed his lips."

Resolutions of regret were passed by the Courts, the American Bar Association, the New York State Bar Association, State and social clubs, and the New York Southern Society, which perhaps lay as near his heart as any of his many interests. A Citizens' Memorial Committee was formed, the list of its seventy-seven members including men of every calling, of opposing political parties, of differing religious creeds, whose close and amicable cooperation was a convincing proof of the strong and impressive nature of the man whose influence they strove to perpetuate, and reflected the breadth and catholicity of his own great sympathy which was as broad as humanity.

This committee,* in its personnel, was one of the most remarkable tributes to personal character the city of New York has ever known, and its activities continued over a period of thirty-seven years. A bronze bust was presented to the Alpha Delta Phi Club and a memorial drinking fountain was erected in Van Cortlandt Park. A small medal was prepared for use primarily in Law Schools of New York, and later in the Trade Schools, as Mr. Sullivan was a pioneer in the movement to establish this valuable system. The medal was later abandoned; a better medium for the purpose, in the shape of a plaque, was substituted and was widely used in educational and public service institutions.

In 1913 the committee established in the American Numismatic Society a fund for purchasing medals designed by either American or foreign artists. There is a continual exhibit in their museum of these acquisitions which is placarded as annual purchases by the Algernon Sydney Sullivan Memorial Fund.

When, in 1925, death and other influences seemed to indicate its eventual dissolution, the committee, with its ultimate object in mind, consulted with the George Peabody College for Teachers, at Nashville, Tennessee, in regard to establishing a permanent award for character, to encourage the development in others of those qualities exhibited in the life of Algernon Sydney Sullivan. Learning that such an award would be considered of value in educational circles, the committee invited the New York Southern Society to become its associate in establishing it in Peabody College. The society having accepted, the two bodies acted jointly in carrying out the design, and with such success that the Memorial Committee thereafter passed and delegated to the New York Southern Society, as its sole successor, its entire authority and responsibility for perfecting the plan of offering the award to other institutions, and for the fund provided for that purpose.

The Memorial Committee then disbanded; its activities were assumed by the Southern Society under the direction of its own committee whose chairman is Mr. Walter L. McCorkle, a former president of the society and prominently identified with the original Sullivan Memorial Committee.

The award, now made perpetual, and extended to include a total of fifteen institutions in ten different States, is the tangible expression of appreciation and esteem for a man who, so closely touching the complex life of a large city for many years, met his problems with a great courage born of truth and right. It is the ultimate recognition of a character which needs no eulogy because it writes its own memorial in the enduring influence of its integrity, its great humanity, its spontaneous sympathy. "For such lives do not cease, but continue forever in the benefits conferred on other men."

Thus, in the inexorable march of progress, may a lamp well tended shine far into the future, and light for many the way so faithfully trod by Algernon Sydney Sullivan, whose manner of life was a daily exposition of an abiding love for God and man.

Speeches by
Algernon Sydney Sullivan

Though the speeches of Algernon Sydney Sullivan were never designed for publication, the decision to include a number of them here is based upon their undisputed quality of exemplification. As this has been the primary consideration, no claim is made for any specific literary value, and it is realized and regretted that any reproduction in print, in losing the intonation of the voice and the magnetism of the speaker, must be necessarily a very inadequate reproduction of the utterances of one so widely known and honored for his impressive orations.

Neither are the speeches expositions of erudite or involved problems of technical character. Their value, however, is definite, in that they indicate, as can nothing else, the unvarying and instinctive tendency of Algernon Sullivan towards thoughts consistently ennobling, and conclusively show him to be a man of spiritual depth, of humanitarian aspirations; a man to whom personal aggrandisement, despite his learning and ability, never assumed the proportions of a primary goal.

Excepting the argument in the case of the Savannah privateers, no record of Mr. Sullivan's speeches in Court is obtainable, yet his eloquence there was famous among his fellow members of the Bar, and his powerful and lucid disputations gave him an enviable reputation.

For the most part, the available speeches and addresses were spontaneous or hurriedly prepared deliveries, voicing what he thought, felt, hoped for. Early in life Mr. Sullivan cultivated the habit of speaking extemporaneously. His temperament and his mind responded quickly to momentary changes in a situation and to the variety of mental and emotional reactions of his audience, so that even a prepared address was seldom delivered as planned. The following collection appears in original and unedited form, that those who wish to study the character and personality of Mr. Sullivan may find therein the best obtainable material suitable for their purpose.

A. M. H.

ALGERNON SYDNEY SULLIVAN IN 1879

An address delivered by Algernon Sydney Sullivan who represented the city of Cincinnati in the national welcome extended to Louis Kossuth, champion of Hungarian Independence, at the City Hall in New York City on December 6, 1851

GOVERNOR KOSSUTH:

The city of Cincinnati, the "Queen of the West," has made it my pleasing duty in her name to congratulate you and your noble companions on release from imprisonment and to proffer you her hospitalities. Her citizens would do more, Sir; they offer you that kind of sympathy which the present juncture demands.

Since your arrival on our shores the citizens of the eastern portion of our Republic have expressed freely their sentiments with regard to Hungary, but this is the first occasion on which the West could announce her opinions.

In the great valleys of our home, the principles of freedom grow with a luxuriance only equalled by the vegetation on our virgin soil. Our sympathies are instantly and continually with the oppressed, and we remember with satisfaction that the first memorial to Congress asking our government to interfere for your liberation, came from Cincinnati. We regret that you did not succeed in degrading and banishing forever from Hungary the perfidious and tyrannical House of Hapsburg-Lorraine.

There are thousands in the West ready to demand that a new principle shall be incorporated among the laws of nations; that is, that every nation shall have the right to govern its domestic concerns. Each age has its necessity and its duty, and ours may be to establish that doctrine.

The government that intermeddles to assist one nation to oppress another is as much the enemy of liberty and happiness as the pirate on the high seas. Every man's hand and every

nation's hand should be against her. There should be no sanctuary of precedent or policy to which she could flee for safety.
Such a foe to human rights should have no salute save male-
diction. This new law must be established. Freedom, humanity, and the Bible, rightly construed, sanction it. We hope
our Government will give its voice and efforts emphatically in
its favor.   We would count all obstacles slight, and to succeed
would act on the principle of the Latin maxim—"*Aut inveniam
viam aut faciam.*"

In Cincinnati thirty thousand German immigrants reside and
in the whole West they are numbered by hundreds of thousands.
These are ardent lovers of Liberty and her sister, Republicanism,
and they hope, with their fellow citizens, to have an opportunity,
by your presence among them, to show their sympathy with
Hungary in a worthy and substantial manner.

I observe that one of our worthiest citizens has already placed
a thousand dollars in the Hungarian fund.

While we honor liberality in so good a cause, permit me, Sir,
in behalf of the West, to state my approbation of the suggestion
made to you yesterday,* and in the name of the multitude of
modest and humble givers beyond the Alleghanies, I beg leave to
contribute a golden dollar to what was so aptly entitled the
"Treasury of Freedom." May it be the first drop of a western
torrent.

It is said that six great battles have marked the grandest
changes in the political and moral world. In the West, we hope
that Hungary's plains will be the seventh battle field, and that
her tricolor, so beautifully emblematic, shall lead to that victory whereby European despotism shall be forever overwhelmed.   May Hungary's awaking from her present stillness
commence a new and happy epoch for the world—when
the great bell of Time shall sound out another and a
glad hour—the hour of jubilee and freedom to the nations.
Then, Sir, the West will continue to unite her voice with the
acclamations of all America, adopting your own fervent lan-

* One dollar donation to a *Treasury of Freedom* fund.

guage, "Hail! To Hungary, to her fame, her freedom, and her happiness."

In handing you the open letter signed by the Honorable Mayor of Cincinnati and Committee of the City Council, permit me to add again my earnest wish that you will visit our city.

❖

Extract from the report * of the trial of the officers and crew of the privateer "Savannah," on the charge of piracy in the United States Circuit Court for the Southern District of New York, Hon. Judges Nelson and Shipman, Presiding

The argument of Algernon Sydney Sullivan of counsel for the defense. Trial began October 23, 1861, and continued seven days to and including October 30, 1861. The jury did not agree on a verdict and were discharged October 31. The prisoners were later admitted to the status of prisoners of war and exchanged as such by the Federal Government. Mr. Sullivan, of counsel for the prisoners, said:

MAY IT PLEASE THE COURT: GENTLEMEN OF THE JURY:

This case has brought to my mind an interesting episode in ancient history, to which I beg permission to refer. For many years the States of Greece had been engaged in bloody civil strife which ended in the discomfiture of Athens. The Spartans and their allies assembled in council to consider and determine on her fate. Animated by resentful passion, the Thebans urged extreme and vindictive measures: that Athens should be razed to the ground, that the hand of the victorious States should fall heavy, and the Athenians be proclaimed exiles from their homes

---

* Reported by A. F. Warburton, Stenographer, and corrected by the Counsel. New York: Baker & Godwin, printers, Printing House Square, Opposite City Hall, 1862.

and outlaws in Greece. This proposal was applauded by the Corinthians and some others, but at that moment the deputy of the Phocians, who owed a debt of gratitude to the Athenians, sang in the assembly the mournful Choral Ode from the Electra of Sophocles, which moved all present in such a manner that they declared against the design. The poem had lifted them from the passion of the hour, and invoked the memories and ancestral glories of their common nation. The spirits of departed heroes now lent the inspiration of their presence, and yielding to it, the members of that council and jury became great Greeks, as of old their fathers were. Marathon and Salamis, Platæa and Mycale, were pictured in the chambers of their souls, with Miltiades, Themistocles and Aristides for their counselors; and then, and not until then, were they fit to render a verdict upon Athens, the loveliest sister of them all.

And gentlemen, before we touch upon the details of this case, may we not contemplate some examples and sentiments which will enlighten and strengthen our spirits as guardians of the important interests committed to our hands this day? I am sure it will be agreeable to you, and to seek them in the annals of our forefathers,

> The great of old,
> The dead but sceptred sovereigns, who still rule
> Our spirits, from their urns.

It may be that a voice like that of the Theban delegate, and like the voice of Corinth, is sounding in your ears, and appealing, by sophistries, and passion, and prejudices, to you to lay the hand of your Government with all possible severity upon those of her enemies who are now in her power and arraigned at her Bar. But I entreat you to lift yourselves to that standpoint from which our ancestors, who founded this Union, who enacted the law upon which this prosecution is founded, would have regarded a case analogous to that of Captain Baker and the other defendants herein. What was the central and distinguishing idea of government, blazing like another sun on the world, which our fathers established and made honorable? Was it not the imperishable doctrine of revolutionary right—and that without special regard to the names, and forms, and paths through which it might be sought? For many other causes they may have pledged their fortunes; there were many for which they periled their lives; but only for this is it recorded by them, "We pledge our sacred honor." It is their incommunicable glory that they consummated their purpose; and if for anything we have a place in history and a name in the world, it is that we have hitherto professed to be the special guardians of that principle among the nations. Will you rise with me to the dignity and affecting associations that surrounded and auspicated the struggle of our forefathers for this principle? Shall their memory be your guiding light, and their honorable purpose that upon which your thoughts will linger? Let us subject our hearts to their influence, for it will not mislead us. And, now, would our fathers with casuistry and technical constructions of a statue which they never meant should apply to such a case as the present, pronounce judgment of piracy and outlawry against any people who were making an effort, by the recognized forms of war, to assert revolutionary right and independent self-government for themselves? Never! And while the page on which our fathers' history is written is lustrous, it would be readorned with all the beauty of immortal splendor, if under it were written today, "That which the American people of 1776 claimed for themselves (the right to 'dissolve the political bands that bound them to another'), they possessed the greatness of soul, in 1861, to acknowledge against themselves, when another portion of the same race sought the same end. Beguiled by the almost omnipotent sophistries of interest and passion, they have nevertheless adhered in loyal faith to their time-honored doctrine of free government. In the faithful devotion of the Sons, the principles of the Fathers have been revindicated. Henceforth the nation must stand unapproachable in their greatness."

Why I make these observations, gentlemen, is that when the officers of the United States ask you today to find a verdict of guilty against these prisoners, they ask you to do that which, shape it and distort it and reason about it as they may, is asking you to lift an impious hand and strike a parricidal blow, conspicuous in the eyes of the world, against the ever sacred doctrine which our ancestors transmitted to us as their best legacy and a part of their own good name. Will you abandon it? Nay, rather cling to it,

> As one withstood clasps a Christ upon the rood,
> In a spasm of deathly pain.

I wish now, gentlemen, to ask you to go with me a moment to the deck of the *Perry*, when she captured the *Savannah* and her crew. Let us recall the historical incidents of the capture, and the preparations for the trial, that we may introduce this case as justice requires.

The *Savannah* was captured on the Atlantic Ocean, about fifty-five miles from Charleston. The Commander of the *Perry*, who at that moment represented the United States Government, virtually said to the defendants herein, "We propose to try you as citizens of the United States, who, by acting under a commission of letter of marque from the Confederate States, have become liable to the penalties of the United States law against piracy." The prisoners at once reply, "If that is true, take us into the nearest ports for trial. They are in South Carolina. You claim that she is a part of the United States, and that her citizens (*i.e.*, ourselves) are amenable to your laws, and that the United States are sovereign there. Take us before one of your Courts in that State and try our case." "Oh! no," say the United States, "we cannot, with all our guns, land upon the shores of South Carolina." "Well, take us into the adjoining State, Georgia." "No; there is not an officer of the United States in Georgia. We cannot protect or sustain a single law in Georgia." "Well, take us to Florida, Alabama, Mississippi, Louisiana or Texas—any place along that extended coast of over two thousand miles." "No," say the United States, "throughout all that coast, we confess to you, Captain Baker, that we have not a

Court, not an officer, we cannot execute a single law." "Well, take us north, into North Carolina, or into Virginia." The reply of the United States is still, "We have no place there. But, notwithstanding, we admit that throughout that territory we have no practical existence; we have no Court; we have no civil functionaries; we have no protection for allegiance to us; we have not a citizen who acknowledges his allegiance to us; we admit that the people in those States have excluded our Government and established another, which is in active and exclusive control. Notwithstanding all this, you are still our citizens; and none, nor all of these facts, relieve you from the guilt and liability to punishment."

The defendants are accordingly put in chains and brought to the District of New York for trial. The witnesses for the prosecution prove all the facts that are in the case, and we stand willing to be tried by them. They prove that the defendants did capture a brig on the high seas, which brig belonged to citizens of the United States. They prove, further, that the defendants at the time of the capture, and in the act, alleged that they did so, in the name and on behalf of the "Confederate States of America," and by authority derived from them, as an act of war between the two Governments.

The authority and intent thus alleged for the capture, were they honestly, or only colorably alleged? Were they a justification of the act, so far as this prosecution is concerned, or not?

First. Was it true that the capture of the *Joseph* was in the name of the Confederate States? The fact is, that when the *Savannah* approached and summoned the *Joseph* to surrender, the captain of the *Savannah* stated his purpose to be as I have repeated; he hoisted the Confederate flag; he wore the uniform and insignia of an officer of the Confederate States; he had, as the paper upon which his vessel was documented, a paper which has been produced before us, and which bears the broad seal of the "Confederate States of America," which authorizes him to take the *Savannah* as a private armed vessel, and, in the name and authority of the Confederate States, to "make war" against the United States and her vessels.   The facts preclude any possible suggestion that the defendants made any false pretence on the subject.   The defendants had every adequate and sufficient warrant for what they did, if the "Confederate States of America" could give any authority which would constitute a defence, or if there was anything in the state of the contest between the United States and the Confederate States which constitutes war.   But, the question will present itself, even if the defendants had this warrant from the Confederate States: Did they intend to, and did they in fact comply with its requirements, or were they abusing and transgressing its license, and engaged in free-booting?   Did they intend to infract the regulations prescribed for their control by the Government of the Confederate States and imposed imperatively by the law of nations upon legitimate privateers, or did they intend to rob and steal?   I think I may safely assert that the law officers of the United States will admit that the defendants intended in good faith to comply strictly and literally with all the conditions of their authority, prescribed by their own Government for their conduct, and also with the code of war in the law of nations.   And not only was this their general intention, but as a fact, their conduct furnishes not a single deviation from these requirements.   I read to the Court and Jury the Regulations published by the Confederates, for the privateers, and which were found to be on board of the *Savannah* at the time of her capture.   They are similar, in all of their provisions, to those usually prescribed by civilized nations at war. In substance, they permitted the privateers to capture the vessels and cargoes belonging to the United States and her citizens, the capture to be made in the name of the Confederate States; they forbade, after capture, any disturbance or removal of the furniture, tackle, or cargoes of the captured prizes, and required immediate transmission, to a proper Court, of the prize, for adjudication.   Did the defendants comply with these terms?   The evidence is too plain that they did, to admit the slightest doubt.

As soon as the *Joseph* was captured, a prize crew was put on board of her and she was sent to the care of an Admiralty Court in a home port, and her papers, books and crew were sent along, that the Court might have the fullest evidence of the ownership and character of the captured vessel, and be able to decide properly, whether or not she was liable to capture. If the defendants had any corrupt or furtive motives, or if they had been indifferent to their assumed obligations, would they have been so scrupulous in furnishing all the evidence to the Court? Did they destroy, alter or erase any evidence, or offer to do so? Did they evince the least desire to have any other than the full facts appear with regard to all their acts? Your answer, with mine, is "No!" And when the vessel arrived in port, observe what proceedings were instituted by the agent of the captors. He did not offer to sell the vessel and cargo at private sale; he did not offer to submit her disposition to the adjudication of any merely State Court; but caused her to be libeled in a Prize Court, constituted on precisely the same basis, and enforcing the identical rules of law with the United States Prize and Admiralty Court, which convenes in the room adjoining to that in which we now are. In fact, I am safe in saying that the decisions of our Courts here are controlling precedents in the Court wherein the brig *Joseph* was tried and condemned as a prize of war. The trial was in a Court known to and recognized by the law of nations. Now, gentlemen, I certainly need do no more than thus re-advert to the facts in evidence to remove from your minds the slightest suspicion that the defendants ever intended to violate the laws of war or the instructions received from their Government when they received their letter of marque.

Perhaps, however, the question may arise whether the defendants did regard the commission under which they sailed as competent and adequate authority to justify their acts; or were they distrustful of its sufficiency? I do not admit, gentlemen, that that is a consideration to which in this trial we should recur, for your decision must rest on other grounds. But, I will not hesitate to say, that it is morally impossible for any man who has heard the evidence, and who is familiar with the course of events in the South, to believe that the defendants did not act in the fullest confidence that the authority of the Confederate States was ample and just authority for their undertaking. Even that one of the *Savannah's* crew who has become a witness for the prosecution, under a *nolle prosequi*, asserted on the stand, that at the time the *Savannah* was being fitted out for her cruise as a privateer, no one in the community of the South seemed to have any other idea but that the Government of the Confederate States was completely and legally established, and that every citizen of those States owed to it supreme allegiance. They believed that a letter of marque from the Confederate States constituted as good authority for privateering as the letters which were issued by our revolutionary fathers in '76, or as if they were issued by the United States. But, gentlemen, we are to proceed one step further, for under the theory presented by attorneys for the prosecution, they virtually admit that there was good faith on the part of the prisoners, and that they intended to comply with the restrictions imposed by the authority which they carried out of port with them. But they say that, inasmuch as the Confederate States were not a recognized Government, they could not confer any right upon the defendants to act as privateers, which could justify them in a plea to the pending charge. That is a proposition which enfolds the real issue in this trial. The difficulties in respect to its solution do not appear to me to be great, and I am satisfied that the more they are examined the less they will appear to candid minds.

Had the Government of the Confederate States a right to issue letters of marque; or, in other words, to declare and wage war? The denial of that right, by the attorneys for the United States, involves them in inextricable embarrassments, and must expose the fallacies which lie at the bottom of the erroneous reasonings of the prosecution.

In the first place, it is substantially an assertion, on the part of the United States, of the doctrine, "*Once a sovereign always a sovereign*"—that the United States Government cannot—by revolution accomplished—by the Act of the States repealing their ordinances of union—by any act of the people establishing and sustaining a different Government—be divested of their former sovereignty. Or, in the language of Mr. Evarts, until there has been some formal acquiescence, some assent, some acknowledgment by the executive authority of the United States of the independence of the Confederate States, there can be no other plea, and no progress in any line of investigation, with a view to a defence of these defendants in a Court of justice of the United States. Upon that point, I beg to be understood as taking an issue as wide as it is possible for human minds to differ; and I am bold to assert that the doctrine cannot be maintained successfully in a capital case of this kind. It is not true that a recognition of the Confederate States by the United States executive, in a formal and distinct manner, is requisite to entitle them and their citizens to the rights belonging to a nation, in the eye of this Court. An acknowledgment of independence would be one way of proving the fact, but is far from being the only way. Proof of such an acknowledgment by a formal State paper would, of course, terminate this prosecution; but, in the absence of that fact, there may be a recurrence to others, which will suffice as well, and satisfy the Court and Jury that the Confederate States must, at least, to a certain extent, be regarded as a nation, entitled to the usual consideration belonging to a nation at war. To show how unreasonable the proposition is, and to illustrate how impossible it is to accept it, let me submit a supposition:

If, for fifty years to come, the United States shall not reëstablish her sovereignty and restore her laws and power over the seceded States, and the latter shall continue to maintain an open and exclusive Government; and if the United States shall still refuse to recognize the new Government by formal documentary record, would the refusal then warrant the United States in capturing Confederate armies of a new generation, and punishing them for treason and piracy? And, if so fifty years hence, would it continue twice or thrice fifty years? Or what is the limit? The difficulties in the answer can be avoided in only one way, and that is, to conclude that the acknowledgment of the independence of the revolutionizing section is of no consequence at all, for all the purposes of this case, provided the fact of independence and separate Government really exists, and is proven. A *de facto* Government, merely, must be allowed by every sound jurist to possess in itself, for the time being, all the attributes and functions of a Government *de jure*. It may properly claim for itself, and the citizen may rightfully render to it, allegiance and obedience, as if the Government rested on an undisputed basis.

This is a rule never denied in the law of nations. History has scarcely a page without its record of revolution and dynastic struggle to illustrate this rule. The official acts of a *de facto* Government affecting personal rights, title to property, the administration of justice, the organization of its society, and imposing duties on the citizens, receive that consideration which belongs to acts of long-established Governments.

The successor does not pronounce the laws of the predecessor null. He simply repeals them, with a clause protecting all vested rights. This principle is correct, even in case of an usurping monarch; but how much more, if it shall appear that the people who are to be governed, have, for themselves, with mutual concurrence and choice, cast off the former Government, and organized a new one, avowing to the world their purpose to maintain it, and at the same time yielding to it the obedience which it requires?

When that state of facts shall occur, and a people sufficiently numerous to enable them to fulfill the duties of a nation, and with a territory sufficiently compact to enable its Government to execute its functions without inconvenience to the world, shall evince its purpose and a fair assurance of its ability to maintain an independent Government, it will be a surprise, indeed, to hear, in this country, that such a people are still liable to felons' punishment and pirates' doom. It is no longer a case of insurrection or turbulent violence. It has ceased to be a tumult or a riot. The war between the original Government and the revolutionary Government may still continue, but no longer can it, with propriety, be said that the army is merely the *posse comitatus*, dispersing and arresting offenders against the law. The

THE GRAND RECEPTION
OF KOSSUTH

1851

"THE Grand Reception of Kossuth. The Champion of Hungarian Independence arriving at the City Hall in New York City on December 6, 1851."—*By the courtesy of the New York Historical Society.*

LITH & PUB BY N CURRIER.   152 NASSAU ST. COR DE SPRUCE N.Y.

GRAND RECEPTION OF KOSSUTH,   GROSSER EMPFANG KOSSUTH'S,

"THE CHAMPION OF HUNGARIAN INDEPENDENCE AT THE CITY HALL, NEW YORK, DECEMBER 6TH 1851."   "DER KÄMPFER FÜR UNGARNS UNABHANGIGKEIT BEY DEM STADT HAUS, NEW YORK, DECEMBER 6TE 1851."

472

conflicting parties must, at least for the time, be deemed two distinct people—two different nations. The evidence in this case and the public history of the day, show that such is the condition of the United States and the Confederate States. In addition thereto, the United States have, by repeated acts, indicated that they so regarded the fact. The principal witness for the prosecution testified that he repeatedly saw the officers of the United States negotiating, through flags of truce, with the officers of the Confederate States; and that always the flag of truce from the Confederate States was displayed with their Government flag, but that fact never prevented the negotiation. This was well known to our Government. We have in evidence, also, the agreement of capitulation at the surrender of the forts at Hatteras Inlet. The representative of the United States signed that official document and accepted it for his Government, with the signature of Commander Barron to it as "commanding the forces of the Confederate States," etc. That was a virtual recognition that there is such a Government, *de facto*.

A few days since our Government published another general order, or document, directing that a certain number of prisoners, captured in arms against the United States, and when fighting under regular enlistment in the army of the Confederate States, should be released as "prisoners of war," because the Confederate States had released a similar number. That was an exchange of prisoners of "war," and another virtual acknowledgment that the Confederate States constitute a Government. Remember that these "prisoners of war" had, if they were citizens of the United States, violated the law in the first section of the statute under the eighth and succeeding sections of which this prosecution is founded. One class were fighting on land against the United States, and the penalty is death by the statute. The defendants here fought on water; and there is the same penalty, if either is liable to the penalties of the statute. Both classes fought under the same flag and received their commission from the same Government. If one class are "prisoners of war" in the opinion of the Government of the United States, so must the other be. It is impossible to recede from the consequences of the virtual recognition of belligerent rights involved in the exchange of these captives, under the chosen designation of "prisoners of war." How, then, doth the dignity of our Government suffer by this prosecution? It evinces an indecision, a caprice, a want of consistency and character on the part of the Government. It is an unfortunate, and I hope an unpremeditated one. The good name of the nation is involved, unnecessarily, by the mere fact of arraignment of these defendants under an indictment; but your verdict of "not guilty" may yet save it.

The Jury will and must accept the construction which the Government has in fact put on the law, viz., that it does not apply, and was never intended to apply, to such a state of affairs as the present revolution has brought about.

Let me illustrate further the absence of all reason to support the proposition that, until a formal acknowledgment of the existence of the Confederate States by the United States, the official acts of the former cannot be regarded as having any validity, or as affording protection to their citizens. Go beyond our own borders, to countries where the sovereign is an individual, with fixed hereditary right to reign, and where the doctrine established is that which I repudiate, "Once a sovereign, always a sovereign," and that the sovereign rules by divine right and cannot innocently be superseded. If the doctrine affirmed in this case be true, that to give validity to the acts of a Government established by a revolution the preceding Government must have recognized its existence, then the world will be sadly at fault. Show me where the King of Naples has acknowledged the kingship of Victor Emanuel? Show me where the sovereigns of Parma and Modena and Tuscany have consented to the establishment of the new government in their territory?

But the people have voted in the new Government, and they maintain it; and Victor Emanuel is, in spite of King Bomba, *de facto*, King of Naples; and Victor's commissions to his army and navy, and his letters of marque, will be recognized in every court in every enlightened nation.

Even in Italy, the Courts of Justice would, when the case arose that required it, enforce the same regard to the existing Government as if the former sovereigns had formally relinquished their claims to sovereignty. Again, I say, the act of the people is entitled to more weight in an inquiry, "What is the Government?" than the seal and recognition of the former sovereign.

As Americans, imbued with correct opinions upon the relation of the governed to the governing, your hearts reject the theory propounded by this prosecution, and concur with me.

To vindicate your opinion you will find the defendants herein "not guilty."

Come to our own recent history. Texas was one of the States of the Union which is called Mexico. Texas seceded from that Union. She declared her independence, and during a struggle of arms became a *de facto* Government. Mexico would not recognize her independence, and continued her intention to restore her to the old Union. The United States, however, recognized the right of Texas to her independence, and invited her to enter into our Union, and did incorporate her in that Union in defiance of the doctrine of Mexico, "once a sovereign, always a sovereign until independence shall be acknowledged." We then denounced that doctrine, but now we seem ready to embrace its odious sentiments. We placed our declaration on record before the world, that Texas, by her act alone, unauthorized and unrecognized by the Central Government of Mexico, had become a sovereign and independent State, invested with full power to dispose of her territory and the allegiance of her citizens, and, as a sovereign State, to enter into compacts with other States.

Have not the Courts of the United States sanctioned that proceeding? Suppose that Hungary, or Venice, or Ireland shall separate from their present empires and establish Governments for themselves, what will be our position? Let your verdict in this case determine.

It is, perhaps, well, now, to recur to the law of nations.

That is a part of the common law of England and of this country. We may claim in this Court the benefit of its enlightened and humane provisions, as if they were embodied in our statutes. There are circumstances in the history of every nation, when the law of nations supervenes upon the statutes and controls their literal interpretation.

If the case becomes one to which the law of nations is applicable, it thereby is removed from the pale of the statute. Such is the present case. In the seceded States a Government has been established. It has been hitherto maintained by force, it is true, as against the United States, but by consent of the people at home; and both sides have taken up arms, and large armies now stand arrayed against each other, in support of their respective Governments. It is all-important to the cause of justice, and to the honor of the United States, to see that in their official acts, in their treatment of prisoners, either of the army or captured privateers, they conform to the rules recognized as binding, under similar circumstances, by civilized and Christian nations, and sanctioned by the authoritative publicists of the world. I will recall your attention to extracts from Vattel, and with the firmest confidence that they will vindicate my views, that the defendants are entitled to be held as prisoners of war, and not as criminals awaiting trial:

Vattel, Book III, chapter 18, section 292:

When a party is formed in a State, which no longer obeys the sovereign, and is of strength sufficient to make a head against him, or when, in a republic, the nation is divided into two opposite factions, and both sides take arms, this is called a *civil war*. Some confine this term only to a just insurrection of subjects against an unjust sovereign, to distinguish this lawful resistance from *rebellion*, which is an open and unjust resistance; but what appellation will they give to a war in a Republic torn by two factions, or, in a Monarchy, between two competitors for a crown? Use appropriates the term of civil war to every war between the members of one and the same political society.

Subsequent clause in same section:

Therefore, whenever a numerous party thinks it has a right to resist the sovereign, and finds itself able to declare that opinion, sword in hand, the war is to be carried on between them in the same manner as between two different nations; and they are to leave open the same means for preventing enormous violences and restoring peace.

Last clause in section 295:

But when a nation becomes divided into two parties absolutely independent and no longer acknowledging a common superior, the State is dissolved, and the war betwixt the two parties, in every respect, is the same with that in a public war between two different nations. Whether a Republic be torn into two factious parties, each pretending to form the body of the State, or a Kingdom be divided betwixt two competitors to the Crown, the nation is thus severed into two parties, who will mutually term each other rebels. Thus there are two bodies pretending to be absolutely independent, and who having no judge, they decide the quarrel by arms, like two different nations. The obligation of observing the common laws is therefore absolute, indispensable to both parties, and the same which the law of nature obliges all nations to observe between State and State.

If it be between part of the citizens, on one side, and the sovereign, with those who continue in obedience to him, on the other, it is sufficient that the malcontents have some reasons for taking arms, to give this disturbance the name of *civil war*, and not that of *rebellion*. This last term is applied only to such an insurrection against lawful authority as is void of all appearance of justice. The sovereign, indeed, never fails to term all subjects rebels openly resisting him; but when these become of strength sufficient to oppose him, so that he finds himself compelled to make war regularly on them, he must be contented with the term of civil war.

Clause of section 293:

A civil war breaks the bands of society and government, or at least it suspends their force and effect. It produces in the nation two independent parties, considering each other as enemies, and acknowledging no common judge. Therefore, of necessity, these two parties must, at least for a time, be considered as forming two separate bodies—two distinct people. Though one of them may be in the wrong in breaking up the continuity of the State—to rise against lawful authority—they are not the less divided in fact. Besides, who shall judge them? On earth they have no common superior. Thus they are in the case of two nations who, having a dispute which they cannot adjust, are compelled to decide it by force of arms.

First clause in section 294:

Things being thus situated, it is evident that the common laws of war, those maxims of humanity, moderation and probity which we have before enumerated and recommended, are, in civil wars, to be observed on both sides. The same reasons on which the obligation between State and State is founded, render them even more necessary in the unhappy circumstance when two incensed parties are destroying their common country. Should the sovereign conceive he has a right to hang up his prisoners as rebels, the opposite party will make reprisals; if he does not religiously observe the capitulations and all the conventions made with his enemies, they will no longer rely on his word; should he burn and destroy, they will follow his example; the war will become cruel and horrid; its calamities will increase on the nation.

Remember you are an American Jury; that your fathers were revolutionists; that they judged for themselves what Government they would have, and they did not hesitate to break off from their mother Government, even though there were penalties of statutes with which they were threatened. And remember, also, that from the beginning of your fathers' Revolution, they claimed that they were not liable to the treatment of offenders against British statutes, but that the Colonies were a nation, and entitled to belligerent rights—one of which was, that if any of their army or navy fell into the hands of the British Army, they should be held as prisoners of war.

Your fathers never admitted that the *Continental Army* were liable to punishment with the *halter*, if taken prisoners.

To be sure, the statute of Great Britain, literally construed, so provided, but the law of nations had supervened, and rendered that statute no longer applicable. Vindicate your respect for your fathers' claims, by extending the same immunities to the prisoners at the bar, whose situation is analogous to that of our fathers.

At the commencement of the Revolution, preceding the Declaration of Independence in 1776, the Colonies became each a separate sovereignty. That became the *status*, with some, without documentary declaration to that effect; but most of them have left on record positive enunciations of their assumption of independence and sovereignty as States, unconnected with the proceedings of any other State.* They entered into a Confederation as independent States, declaring, however, distinctly, in a separate article, that each State retained its own sovereignty, freedom, and independence, and every power of jurisdiction and right not expressly delegated to the United States in Congress assembled. And at the close of the war, when the treaty of peace was made, recognizing the independence of the Colonies, each State was named individually. I have never been able to discover when and where, since that period, any State has surrendered its sovereignty, or deprived itself of its right to act as a sovereign. The Constitution suspends the exercise of some of the functions of sovereignty by the States, but it does not deprive them of their power to maintain their rights as sovereigns, when and how they shall think best, if that Constitution shall, in their judgment, be broken or perverted as a delegated trust of power.

Listen, therefore, to the better voices whispering to each heart. Remember, the honor and consistency of the United States are involved in this case. By a conviction of the defendants, you condemn the Revolution of your ancestors; you sustain the theories of the worst courtiers who surrounded George III in his war to put down the rebellion; you will appear to the world as stigmatizing revolutionists with the names of outlaws and pirates,

---

* An interesting fact, not published previously, I believe, has been communicated to the public recently by Mr. Dawson, of New York, a historical student and writer of great research and culture. He has found an original minute in the records of the General Court of Massachusetts, whereby, as early as May 1st, 1776, the sovereignty and independence of that Colony was declared formally. (Copy of footnote on page 230 of the printed volume of records.)

which is the phraseology applied to them by Austria and Russia; you will violate the law of nations; you will appear to be merely wreaking vengeance, and not making legitimate war; you will henceforth preclude your nation from offering a word of sympathy to people abroad who may be struggling for their independence, and who have heretofore always turned their hearts to you. You can never, having punished your revolutionists on the gallows, send an invitation to the unfortunate champions of independent Government in the old world. Kossuth will reply: "The American maxim is that of Francis Joseph, and of Marshal Haynau." You cannot say "Godspeed!" to Ireland, if she shall secede. No! as you love the honor of your country, and her place among nations, refuse to pronounce these men pirates.

Tell your Government to wage manly, open, chivalric war on the field and ocean, and thus or not at all; that dishonor is worse even than disunion. Stain not your country's hand with blood. If I were your enemy, I would wish no worse for your names, than to record your verdict against these prisoners. Leave no such record against your country in her annals; and when the passions of the hour shall have subsided, your verdict of acquittal of Thomas H. Baker and the other defendants herein, will be recalled by you with satisfaction, and will receive the approval of your countrymen.

❖

Algernon Sydney Sullivan presided at the reception given by the Arcadian Club in 1874, to Dr. Isaac I. Hayes, the Arctic Explorer. Introducing Dr. Hayes Mr. Sullivan said:

When, as tonight, amid the placid scenes of Arcadia, a vista is opened through which the eye catches glimpses of latitudes where millennial winters have piled ice onto ice—mountains which prop the incumbent sky; where all the weird and tireless spirits of the tempest emboss the hills with frosted crystal; where every

promontory becomes a lens which holds the hues of a rainbow
visible prisoners in its bosom; where the elements contend as
demons to keep hidden their guarded secrets; we turn to each
other and ask who are these, the bold adventurers whom we
discern toiling through that arena of peril? Are they, indeed,
the very demigods of Grecian fable who realize to our senses that
the lustre and heroic inspirations of classic antiquity re-embody
themselves over and over again to each age which is willing to
fight the dual tournament for refinement on the one hand, and
against materialistic tendencies on the other? Is there here
recounting itself a new Iliad of contest and a fresh Odyssey of
adventure? Is it fancy, or do they with stately step actually
pass before the enthroned genius of all science with sentiments of
proud self-devotion, exclaiming *Morituri Te Salutant?*

Noble band! Ye need no heralds! Hail! And honor! To
Perry and McClintock and Franklin and MacClure and Osborne
and Kane and Markham and Hall and all their co-laborers, last,
and chief to us, our guest this evening, Dr. Isaac I. Hayes, whom
I now introduce. As we welcome him, let us announce our
earnest wish, and as we believe, the wish of all New York, that
the Congress of the United States shall promptly and liberally
equip an expedition to the North Pole and entrust its command
to him as the true master of the situation.

❖

*An address delivered in 1875 by Algernon Sydney Sullivan in the
lecture room of the original Church of the Strangers, New York
City, for the benefit of the work of that church*

The Disposition Becoming to a Neighbor.

Only that history is true history which might also be fable or
poetry. A good test of perfectness in either is—would it be translatable into the other and retain its individual lineaments? A

Greek said: "A picture is a silent poem, a poem is a speaking picture." So every action which has significant character at once incarnates itself in the personal consciousness of all humanity. As soon as it is discerned the whole realm of nature is in harmony with it, and each man recognizes it, so that irresistibly he exclaims, "'Twas I did, or felt, that." This absorption of all into one, this enlargement of one into all, this discovery of an ocean's tide in each raindrop, this time-beat in the vein of each individual with the pulse in the life-current of humanity as a unit, is the only stairway to science, to art, to poetry, to religion, yea, to continued existence of our race itself. But though this is the threshold of all truths, it is also the goal of all truths. The philosopher cradles his earliest enquiry in it, and after long and curious cycles of speculation he ends his pilgrimage at the same shrine, with confirmed and enlarged views of the dignity and the unity of humanity. It is notable how the spirit of modern enquiry is engrossed with labors to illustrate this truth.

The students read on inspired pages, "The whole earth was of one language and of one speech," and straightway they begin research to analyze the different families of language. With delight and surprise they disclose hundreds of roots, identical in form and nature, which remain as constituent elements in different languages that have no traceable connected origin. They are discovered not to be interjections, nor can they be imitations. Says a beautiful writer, "Historically studied, the science of language leads us up to that highest summit, from whence we see into the very dawn of man's life on earth, and we perceive that no amount of variety in the material or formal elements of speech, is inconsistent with the admission of one common origin." The heart of man answereth to man; the language is like the ring which comes from striking different pieces of the same kind of metal.

Let us tonight turn our ear to catch the tone of one poor human heart, which echoes to us from the shadow-caves of the old centuries. As it vibrates let us see if our hearts be consonant. It seems to come from a lonely desert between the Mount of

JEREMIAH SULLIVAN
Judge of the Supreme Court of the State of Indiana, 1837–1846

Olives and the Plains of Jericho. Outlaws lurked there, and their frequent crimes had given it the title of the *Bloody Way*. A Jew, with staff and girded loins, goes down that road. Suddenly he is attacked, he is wounded, he is stripped, he is left half dead; his cry could reach no friend or neighbor; his scattered thoughts flit homeward to wife and children.

Pitiable plight indeed! Is it hopeless? No, he lies near the highway, and soon enough to save him some wayfarer will come with means of relief. How wistfully the eyes of the fainting sufferer glanced along the plain towards the mountain. At length he beholds a single traveller and a smile of hope brightens his eye. It is of no moment that it is a stranger; it is a fellow man and that is sufficient. "My distress," says the sufferer, "my destitution will melt away every bar, and the mute appeal of my wounds will be irresistible." As the stranger draws nearer, the wounded man, faint with excess of joy, closes his eyes as he hears the sandals sound on the stones near him and in an instant he expects the tender hands to lift him up and helpful sympathy to almost restore him. A moment! And do his startled ears tell aright? The steps go away from him! He looks, and the pangs of his despair feel a new quivering as he beholds the tunic dress, marks of the Sons of Aaron, which is on the shoulders of him who carries hope away as he passes unheeding, by.

Dismayed, he becomes lost in doubt. Have my senses deceived me? Mine own countryman, my teacher, my judge—to pass me by? What a shadow of dark thoughts settles down upon his soul, and then what wild fancies fly around him on fever born wings! At length the road shows another man upon his journey. The wounded sufferer has gone through that experience that withers the heart. He waits now with hesitation; he desires; he dares never cherish hope in man as formerly. The pilgrim is a son of Levi. He has finished his weekly course of service in the Temple and now is returning to his family in the country. Perhaps he has yet lingering in his ears the Psalms of the holy service. His thoughts are full of his peaceful home whither he journeys. The half-dead sufferer watches; the Levite is at the place. Oh! Blessed opportunity! He comes towards me! He is moved by compassionate interest! He looks upon me! Ah! That will be enough; he will save me. But no! Surely phantoms mock me! He too passes by on the other side.

Alas! My poor, bleeding, abandoned, despairing brother, thy groan as it struggled from thy bosom is audible now, and thou still liest in the desert,—and that desert is here! The Plains of Jericho are around us tonight. Son of Levi, child of a devout family! Stop, turn back! Bethink thee what thou hast passed by. Thou has passed away from thy better self; thou art passing away from thine inheritance as a minister of charity; thou art putting in the caves of thy memory a hideous spectre. Thou art putting lead on all thy winged hopes; thou art summoning fears to hover between thine eyes and thy children's future. Thou art passing away from the loving Father of all who is beside thy stricken brother.

Thou art planting a thorn where a lily wished to grow in thy heart. Thou art biting with wintry winds the breast which the bandits almost drained. In the great division which is taking place thou art enlisting on the side of the unmerciful. Thou art dethroning as thy King the Divine, and setting thy choice on selfish fears and selfish convenience.

Thou sayest to the parched desert, "Our kindred bosoms shall open with no sweet fountains."

Thy lips were sealed; thou hast not made any professions, but this incident by the way has unmasked thy nature!

> He that good thinketh, Good will do,
> And God will help him thereunto,
> For was never good work wrought
> Without beginning of good thought.

The frowning rocks which are the scene of noble actions seem to enwreathe themselves with beautiful fancies. Nature is never dead and inharmonious to a soul overflowing with benevolent feeling. Bleak and voiceless were the stones and the earth and the sky, that day, to our Levite. With sensibilities deafened to all nature's sympathies his sandaled foot plashed in the sand, leaving an impress there to be levelled out of sight by the first gust of wind. 'Twas a true symbol of his heart. It was not granite—a sight of wretchedness stopped him. He came across the road, he actually contemplated the case. The angels pressed their pinions on his heart but its earthly dust held the image only for an instant, and he passed on out of the golden sunbeams of charity into the cavern of selfish musings.

My lecture this evening is to crystallize for you and myself one idea,—the looking, and then the passing. It is that supreme moment of debate, which all New York holds with itself daily, in which I would have my one word take voice.

It happened that near midnight a messenger came for me to visit a man in a prison cell. He sat close to the grating and, resting his face upon his hands still crimson with another's blood, he told his story. It was full of that interest which blazes out of man's wrongs and man's pride and man's revenges. I said little, for I was oppressed by the scene and all the circumstances. As I turned away I saw a poor woman being led into the basement, and I followed. The room was not large, was lighted with gas, had a well-heated stove, and along one side was a raised wooden platform sloping to the wall. On the platform without bed or pillow, save a little bundled clothing, seven or eight women were reclining. On the floor were four groups, each of women and children. The women were crouched in that posture which tells so plainly of wretchedness—the head almost upon the knees —and each child with body on the floor, nestled its sleepy, forlorn, but trustful little head in its mother's lap, and clutched its little hands in the mother's dress. The similarity in the appearance of each group was striking. The listless mothers were strangers and apparently took no notice of one another. The resemblance only arose from their having walked through like paths of poverty and trial. The maternal instinct and love were there, but they made little positive expression. The woman exhibited herself in each case, a resigned, patient, enduring prop. She expected of course the children to cling. She was ever ready; but it was painful to discern in all that it was felt to be a mysterious destiny. Submission was there, but the joy and the life had gone as brown leaves in a chaplet. The bundling of two large cloths upon the babes told well enough of the mothers' brooding care to keep away the cold from the tender limbs, indifferent to appearances.

I was in the room for homeless wanderers, at the station house.

One of those women was a widow whose husband had been drowned a year before. Left in destitution she had struggled with true woman's courage to support herself and children. Herself of good family and a once comfortable home, the trials of life seemed not to have been received with bitterness. In the past she had borne her burden well, but when I spoke to her she was in gloomy despondency to the very nethermost depths. After a period of unusual distress and sickness she had addressed her first appeal for help to one who she had supposed would give ear. Had he stayed away she could have borne it. But herein was the gall and agony and prostration of it all; he came to the place, awakening hope. He looked; expectation nursed, he syllabled words of sympathy; for a moment sweet as the sunrise music of Memnon's statue, and then—he passed by on the other side. He went away with a promise never fulfilled, and the bleakness of the desert widened in her heart until it reached the horizon.

It is not sorrow which breaks the heart; it is the sense of help withheld where help is seen to be needed and possible. I have sometimes thought the explanation of it was here. The sufferer has all the chords of nature highly wrought. His desires have produced a glamor in which his own imagination has made a deceitful flattery of himself. Impressed with the happiness which could come to him from the good deeds of another, he fancies what happiness he would feel in relieving others. Indeed he thinks the human breast—his own precisely like others—could feel no otherwise, and for one brief hour his estimate of humanity includes much of divinity. Beings of a higher order bend down near man.

How near he touches on the Angel's wing!
Which is the Seraph, which the child of clay?

Then, when the disappointment befalls his expectations, his
first sad look at his fellow man is followed by introverted thought,
and he loses faith in himself.   What more is left for him to lose?
It is a curious illustration of my notion that human nature
cannot maintain an unshaken will under suffering, if hope passes
by on the other side; that perhaps the grandest of all Greek
tragedies impersonates the elevated claims and aspirations of
humanity under the myth of a divinity whom he calls Prometheus.
The grand genius of Aeschylus, which "always did right without knowing it," as his contemporaries said of him, realized that
the scheme of never-ending suffering and never-ending resolution required a God.   He knew no other scale for the measure-
ment of this matchless power.   Exiled to a naked rock on the
shore of the encircling ocean, he places this self-devoting divinity,
chained fast by inexorable power beneath the rendings of a vul-
ture.   The poet even fortifies his resolution as he atones for his
disobedience, by attributing to him the consciousness that that
disobedience consisted in the benevolent attempt to give perfection to the human race.   We have the first silence of Prometheus,
while he is chained down under the harsh inspection of Force,
whose threats serve only to excite a useless compassion in Vulcan,
who carries them into execution; then his solitary complaints;
the arrival of the tender Ocean Nymphs, whose kind but dis-
heartening sympathy induces him to give vent to his feelings, to
relate the causes of his fall, and to reveal the future; the visit of
the ancient Oceanus, a kindred God of the race of Titans, who,
under the pretext of a zealous attachment to his cause, advises
him to submit to Jupiter, and who is on that account dismissed
with proud contempt; the introduction of another victim of the
same tyranny from which Prometheus himself suffers; his prophecy of himself that he is to receive a deliverer after many ages;
and at last in the very act of still refusing to disclose his fateful

secrets, the earth yawns, and with the rock to which he is chained he is swallowed up into the abyss of the nether world.

It is, then, this principle of evil agency, which feathers every shaft in the quiver of indifference to others' want that, by contrast, lifts work like that of the woman's free dormitory to the rank of a grand moral power.   It matters not that its rooms are few and small.   Roofless, homeless, wandering sister, whoever thou art, and wherever in this cavern-filled desert towards Jericho, whether thy cry be aloud, or thou art still and stunned at thy desolate state; whether the million-handed Briarens of New York have left thee half dead, or thou art a waif drifting from another wreck; whether it be thy weakness or thy errors, *There's a light in the window for thee.*   Even, my sister, shall thy weary limbs fail to reach the doorsill, still the beacon was waved to thee, a loving, kindly message.   Thou has not been passed by; give not place, therefore, to bitter thoughts of others, and cling closer than ever to hope and trust in thyself.

In our journeyings in life's desert places, we must not forget the hearts whose mourning drapery hides itself from the world. Let me leave with you the picture of one of them as she draws it herself.   Such as these pass not by, my friends.

❖

In the Tilden and Hendricks Democratic Campaign, a great Ratification Meeting was held in New York City, on the night of November 2, 1876.   Algernon Sydney Sullivan was chairman and presided at the grand stand in Union Square.   He opened the meeting with this brief address:

FELLOW CITIZENS:

The beauty of this autumn night, the magnificence of yonder passing pageant, cannot divert our thoughts from the serious object of this assembly of the people.   You have had only too much ground for complaint of bad administration of your Government. It is not merely burdensome taxes, official frauds, and profligate waste that you complain of. A free people can endure much of these and yet not feel downcast. To rouse men to the pitch of excitement we witness at present, the popular heart must have apprehensions in regard to the highest interests of the State and as to public morals.

That these are in peril; nay, that they have been hurt and stained by the Republican Party is the real indictment we bring against them. They have poisoned the very founts of the political system. They have wiped out the salutary and proud faith in the minds of the people that their Federal Government was the type of honor and justice and fidelity to the laws and constitution.

They have brought the heads of good citizens low in sorrow and shame. They have not shrunk, in these latter days, from laying impious hands upon our sacred ark, the ballot box, and when the ballots of our people next Tuesday drop from their hands, it will not be as in the good days of old, like the silent snowflakes, to execute the will of freemen and (I speak with reverence) the will of God; but, the tramp of armed men and the click of firelocks will make ominous echo. Soldiers of the American Army! When you march with your bayonets to violate or obstruct the freedom of the polls, muffle your drums! For you move to the grave of your country's liberty! Encrape your standards, and let the blare of your trumpets sound the dirge! For your swords are at Freedom's throat.

I beg the federal authorities to pause before it is too late. I invoke inspiration from the noble souls who seem to look encouragingly upon us from yon majestic statue of Washington, from this nearer statue of Lafayette, and the third in the noble group, which surrounds our platform, the revered Lincoln.

My friends, let us, in the example of these departed and heart-enshrined patriots, do our duty. Tilden and Hendricks represent patriotic duty. I hope and believe in the people, and I see many auspicious signs. Elect Tilden and Hendricks and we will have a rescued constitution, a purified official life, disenthralled states, peace between all sections, a free ballot box and a redeemed national name. For the pean of such a victory we may adopt Whittier's lines:

> Ring, O Bells,
> Every stroke exulting tells
> Of the burial hour of crime.

❖

Another address made by Algernon Sydney Sullivan in the Tilden and Hendricks Campaign, 1876

FELLOW CITIZENS:

The best hopes of our country are now identified with the full success of the St. Louis Convention. That body reviewed the widespread extravagance and corruption in legislation and administration, and it pointed out how much of this was due to the fact that the Republican Party had fallen into the clutches of corrupt men, and how much to the fact that the party had become incurably diseased of false political theories. It depicted the results in growing social demoralization, and in burdens upon the property and industries of the people. It proclaimed its purpose to stop this waste, to punish and root out this fraud, and to have the Government managed according to a wiser and purer political code, which it then published. As to that platform of principles, I will say, I have read much in books of the opinions and recommendations of the best public men, their speeches and carefully prepared state papers; I have listened to the eminent and patriotic men of all parties, in my time, and I have never heard or read a declaration more entirely expressing a lofty, honorable and wise public policy than that of the Democratic platform.

CHARLOTTE RUDESEL CUTLER
Wife of Jeremiah and Mother of Algernon Sydney Sullivan

"He who aims at the sun may not hit it, but he will shoot higher than he who aims at a lower mark," is an old Persian saying, and it is an inspiring maxim for us. As became men who were in earnest, the democracy then asked themselves who, if made chief magistrate, will most faithfully execute the laws, be a terror to evil-doers, and bring to an end the shameful abuses which the Republican Party has inflicted upon us. More than the fate of a mere party hung upon the answer to the question. It involved all that ennobles and justifies party life, the preservation of any civil government worthy of a free people. The reform Democrats showed their courage and confidence in the high spirit of their party. Its aim was reform: reform in men, in platforms, in measures, in official usages and theories, in parties. Yes, reform in our party. They turned their eyes to a Democrat who is a more intrepid reformer than Bristow, one who has clearer, broader and more practical purposes than the self-styled independent reformers, who, at the call of Mr. Carl Schurz, met at the Fifth Avenue Hotel; a man who was, and is, independent even in his own party; a man who is always honest; a man of extensive information in public affairs, and familiar with the best lessons of political science; and a man thoroughly imbued with the spirit of our American system of government. Above all, they recognized a man who is almost fanatical in his creed, that social purity and official honesty are the only conditions upon which our institutions can endure. They knew that this man had been tried in public station, and had proven by action as a reformer what he would do and what he can do better than any other man in this country. Need I otherwise name Samuel J. Tilden? The democracy of New York ratifies his nomination and will bear him and his cause onward to triumph.

My Fellow Citizens: Contrast this with another picture, the Republican Convention at Cincinnati. They refused to enter the fight against corruption, much less to lead it. Benjamin J. Bristow, a tried and practical reformer, was a candidate before them. His nomination would have meant washing their hands of the present corrupt system, and taking the control of the

Government away from the friends of Grant and of his systems. Words would not do that. Their acts must be significant and unmistakable. Professing to have crossed the river to stay on the reform side, a distrustful people expected them to prove their sincerity by burning the bridge behind them. The representative men of the party were all present, they who made it that which it is, and who are now to decide what it shall be in the future. What stand did they take? Did they manifest the heart, the hopes, the pluck of reform? Did they condemn a single measure in the past? Did they denounce a single criminal in the ranks of their party? Did they assert that with a new lease of power they would do otherwise than in the past? No candid man affirms they did.

The man who held the heart and the strength of the convention with himself was ex-Speaker Blaine. He had constructed this model platform: *In your public office, as Speaker of the House, make serviceable decisions for the rich lobby, and use them as a plea for financial favors in return.* He and his devoted followers were the blood and bone of this national council of the party. The few friends of reform were pushed to the corner. Scarcely one sixth of the convention voted for Bristow. The friends of the present corrupt system triumphed. Bristow and his system were spurned. The ruling cabal said we will have a candidate acceptable to us so we shall not be disturbed. They designated Mr. Hayes, a man of estimable personal character, but they never intended to have a Hayes administration. *Stat nominis umbra,* and that name is *Grantism.* When they rejected Bristow, they declared we reject any man of whom he is a type. Men who punish revenue frauds "need not apply." This qualification for candidacy they made only too plain. This was not chance, for the Convention knew how to be ambiguous when they extended it.

Let me illustrate: Last year our Chamber of Commerce held an election for President and other officers. Samuel Babcock was at the head of the Hard-money Ticket, and George Opdyke led what was known as the Soft-money Ticket. Mr. Opdyke was defeated, but he adheres to his financial theories; and we know he is a very intelligent and earnest man. Recently an old merchant met him and said, "How is it, that you, a 'Soft-money' man, support Mr. Hayes on a 'Hard-money' platform?" Mr. Opdyke denied that the Cincinnati platform is a "Hard-money" platform, saying that the "Hard-money" amendment was voted down. Thus we have it, the "Hards" and the "Softs" each interpreting the Cincinnati resumption plank in harmony with his own wishes, and all equally honest. The fact is, the Convention intended to cover their financial plank with a very large chameleon to suit differing eyes.

On the other hand, the democracy intend to move unswervingly towards resumption by economy, preparation and wise finance, and to keep the public honor unsullied by a single stain of repudiation, under which the Republican party have clouded the fair fame of the country.

When I hear some of the Republican orators promising reform with the election of Hayes, in view of the record of their party and its present condition, I can only call to mind a story told by my friend W. J. Florence, the comedian. Jerry Houlihan was a waiter in a Dublin chophouse; Jerry's only fault was an inordinate desire for whiskey, and this unlucky circumstance had caused the poor fellow to lose his place at least once a month. But being a good servant when sober, and a great favorite with the college boys who frequented the place, he was reinstated at their request. One evening, Jerry being decidedly groggy, a group of collegians determined (if possible) to bring him to a sense of his degradation. To accomplish this, one of the party picked up a newspaper, and in Jerry's hearing read an imaginary paragraph as follows: "Thomas Johnson, a waiter at the Blue Boar Tavern, met with a terrible death. Last night in his endeavor to blow out a candle, his breath being highly charged with alcoholic gases (he being a confirmed drunkard) at once communicated with the flame, and the poor fellow was burned to a cinder. He leaves a wife and family to mourn his untimely end." "I beg your pardon, gentlemen," said Jerry, "but do you mean to say this man's breath took fire from trying to blow out the candle?" "Yes, Jerry, it is a common occurrence." "Oh! Murder!" says Jerry, "and how many times have I disgraced meself and me family by me love for the drink!—I am a reformed man from this minute." "That's right, Jerry," echoed the party, "reform before it's too late." "I will, gentlemen; get me a prayer book." One was brought from a servant's room. "Now, Jerry," said the gentlemen, "don't flinch, old boy!" "I won't!" says Jerry; "for here I swear upon this Holy Book, that from this blessed minute, for the balance of my life, I'll never try to blow out a candle."

Under all the circumstances poor Jerry must have been a delegate in the Cincinnati Convention, to draw up its platform pledges of reform.

❖

An address by Algernon Sydney Sullivan before the Young Men's Hebrew Association, November 14, 1877

The Influence of Orientalism on American Thought.

The day is not remote in this country when speculative inquiry and every form of philosophic investigation will find their largest theatre. This activity will be in a large degree controversial; partly because that is the law of advance in truth, and partly because from every source science is ushered upon our attention in a dual form, questioned as well as questioning. We must take one side of the issue or we must comprehend both with a view to reconcile and harmonize them. These questions to which I allude have a genealogy. They are, under new forms, or enlarged development, manifestations of queries which were in the germs of thought in the earliest age of our race. So far as there is literature we can trace them.

The metempsychosis of error or of truth is itself a subject of profound study, and as instructive as it is curious. The first labor of any thinker is to trace from its earliest beginnings and through its changing phases to its present form the postulates upon which he purposes to add his own reflections. If, besides discovering the modifications to which a given thought has been subjected, he may happily have found when and where it germinated, and that one of the conditions of its birth was the nature and character of the race by whom it was evolved and announced, we see at once how important in the field of enquiry becomes the history of race. I say the history of a race because the events of that history may blend with and color the idea in its progressive development.

These considerations will have peculiar force in America. Inheriting its ideas from the literature made up not only by individuals of separate nations, but from nations who themselves were of the blood of commingled races, our country is to be the point for a new assembling for all peoples and under circumstances so changed from the condition under which unions have taken place in past history, that the relative strength, virtue, creative power and wealth of endowment of each will be left to be tested anew. We may see the gradations made in the past reversed. We may come together not by war, and there will be no element of conqueror and conquered to give advantage to one opinion. There will not be the case of a migrating people, moulded by the laws of a distant climate, settling among a resident population already strengthened or enfeebled by its climate, to contend under this inequality for supremacy.

Here, the climate and physical laws will be new to all and alike for all. It is a common advantage or disadvantage. Here, there will be no question of caste, or even of toleration, to operate with its repressing influence upon sensitive natures, of ten more disastrous than violent persecution. All shades of opinion, provided they do not antagonize society itself, exist by absolute and equal right. They will be *fancy free*, and not as is sometimes said, *tolerated*. The idea of toleration, in the usual sense, is itself intolerable and hateful. There will be, in this country, an opening of the lists for the freest intellectual combat mankind has ever known.

The history of the world furnishes no instance of a nation absolutely free from external influences upon its civil and social life. Attempts at isolation did not avail. It was realized only in measurable degree, and for limited periods. The difference in degree changed the facts for observation, just far enough to assist the philosopher, by his comparisons, to verify and measure more accurately the force and character of the influences which are supposed to modify national ideas. China, with non-intercourse or limited intercourse, we usually quote as furnishing the standard, which may be called zero, from which to mark the gauge for all people between themselves and the nations that most freely visit, and are visited by their fellowmen. But even the nations which appear to have been the most fixed, and for the longest periods secluded and unchanging, nevertheless find their historic page recounting the events of their old migrations, their conquests or their subjugation, involving a commingling of races or other change in influential surroundings. When closely studied, their interior history is the usual chronicle of contending forces working out the problem of what the resultant national character shall be.

The positive influences which change and bend sentiment in the minds of men will be seen to be as traceable as the simple fact in nature—that trees by the sea incline all in the direction of the prevailing winds. For our purpose tonight it is needless to speculate upon the qualities in the human mind by virtue of which it ceases to be master of itself, changing with its surroundings. The fact is visible. To trace its course, its law, and above all, its limits, is a task in study as fruitful in interest as it is important. You have heard it explained, perhaps, by the illustration borrowed from an eminent physiologist: "Some believe that every impression made upon the material substance of the brain produces a permanent change in its structure, and that one impression never completely effaces another; that the mind can, as it were, see all of them, and that what the mind or soul thus bears, death itself can not destroy."

Dr. Draper's explanation of certain physical phenomena are adduced to give countenance to the theory of permanent impressions upon the brain structure. He says: "If on a cold, polished piece of metal, any object, as a wafer, is laid, and the metal then breathed upon, and when the moisture has had time to disappear, the wafer be thrown off, though now upon the polished surface the most critical inspection can discover no trace of any form, yet if we breathe upon it again, a spectral figure of the wafer comes into view, and this may be done again and again. Nay, even more, if the polished metal be carefully put aside, where nothing can deteriorate its surface, and be so kept for many months, on breathing again upon it, the shadowy form again emerges. Or, if a sheet of paper on which a key or other object is laid, be carried for a few moments into the sunshine, and then instantaneously viewed in the dark, the key being simultaneously removed, a fading spectre of the key on the paper will be seen, and if the paper be put away where nothing can disturb it, and so kept for many months, if it then be carried into a dark place, and laid on a piece of hot metal, the spectre of the key will come forth. In the case of bodies more highly phosphorescent than paper, the spectres of many different objects, which may have been in succession laid thereupon, will, on warming, emerge in their proper place.

"Indeed," said the professor, "I believe that a shadow never falls upon a wall without leaving thereupon its permanent trace, which might be made visible by resorting to proper processes. But, whether the impressions of sense be permanently fixed in the brain or not, there is no reason for supposing that any perceptions which the mind has once taken notice of can ever be lost."

Without adopting any physiological theory, it is enough for us to consider that all experience seems to consist in recalling the remains of old ideas upon which the image of a new idea is printing its spectral form, and both make up for us the present existing reality. All combined, they are our conscious selves.

The effect of today is a cause with tomorrow. Events, to our consciousness, stand to each other in the order of perpetual pro-creation. Each Present is the womb of every Future. The Now foretells and ordains the Hereafter. The minutes, as they pass, are audible with prophecy to the intelligent listener, delineating coming events. Now unite to these thoughts that of Race with its transmissible physical qualities—the well-known facts of hereditary capacity and tendency of thought; of unbroken repro-duction of the same temperament and disposition; of the same appetites, the same passions, the same love of order, or of its oppo-site; the same dominance of spiritual or of material taste; the same elevation or dethronement of the sensual; and, above all, the notion of the destiny of man and of his origin—the most absolute and lasting of all the conceptions of the human intellect; and we begin to see how the problem of humanity, as it shall be investigated and worked out in America, will never be perfected without the moulding influences of transmissible race tendencies. These must be recognized as factors in making the result, but they must be ascertained and defined, combated or encouraged; and where they constitute the equipment fitted for the grand achievements that are at hand, the living representatives must accept the honored trust. They must quit themselves like men. The despositaries of a truth must never hide it. As a kind mother America summons, as an absolute sovereign she commands, each of her children and subjects to bring their trib-ute to her intellectual storehouse. May I suggest to you, young gentlemen, something which she expects of you? May I try to point to a grand mission which the hour and the field set before you?

In the movement of humanity, the problems of life, as I said, have not changed, but men have not always recognized them alike or concurred as to their due rank in importance. Remem-ber, so as to keep this distinguishing character clear, that European civilization is a complex creation; a resultant, not of its own evolution, nor holding only to its traditions in common with the entire human family, but seeking and receiving at important

Drawing by W. E. Mears

THE SULLIVAN HOME IN MADISON, INDIANA

Showing the original house built in 1817, and the later additions at the rear

epochs, fresh combination with Asia. Migrating nations would take on many modifications in an European home. Their characteristics seemed as distinct and firmly set as if they were original instead of being in a large degree adopted. The migrating nations had merged. There was a discernible fact which properly might be called European character, at the period when the settlement of America began. The European nations had become the masters of the world and of its wealth, by their arms and commerce. Like masters they were dogmatic, absolute, and intolerant. They were repellant towards aggressive influences from beyond themselves, as to religion, literature, art or civil polity. That is human nature. The sense of equality must be present in order that example or precept may have potency. Among themselves, by inter-travel, European nations were gradually assimilating and having all things in common respecting knowledge, arts, social morals and ideas.

They are now ceasing to be foreigners in respect to one another. By general acquiescence, one language was adopted as the common vehicle for diplomacy and social intercourse to a degree which makes the literature in that language a depositary and herald to the whole continent of those ideas which otherwise would dwell at the home of their origin. The students of a continent became embraced in one family of letters. Approximation is growing to assimilation so that we may almost say there is one European nation.

The attrition of ideas which is witnessed is the controversy of a people among themselves. They liken themselves to the disputations of different schools connected with the same academy. But although Europe has thus become so individualized, and apparently is original, yet no one forgets the ethnological discoveries of the last century due to the English scholars in India and to the philologists of Germany. They demonstrated that "The ancient idioms of Brahminic India; the dialects of Persia; the Armenian, the Greek, and Latin languages with their derivatives; the Slavic languages, the Germanic and the Celtic formed a vast whole, radically distinct from the Semitic group." This they called the Indo-Germanic, or Indo-European.

Here we have the assurance to expect that similar language will be found to have its never failing counterpart, similar thought and similar methods of thought. A word is the publishing of a thought by articulate sounds. The same word with different peoples denotes unity of character and of thought tendency, as the same tone in two pieces of metal indicates similar structure and elements. But add to this the demonstration by Comparative Mythology that all the Indo-European nations had originally with a similar language, a similar religion, of which each one in departing from the common cradle has carried away the scattered fragments.

This religion is the worship of the powers and phenomena of nature, tending by a species of philosophical development to a species of Pantheism. The Semitic races obeyed entirely different laws. Semitic spirit was, and ever will be, positively Monotheistic; and, as such, there never will be in its history a moment when its antagonism will not be discernible to the spirit of pagan belief which, in matters of faith, science, art, and philosophy, lurks in the traditions, instincts, and thought tendencies of the Indo-European races, ready ever to rise unbidden and clothe themselves in the robes and phrases of professedly new ideas, but in fact vitalized with the false energy of its veiled generic type.

The important truth remains, that today, as veritably as in the distant past, the Semitic peoples and the Indo-Europeans are entirely distinct and different. European criticism and philosophy impatiently undervalues and decries Asia. That verdict of the West against the East has been so reiterated that we have almost come to assume it to be true as a matter of course, and that the Orient was to be disregarded, or rudely pushed aside as having no place or justifying no expectations in the uneasy, sometimes despondent and sometimes hopeful inquiry from nature, "What is truth?"

Beneath American skies the two rivers of thought may be confluent; they will never mingle. One or the other; one, not the other, holds the true elixir, and with that which is true our fountains must be filled.   The two represent the opposing poles of thought as to man's origin, the sanction that determines his duty, and his destiny.   The races, by the very laws of their being, are face to face, having nothing in common in their manner of feeling and thinking as to the corner stone of all philosophy. But, as Renan beautifully says, "The march of humanity is advanced by the struggle of opposing tendencies; it is in the aggregate that all these contradictions harmonize, and that perfect peace results from the shock of elements apparently hostile."

Shall that resultant civilization and philosophy known in Europe, and which we call European — that combined contribution of so many races of divine origin, education and travels, of different climates and wars, which has migrated once more to expand on this continent where no inhabitants were to be pushed aside, be amalgamated, like stems taken from a thicket and here set out wide apart as in a prairie — shall it continue to develop in the direction of its present tendencies, seeking after nice combinations, the harmony of opposite things?   Or will it in its beliefs, loosen its hold on one type of thought, and gradually build on one of the two simple and original elementary tendencies exemplified in the opposite beliefs of the two grand race divisions we have been considering?

Neither will ever rest satisfied with subjection to the other. Yet one, the right one, must dominate to refine, to elevate, to humanize mankind.   It is no idle question.   It is full of import for good or for evil, as it shall be determined.   It means to affirm or deny the opening sentence of the unapproachable history of all histories: that book, the gift of which to mankind by the Jews places them in the just estimation of all at the head of the human family as benefactors.   In that priceless heritage, the truth that comprehends all truth, claims first place for mention.

"In the beginning, God created the heavens and the earth."

"And God said, Let there be light: and there was light."

"And God divided the light from the darkness," and so on, with the grand old story of the Divine Power establishing the firmament, separating the earth from the waters, making the earth fruitful, creating the sun, moon, and the stars, the fish and the fowl, the beasts and cattle, man in the image of God; making the appointment of food, and ordaining the Sabbath.

It is as strange as it is true, young gentlemen, that today in Europe and America, the one aim and end of all the intellectual activity is to attack or defend the integrity of that terse and awfully sublime passage of Mosaic history. In numberless ways the conflict shows itself. We see it and feel it every hour. Only this week we have had a most interesting confession of its pressing claims in the publication of a very learned book from the pen of Professor Charles W. Shields, of Princeton, entitled, "The Final Philosophy: or System of Perfectible Knowledge, Issuable from the Harmony of Science and Religion." What echoes of intellectual and theological strife in the past, and of today, awaken at the reading of this title, "Harmony of Science and Religion!" Not a lecture room on either continent, nor a chemist's laboratory, nor a printing press; not a library, not an editor's desk, not a student's shelves, that does not teem with signs of this controversy. The professor, the preacher, the physician, the poet, the historian, the physicist, the geologist, the student in every department racks his mind with enquiry and argument. It enters the field of social morals; it affects for each individual his sense of his destiny, his notion of duty, and the standard of true dignity for the human family. The controversy progressed through centuries with ever varying phases, until the circuit, in the terse language of the writer last named, may be summed up, "Theology, having begun with a vain attempt to suppress reason by authority, had ended with a defensive struggle for her own life; whilst philosophy, having begun with a legitimate revolt of reason from authority, had ended with a wild assault against the citadel of the faith."

Observe, I am not speaking of any particular phase of theological doctrine. It would be gross presumption and impropriety for me on this platform to permit my observations to turn upon so limited a view. With the phases of faith I have nothing to do this evening, except as to the one sublime thought always held to by the Semitic race, the existence of One Supreme Being, infinite and eternal, and unchangeable in His being, power, holiness, justice, goodness and truth. He made the material universe, and ordained all its laws. From his hand sprang all moral intelligence and all moral nature, and all moral law. Knowledge, and the mind that can know, and the laws of investigation, of observation, and belief, subject and object, are they not alone and all of Thee, Oh! God?

The Indo-European races, so far as they have adopted that creed, have felt the power of the truth under the influence of Semitic teaching, and, may I not impressively add, of Semitic example. I deplore the prevalence of what is politely called "Modern doubt." I do not believe in or hope much from anything save strong, radical, abiding faith. No nation of doubters was ever, or ever will be, a power in the world. No doubter will ever reign over the intellect and heart of this world. He will be a guide, he will be a beacon, he will be a teacher, but he will be only like the ship which, though it may bring comforts and embellishments to your home, will never be the home itself, with hearthstone and rooftree, where the heart will seek its rest. Yet never was there a period when Materialism and Pantheism, in Protean shapes, so boldly and so dangerously attempted to proselyte the intellect as at present. They shake the faith of the pious, they set up a new altar—*Knowledge for its own sake*—as the ultimate good and as the development of its highest sphere of our common humanity. In their careering fancy, they even take credit to themselves that they have schools of faith, as to whether their doctrines involved Atheism, Deism, Infidelity, disbelief of any supernatural agency, or simply a groping scepticism which they call a philosophic spirit. In all this, gentlemen, I find myself moving away from them. It seems to me that the old pagan spark is reviving itself in their souls. I know not whither it may lead me, even if I follow as an inquirer. I know that in all science, and in all philosophy, and in all art, and in all civil order of government, and in all manhood; in all that is lovely and of good report, in all that will endure and not perish, there is and must be a principle, and elementary foundation truth.   After the limited study and reflection which I have been able to give to such subjects, I believe the truth in all this maze was in the ancient oracle entrusted to the renowned and privileged sons of Abraham.   I am not speaking of mere Judaism as a theology, but as a science.

As I believe that in error, race will assert itself in a tendency to that which I believe to be a pagan philosophy, I count upon the orientalism of the Semitic races as the ultimate touchstone which will try to overthrow all this false philosophy.   It is one of those instances where conservatism is the truest progress.   To me it has been inexplicable how the Jew of modern days, the Jew in America especially, can content himself in quiet while the *Heathen rage* and *The people imagine vain things*.   Your race, it is now estimated, numbers more than half a million in America. That which was committed to your fathers was not for a day, or for an age, nor for a century, but for all ages, and for mankind. In this conflict of the active minds on this new stage, the friends of truth have a right to look to you to announce your side, and to see you champion it boldly.   That you will do it efficiently if you undertake it, who doubts that knows the courage, the genius, the eloquence, the poetry, the endurance and fortitude of the Hebrew race.   The very varied gifts of spirit and of speech which you inherit are the dowry which declares your duty.   So far as the Monotheistic faith has been accepted and professed, reënforce it. Your race never had a Mythology, you never knew a Pan-Theistic theology.   You kept the archives, you were the *Book people* of the Semitic race.   With the merely theological aspect of your faith I have no right to meddle.   I bow before it with the profoundest respect and reverence.   But, just as in Rome and in Greece, Mythology was a part of the Statecraft, was the guide of their poetry, was so mingled with their philosophy that Socrates, for instance, in the grandest hour of his grand life, in the moment of finishing the drama of his dialogue upon immorality as his latest dying words, directed the sacrifice of the cock vowed to Aesculapius.   Error as to the primal law of creation will poison not only all physical science but ultimately all our poetry, our social morals, and our civil polity.

Now, what sphere of action does this view open to the young men of this Hebrew Association in New York? You little think how much you are observed. You do not realize how much notice is taken of any true efforts by your race to participate in the active discussions of the day. You do not realize with what power your opinions come, provided you are consistent and loyal to the patriarchal traditions and the Sinaic revelations. When you enter the arena, it is not only fancy that invests you with historic halo. The mind of man is so constituted that the vivid memory of traditions with a people of old traditions, operates with them as if another people were present. The voice of the past is heard, and each generation through which the tradition has been handed seem to have imparted additional value and sanction.

It is as if one after another of the succeeding generations had said, Our fathers gave us this, it was their support and staff from the cradle to the tomb. We have leaned upon the same support; we have tested it in adversity and prosperity; we have compared it with the creeds of unbelieving gentiles, and how, when we in our turn in the great procession are drawing near to the house appointed as the final home for the living, we call to our pillow our first born and our whole household, and transmit the precious heritage of a true belief to them.

With this mystic power of antiquity, with the vindication of the truth by the martyrdoms of generation after generation of your people, you can speak. Will you do it? It opens a new destiny for you. It is not proselyting for your special worship. It is standing forth to battle the challenging Philistine. If faith be wrecked in these modern days, it will not be one people alone who will suffer. Unbelief comes in like a tide when once the dykes are down, and hovel and palace, pleasure ground and the tilled fields alike are submerged. The flower and the fruit, the trunk and the root all alike decay.

Renan, in one of his lectures upon your race, said the European alone conceived the idea of a state that contained the principle of freedom, that is a state with a balanced constitution to check despotism on the one hand, and anarchy on the other. I conceive that the true idea of law, and the true spirit of obedience to law, binding it voluntarily as a yoke about our necks as citizens, so directly depends upon a living belief in a supreme and personal God, the creator and the object of reverence and authority, that to build up and maintain that faith in the minds of the people of this land is also to make, and in the best sense to maintain, the State.

❖

Address of Algernon Sydney Sullivan at the Fourth of July Celebration at Chestertown, N. Y., 1878

If the eyes of an untutored man, blind from his birth, were opened for the first time when he stood on the banks of one of your lakes rippling in the breeze, sparkling beneath the sun, and mirroring everything around and above him, he might well exclaim, "Truly I have seen water in all its beauty!" Bandage his eyes, however, and wait until the afternoon shower is passing into the eastern horizon, and then open to his vision the trailing garments of the retreating clouds at the moment when the sun floods them with his ambient gold, and the rainbow adds an unspeakable magic to the sky.

Think you our novice would easily realize that this was only a revelation of another power of beauty, under new conditions, belonging to the same element which brimmed the lakes? But when he did learn that lesson, he would have learned a fact which finds its simile in the wide firmament of truth. I propose to make some test of its use for inquiries that crowd into our thoughts on an occasion like this. Each nation has its distinctive and individual character. That character is fixed by the law

Drawing by W. E. Mears

THE DOORWAY OF THE SULLIVAN HOME IN MADISON,
INDIANA

of its being. Its inner life has thus manifested itself. Its constructive genius has followed its bent, and has demonstrated its capacity and its scope. Its aspirations fulfil themselves by work, which, it may be, is done without actual consciousness at the time wherefore it is done. The nation was influenced by some physical circumstances, its traditions, its pedigree, the state of surrounding nations; its wars, its commerce, its resources and its growth. What it did, and endured, makes the historic picture and reveals the national character. You can weigh and measure its religious character, its grasp upon morality, its courage, its prudence, its thrift, its energy, its standards of excellence and glory, its purposes and its hopes; its ability to learn and utilize the force of nature, its breadth and grandeur, its pettiness or its vices. But how are you to discern all these? The mere narrative of events will not teach you. The relation which these events mutually bear, whether as cause or effect, must be investigated. The philosophy that enlightens the true historic Muse must be invoked.

The mere story of routine life will not help you. The thing is to ascertain and trace the ideas of which these every day actions are but the outward counterfeit presentment.

The storied facts make the broad expanse, which we may call the history, held in a body like the waters of a lake. It seems filled with motion and life, but the fact remains, nevertheless, that while there, the mud from its bottom is always the limit which your searching vision reaches, alas! only too soon. The mind asks, is all this of the earth earthy? Or, can these actions unmanacle themselves? Have they kinship with the morning? Can they ascend to the stars? Will they marry with the rays of the everlasting sun and their womb bring forth brightness and beauty?

Will they hold on their brow a bow of promise to the world amid the passing storms of life? Is there that quality in and through every drop that it can sublimate itself, and amid the airy regions of fancy take into its bosom the light of heaven, and, if one may so speak, furnish the prism without which even that light lacks the medium for display of its intrinsic splendor?

These enquiries, if answered fairly, will disclose the essential merit of any nation. Let us answer candidly for ourselves in respect to our own beloved land.

First, we recognize the cornerstone of our institutions to be the civil equality of all men. The point I wish to note under that head is that the acceptance of that doctrine attests, as imbedded in the national character, a sentiment of justice and philanthropy. Each man realizes that the utmost claim he can make for himself he makes for every other citizen; and that whatever he denies to every other, by the same expression, he must deny it to himself. Of necessity he is, therefore, all the time training himself to observe the true laws of happiness in society. For that happiness and prosperity will be found to depend upon rules which can be ascertained and defined.

Those rules are stated by an answer to two questions. What acts destroy the welfare of others? What acts promote the welfare of others? The answers constitute the law of the Commonwealth. They are the law as much as if precisely stated in a statute book. In every case the answer must always decide *for* just measures and *against* unjust ones. The training, therefore, of citizens in such a republic is to develop the highest faculties that can adorn human nature—love of justice and of truth. More than anything else, it is this educative faculty that is inseparable from our institutions that ought to endear them to us. A noble manhood is ever being modeled as the type of citizenship. A forbearing, self-postponing manhood, which springs out of each individual's own self-respect. It formulates itself thus: my own dignity demands the acknowledgment from other of certain rights because I am entitled to the full measure of the estate that is the common inheritance of all citizenship. In that very assertion, I have showed my creed, and conceded the title of all others to share it. I have exhibited that spectacle than which nothing in human conduct is more sublime; I have cheerfully, voluntarily bound the law as a welcome yoke about my own neck. Obedience to law becomes a part of my life.

Obedience, not enforced by penalties of a superior. It is not from dread of the lawgiver. It is my own will.

Can there be a question as to the value of political institutions which thus open the springs of love of law? How strongly, too, led by this sentiment, any man will be influenced to reverence the Supreme lawgiver. In this view, then, we find a quality in our political system that elevates the national character; the system is not the mere mechanical machinery to regulate affairs by repressing and restraining men.

Humanity itself is elevated. It aspires to accord with the maxims of universal right and of supreme wisdom. Every law points heavenward, and the page which sketches the character of a people developed under such influences is a page not only luminous, but encircled with the rainbow of truth.

A political inheritance like ours engenders a sense of guardianship in the mind of every citizen. He is by virtue of his citizenship a trustee. He has learned that the maintenance of the true principles of his government, ensures his happiness more than any wealth he could attain. He measures by a true standard the relative claims for his pursuit of those things the word offers. When he has weighed and counted them well, he considers that there is no heritage he would transmit to his children at the expense of this political equality. In that gift more than by any other means he insures the possession of all the other benefits to be attained in life, and he secures to them that condition which guarantees the fullest and freest enjoyment of whatever possessions they may acquire. Few sentiments are more ennobling to our nature than that of fidelity to an honorable trust. It exalts and dignifies manhood. The wisest rulers of men have acted upon it as a maxim. For confirmation we need but study the results that followed the action in this direction of Frederick the Great when, after a regiment in battle behaved badly, he redeemed them to his own and their glory by conspicuously trusting them again, and in the very crisis of his fate. History tells how splendidly the result vindicated the wisdom of his course. Such reaction arises from a principle planted deeply in

our nature.   Realize, then, the elevating influence upon national
character, where this feeling of a trusteeship of liberty continually lives in the breast of the people.

❖

At the public obsequies of Bayard Taylor, in the City Hall of New
York, March 13, 1879, the obituary oration was delivered by
Algernon Sydney Sullivan

Stilled for an hour in presence of these solemnities, be the
turbulent pulse of our busy city! Yon stately incoming ship
with flags at half-mast has sailed the sea as part of a grand
funeral cortége. Germania sends back the remains of her beloved and adopted son to the tender hearts of his brothers in
America; and with a funeral pomp, not marred by the mere gauds
of show, 'mid the tide of song and choral strains of a hundred
voices, the precious trust has been borne hither today.

We have the sable plumes; we have the bier; we have the
o'erspreading pall and the entwining cypress; but not one, nor
all, can oppress this scene with gloom.   Our fancy soars beyond
the pale form we have here enshrouded, to joyous converse with
its now enfranchised spirit. With guards of honor we have lain
him in our most august chamber, whose walls are lustrous with
portraits of eminent public servants.

But this ceremony does not resemble any that preceded it
within these halls, for heretofore they were the names of soldiers
and sailors and jurists which were here enlaureled.

Today's obsequies, on the other hand, turn into a festival
to the Muses.   For the first time here they rise into a public
recognition that "The chief glory of every people arises from its
authors."   By this action we do not only proudly do homage to
the genius of a personal authorship, brilliant for individual fame,
and enriching the poetry, the philosophy, the culture and morals

of our race, but the occasion has widened by its intrinsic character, and its associations, into a triumphant enthronement of Literature itself. It betokens and it announces on the part of New York the new birth of a civic pride in the distinction of our nation's poets and men of letters.

When Bayard Taylor left New York for Berlin he had more than a Government sanction. From the people he went forth accredited to the Republic of Letters. The Muse had passed through the chambers of his soul and endowed him not only with lyric gifts, but with unexampled power to feel and interchangeably interpret the poetry of the German and the English speaking races.

By him, the mysteries, the soul-revelations, the wondrous observations and prophecies of the great drama of life, which shine in Goethe's *Faust*, had been more than translated. They had been reëmbodied in English verse, unshorn of original truth or meaning or native rhythm. In his work Taylor had the inspiring touch of Goethe's soul upon him. To write of that extraordinary man a full and worthy biography was not only Taylor's assumed and partly completed task, it was also the hope of Germany as she welcomed him, and the tacit but emphatic commission to him from the scholars of America. Think of the elevation of soul with which in his closing days he wrought in those precious labors. He knew so well that Faust was a life-long growth, and that, as he said, "The most satisfactory commentary would be a biography of Goethe written with special reference to this one work, when, becoming familiar with its history, the reader would find the compressed meanings expanding into breadth and distinctness." Mr. Taylor felt that his biography of Goethe was in that form to be another revelation of the poem itself. Goethe's mind-life was to unveil all its movements and the births of its majestic poetry.

But alas, for our friend! He was not to complete his task. With his habits of labor on him, and his enthusiasm aglow, he was busy when the wing of Death's angel touched him.   As he lay a-dying, wishing still to work, probably his thoughts recalled the experience of Goethe, who continued to labor, says one biography, in his vocation as a poet with unabated diligence, and apparently with unabated faculty, until the hour of his death, which overtook him as if with the pen in his hand.   And when at last lain prostrate, "Faithful to his principles, he continued to occupy himself, that he might not give the thinking faculty time to grow inactive.   Even when his voice became mute, with his hand he traced characters in the air."

Oh!   What a lyric from out the shadows of death was there lost to mortal vision in those illegible traceries in the impalpable air!   Would that we had spirit-power to capture those winged thoughts!   Would that Aeolian harps would echo the numbers to longing ears!   Would that we had Bayard Taylor's dreams about them!

But his voice we shall hear no more.   His manly form and character-expressing features remain for memory alone.   But there are deeper memories with us of his social qualities, his enthusiasm for his work, his ingenuousness in his own estimate of himself, his sensibility to criticism, his modesty coupled with independence and dignity; his freedom from pretension, his cool reflection, the fixedness of his principles, yet with toleration and liberality abounding; his freedom from discontent without grudges against fortune; his frank utterance of his desire for fame, his constancy and warmth in friendship, his good sense, his pleasure in his work, his faculty for despatch in work, his acquired knowledge, his craving curiosity, his courage and enterprise, his love for the arts, his hopefulness, his high aims in existence, the pure character of his muse, and his irresistible impulse to poetry

It was his inner heart from which, a few months before his death, flowed the lines:

I am a voice, and cannot more be still
Than some high tree that takes the whirlwind's stress
Upon the summit of a lonely hill.

Be thou a wooing breeze, my song is fair;
Be thou a storm, it pierces far and shrill,
And grows the spirit of the starless air;
Such voices were, and such must ever be,
Omnipotent as love, unforced as prayer,
And poured round Life as round its isles the sea!

His first book was a collection of his poems in 1844 when he was but nineteen years old. His thirty-five intervening years have been crowded with intellectual labors, and his writings have increased in interest, in brilliancy, in artistic completeness and force. His poems, his novels, his journals of travel, his essays, his lectures, his magazine and newspaper writings attest his hardly equalled industry, and of his books the best critical testimonial has been, generally for each in its succession, "His latest volume is his best."

By happy coincidence it does seem as if his closing volume was a summing up of his soul history and aspirations:

Thou has sung with organ tone
In Denkalion's life, thine own.

The proprieties of the time and place forbid that I should attempt a memoir or a critical review, but there remained welcome theme enough in the tribute of personal affection, and in this popular coronation service to the memory of our beloved minstrel.

Our hearts move in cadence with Goethe's Epilogue in memory of Schiller:

He was our own; let grief's loud utterances
Be hushed before this proud distinction.
Though, after life's exhausting struggles
A welcome haven here he found,
Still onward, upward strode his spirit pure,
To realms of light, of worth, of truth,
And coarse reality, mankind's all-potent master
In shadowy impress merely crossed his path.

As his friends now again lift up the bier to take it onward beneath the shelter of the parental rooftree where, waiting for their dead, are the aged father and mother who fondly have hoped that it might be the course of Providence for this their son to close their eyes; we can only bow our heads in sympathy with their breaking hearts, and in low voice murmur, "Oh! Beloved friend! Oh! Inspired Poet! Repose and Honor to thee! And most tender Farewell!"

❖

Address at the unveiling of a statue of General Custer at West Point, on August 30, 1879, by Algernon Sydney Sullivan, Chairman of the Citizens' Committee which presented the statue to the United States Military Academy

GENERAL SCHOFIELD, LADIES AND GENTLEMEN:

It is the good fortune of some soldiers to be with their death stroke swept along at once into the land of legend, and to have their names enveloped with the purple mist of song. The condition of this gift is not the vastness of the army in the field, nor that the fate of empires be at stake, nor that victory shall be gained, nor that the slaughter shall be great; but there must be something in the circumstances which awakens, and some quality in the soldier's action which reposes on, a universally distributed moral sentiment. Countless individual soldiers have rushed alone against an enemy's lines, but when Arnold Winkelried, at the Battle of Sempach, gathered into his bosom the sheaf of Austrian spears, who does not perceive the moral more than the physical force and courage which made way for liberty, and broke the Austrian phalanx? To hear of it is to taste again that inexhaustible fountain at which humanity so long has drunk its heroism. The deed was strong, as it was an expression of spiritual power and the purpose behind it. All

Switzerland's great will was to be pronounced, and Arnold emphasized it by action. The act was a timely and eloquent declaration. Death was simply the herald to proclaim it. The actor had preferred something to life; and that something was the ideal of his army comrades, and the faithful fulfillment of the trust which for the time being fell upon him. Thoughts like these come upon us at this hour, like the shadowy shapes that are lengthening towards us from yonder old Fort Putnam, and the breezes that flutter these leaves are articulate with whispers of heroism in American soldiery.

But the name which we have come to enlaurel will ever stand bright and high in the honored roll. It is that of a soldier, to praise whom detracts from none. We express the tribute of those who themselves have honest desire for distinction. It is like the highest military reward known among the Romans. That was not booty nor advancement, nor even the *corona triumphalis*, but the crown of grass picked on the scene of the splendid deed of valor, and awarded by consent of the army. Other rewards were given by the General to the soldiers, but this the soldiers gave to their leader.

These ceremonies are in honor of the gallant American soldier and West Point officer, General George A. Custer. More than three years ago, on the field of honor, he fell with his entire command, one and all fighting a brave and desperate battle to the last; he a worthy leader of noble soldiers in a border conflict with savages; face to face with a war which put in peril frontier settlements and unprotected emigrants. The one duty upon him as representative of the army was, to use the first opportunity to strike the foe. The sight of the enemy was to be accepted as the signal for instant battle. To that idea and popular expectancy Custer was loyal. Defeat to him in such action and in such exigencies was victory for the cause of which he and his command became champion heroes and martyrs.

There was much in the conflict of that bloody valley where those soldiers fell and are buried, which invests the officers and men with the character and halo of typical American soldiers.

We take General Custer as their leader and representative, his statue in bronze we erect as an enduring remembrancer. It was the wish of those who have caused it to be prepared that it should stand on the grounds of Custer's much loved West Point. There it is, a statuesque figure now to be unveiled, where, in the attitude of the fighting soldier at the supreme moment of a hand to hand death grapple with a savage foe, it will henceforth be present with the Army of the United States.

General Schofield: To you as superintendent and representative of the United States Military Academy, and, to be preserved here, in trust for the army and people of the whole country, in accordance with instructions of the Committee which I have the honor to represent, I deliver this monumental statue. As I thus dedicate it, I have no words of apostrophe to our dead hero, or of suggestion to the cadets who hither shall gather for centuries to come, I trust, which so press for utterance, as those of a friend and poet whose verses have not yet been published:

Oh, Custer—gallant Custer! Man foredoomed
To ride, like Rupert, spurred and waving plumed,
Into the very jaws of death and hell,
That Balaklava scarce could show so well—
Thou who, with flashing eye and smile on lip
  Could ride the Rosebud's ride of fire and death
  Without a tremor or a shortened breath,
But joyous as one goes a bridal-trip—

The days of Chivalry are with us yet!
To thee, and these like thee, we owe the debt
Of teaching those who follow in that road—
Needing the spur, but brooking not the goad—
  How much of all that won the world's applause
  Of old, when battling out some glorious cause,
Is with us still, when thou, and such as thou,
  A duty to be done, whate'er the cost,
  And all still won, when honor is not lost—
Ride into death with calm and fearless brow!

Ah, if the Days of Chivalry are gone,
We have an afterglow that shames the dawn;
And in the night to follow, proud and high
May shine such planets in our upper sky,—
Born of the noblest Mother of them all,
    The nurse of heroes and the nation's pride,
    Clasping St. Cyr and Sandhurst, o'er the tide,—
Whom in our common speech "West Point" we call,—
That men shall say: "Let the Dead Past be dead:
Give us the Living Present in its stead!"
And as the rolling years in centuries fall,
Place high the Glorious Future over all!

       Chivalry's Afterglow, Henry Morford.

❖

*Address delivered by Algernon Sydney Sullivan at the first public
rendering of "Columbia", offered by the author and composer,
Patrick S. Gilmore, as a national song for the people of the
United States, Christmas Day, 1879*

Deep and intelligent love of country is a passion that must
ever create poetry and music; and an offering to the patriotism
of the country of a national song, founded on history, is by no
means, ladies and gentlemen, an insignificant fact.

Your sympathy with such an offering, your desire to witness
and unite in it, attest a creditable appreciation by you of the
worth of such a high and honorable endeavor. It is in its
poetry that a nation discloses its highest aims and enthusiasm.
Thence you learn what the nation thinks of law, of freedom, of
excellence in character, of the true standard of greatness, and of
God. If it be degraded by low and material influences, a nation
never will sing lofty spiritual songs. Let us then keep in mind
that the service of this Christmas afternoon—which is not to in-

troduce an elegant ode, with florid brilliancy, or a classic lyric, but in simple phrase and measure to embody the sentiment of the American patriotism in a people's song—will be tested by the inquiry, "With what images does it fill the mind, and what feelings does it stimulate?"

When we speak of a song founded on History, we recall a great truth. The poet is, in fact, the true historian. He alone sees truth beneath its veil. History, ordinarily so termed, describes the vesture, but the vivified agent beyond and the soul that warms and colors it are discernible only by the aid of the Muses. The heart, just as all men carry it about with them over the whole earth, and through all time warmed by passions, moved by sympathies—the necessities of its nature, and alive to all truths that are general and not local and incidental—flashes out of its own knowledge, feelings, sufferings and designs; and that gleam is poetry that comprehends the history of man. It shows what he is in all the varying circumstances wherein he lives; it shows what he is doing to change the circumstances. Such poetry is a mirror which not only reflects a faithful image, but which itself takes on beauties from the image in its bosom, and bestows its refulgence as a new enrichment upon the object before it. It is the oriental crystal of the fable; you look into it, and all that ever glanced upon it looks out upon you.

With it there is no such thing as a never-returning past. To it all events are discernible in each event; nothing is transitory. The laws of birth of all that is fine in human nature are known to the poet. He can describe it; he can summon it, and make its embryo wings flutter in the bosom of his fellow man.

Of course a sentiment so elevated and akin to piety as patriotism has made poetry its handmaid. Patriotic melodies, at times, have the power of a sanctuary song. Their effect is illustrated in the history of every nation, ancient and modern.

Who can read the famous "Scolium of Callistratus" and not be transported to the Panathenaean festival when the myrtle-wreathed sword killed the tyrant and gave equal laws to Athens? Methinks I can hear her people at all their festive meetings

chant to their beloved Harmodius, in the Islands of the Blest,
immortal with

> . . . the glorious dead,
> Achilles, fleet of foot, and Diomed.

The French Revolution flamed into songs, and the *Marseillaise*, in its turn, re-kindled the revolution to hotter fires, the
embers of which the song seems ever to relume.

English writers admit that the bold and loyal spirit of their
army and navy have in trying times been kept alive by its songs,
and that the national character has to some degree been formed
by them. One writer said that the four or five national airs of
England which the people sing with honest enthusiasm, form
part of that invincible armory of defence which is found in national character. So firmly are they fixed in the British heart
that you hear a Briton say, "They are of the very genius of our
constitution, and it is only in a country of freedom that they
would possess an interest so warm and universal."

The names of these songs should have mention here today,
and they readily recur to us in the order of their popularity.
First, as an expression of British loyalty, and probably the most
popular song in the world, is *God Save the Queen*. It is one of the
curious facts of history that this grand song is none the less
effective, though the verses in their origin were a Jacobite song
written during the Rebellion of 1715 and used as an expression of
most intense hostility to the royal house now upon the throne.

But, besides this, the British have a splendid quartet of national songs in *Rule Britannia, Briton's Bulwarks Are Her
Wooden Walls, Britons, Strike Home,* and *Ye Mariners of England,*
each of which deserves comment, if time permitted now.

No one more cheerfully than we Americans can acknowledge
the excellence of these songs, or better understand how they
elevate national pride and loyalty.

And now, how has it been in our own loved land? Our
fathers tell us that from the opening of the struggle for independence many patriotic lyrics were published, and that the

enthusiasm of the people was greatly aroused and sustained by such songs as *The Rallying Song*, beginning:

> Freedom's sons who wish to shine
> Bright in future story,
> Haste to arms and join the line
> Marching on to glory.
> Leave the scythe and seize the sword,
> Brave the worst of dangers!
> Freedom is the only word—
> We to fear are strangers.

Equally inspiriting was *The Green Mountain Boys' Song*, with its refrain:

> Then draw the trusty blade, my boys,
> And fling the sheath away—
> Blow high, blow low, come weal, come woe,
> Strike for America!

In the passing century, since the happy issue of the Revolutionary War, the Muses have again and again been invoked for song and music for a national ode.

But while it is true that the ardent nature of the people has found voice in the verses of *Hail Columbia, America*, and especially at trying and at exultant moments, in the prayer and proud assurance of the refrain,

> 'Tis the star-spangled banner, oh, long may it wave,
> O'er the land of the free and the home of the brave.

And although we hold these, and many other American odes, as among the nation's treasures, it is still true that we have nothing yet that is adequate to the requirements of a national hymn. And it is further to be noted, that even as to these of our more favored songs, the music was not co-inspired with the words but are all adaptions.

An old French air, known as *Anacreon in Heaven*, was the tune to which Key adapted *The Star-Spangled Banner*.

Hopkinson wrote *Hail Columbia* to suit a tune known as the *President's March*. And our own, and ever-to-be-admired *Yankee Doodle*, is an old and once-ridiculed English air.

Today, it is our good fortune to christen at one font, both the words and the music, in which it is hoped patriotic feeling may find inspiration and expression.

As I understand the vision which inspires this new song of *Columbia in History*, it turns my sight three centuries back. It is sunset. Upon the deck of a little vessel sailing western seas where Europeans had never before ventured, I hear the mariners sing *Salve Regina*, the vesper hymn to the Virgin. I hear Columbus addressing them and pointing out the goodness of God leading them across tranquil oceans and guiding them to a promised land. The next morning I see that intrepid Admiral landing on one of the islands of the new continent, upon his knees thanking God with tears of joy; ending his voyage as he had recorded the beginning in his journal, *In Nomine Domine Nostrum Jesu Christi*. The banners carried ashore were emblazoned with the Cross, and that must ever remain the first fact in an American history whether written in poetry or in prose. The island which the rising sun revealed to view was over-splendored with a brighter glory—the living Light of the Cross.

In the spirit of this song, I look a century later. I see another small vessel in a northern latitude at mid-winter approach the icy shore of the same continent. It is the *Mayflower*, and from her decks a few Pilgrim immigrants land.

They plant for posterity a State, the end of which was religion, the rule of which was equal laws; the object, the common good, the glory of which was to be Freedom. Before landing they formed a body politic—*In the name and presence of God*.

Borne onward again by this historic song for a century and a half, we are brought into the majestic presence of Washington, amid the scenes which marked the achievement of American Independence.

Again, with nearly a century's flight, the vision is all o'ercast with the night of a frowning Providence, only that the day star shall soon arise to see civil war ended, and man's slavery extinguished.

Borne on further by the tide of this song-review, which of the millions of loving hearts that shall chant this song of Columbia will fail to guard her peace and liberty?

And more than that, who will remain unimpressed by the spirit which springs out of this song, that

. . . man to man shall e'er be just.

Why shall it not inspire us all with a new devotion to advocate the rights of the feeble, and plead for the sufferings of the poor?

For myself, I believe that the duty, the strength and the glory of our country, will be found in that path. I feel it, and I mean it, that that duty in one immediate practical shape is for the education of the lately emancipated slaves, now fellow-citizens with us.

It now only remains for us to recognize the propriety with which the *Columbia* song concludes in ascription of praise to Him, "The King of Glory on His Throne," and in invocation of His blessing.

❖

Application for the admission of John F. Quarles, a colored lawyer, to practise at the New York Bar, made by Algernon Sydney Sullivan to the Supreme Court of the City of New York, May 10, 1880

May it please the Court, Mr. Quarles is an applicant for admission to the Bar of this State as an attorney and counsellor at law, and I move that he be now admitted by this Court. First, having been licensed a lawyer in Georgia, he removed to Washington where, in 1872, he was admitted as attorney and counsel-

SOCIETY PEOPLE
AT A "FIRST NIGHT" IN
WALLACK'S NEW THEATRE

From the New York World
Sunday, December 7, 1884

"THE cartoon depicts a representative New York audience as it may be seen on many a night at Wallack's Theatre. The present noticeable assemblage has gathered to pay tribute to the veteran actor, Lester Wallack, whom the artist has caught in one of his favorite poses, with that jaunty, nonchalant air that causes one to forget the many years he has left behind him. Directly beneath the actor the none less veteran Lewis F. Baker wields his baton with all the ardor of youth, when he made Laura Keene famous. In the first row of the audience, beginning at the centre aisle (bottom of the picture) and moving towards the boxes, sit Algernon S. Sullivan, Gen. Daniel F. Sickles, Gen. Alex. Shaler, Charles J. Osborne, Henry Clews, Gen. Lloyd S. Aspinwall, Rufus Hatch and the Marquis de Leuville.

In the second row, also beginning from the bottom of the picture, are Henry Berg, Clarence Seward, Pierre Lorillard, De Lancey Kane, William P. Douglass, Henry Sims, D. O. Mills, Wright Sanford and Jose Mora. The third row begins with Dr. Hammond, whose arms are characteristically folded. Beside him sits a lady, and then come in the same order Theodore Havemeyer, Judge Barrett, Sidney Dillon, Judge Arnoux, William Winter, Gen. Varnum, ex-Mayor Cooper, and Joseph Keppler. Mr. Frederick Coudert, the gentleman with the Dundrearys on the extreme right of the picture, seems to constitute a row all by himself inasmuch as he sits on a line with none of the others. Possibly he has secured a camp stool and planted himself in the aisle. Immediately at his back commences the fourth row with George Gould and continues with Jay Gould, of the same tribe; S. L. M. Barlow, Jesse Seligman, a friend, George W. Ritchie, Dr. M. J. B. Messemer, Herman Leroy, D. D. Withers, Peter Marie, Fred F. Gunther, Robert Bonner and Superintendent Whitney, of the Society for the Prevention of Crime.

In the fifth row, beginning with Herman Oelrichs, who sits behind Jay Gould, William K. Vanderbilt, William M. Connor, Col. George Bliss, Judge Brady, David Dudley Field, Frank Work, W. A. Croffut and four others, regarding whose identity history is silent. The audience seated beyond the fifth row are supposed to be lost in the hazy distance, with the exception of Robert L. Cutting, who sits behind Herman Oelrichs and W. Chase, F. S. Church and James L. Ford, one row further back. The proscenium box nearest the stage is occupied by August Belmont, his son Perry, two ladies and an unknown friend with a monocle; the second box, by William H. Vanderbilt, his uncle Jacob, familiarly known as "Capt. Jake"; his son Cornelius and two ladies.

In a line beneath the Vanderbilt box will be readily recognized a number of men about town and journalists. The names in the order in which they stand are Lispenard Stewart, Frederick Gebhard, Augustus Heckler, Amory Hodges, Joseph Howard, Maurice Minton, Joseph Parkes, J. W. Keller, and last but not least—in the far, far distance beside the rich plush curtain—Wm. R. Cutting.

Every theatre-goer will readily recognize the faces in the cartoon, and at the same time will observe how thoroughly cosmopolitan the audience is. Some are leaders in society and often head the sets in a German. Others are familiar to the turf and other gentlemanly sports, while many are distinguished for charitable labors."

SUPPLEMENT. No. 2.
SEXTUPLE SHEET.

SUPPLEMENT. No. 2.
SEXTUPLE SHEET.

THE WORLD SUPPLEMENT.

NEW YORK, SUNDAY, DECEMBER 7, 1884.

Society People at a "First Night" in Wallack's New Theatre.

lor in the Supreme Court of the District of Columbia. He practiced in the courts of the district until he was appointed in the Consular service of the United States, which has caused his absence from the country. Since his return he has become a resident and citizen of New York. I present to you the proper certificates and evidence to sustain this motion, in accordance with our law and the rule of the Court. Although such motions are usually *pro forma*, for special reasons I depart a little from that custom. Mr. Quarles is a colored man born a slave, and the first of his race who, within my knowledge, will have become a member of the Bar in the city of New York. On behalf of that Bar, distinguished for character, learning and liberal accomplishments, I welcome Mr. Quarles in advance to his full equality in the franchise of the profession, and I assure him that his entrance to its ranks is observed by the Bar with cordial and respectful interest and most graceful good wishes.

❖

Algernon Sydney Sullivan's response to the toast, "The Stage and the Bar," at the farewell breakfast to Edwin Booth, June 15, 1880

No one, better than a lawyer, knows that the alpha and omega of all the activities of life are dramatic in element and form. If nature has given him any poetic dowry, his daily forensic experience is an art study, framing out of the movements of the hour a true dramatic law, as inseparable from humanity. The Bar exalts the stage, because the stage devotes itself to transmitting into artistic forms the exhaustless beauties and instruction which come through the dramatic sense. And now, when the students and workers in all the fields of thought, go through the laurel groves and come hither with the plucked branches glistening with the dew of a June morning, the Bar presents also its leafy crown, and with it, to Edwin Booth, a recognition of his honors worthily won and becomingly worn.

❖

An Address made by Algernon Sydney Sullivan at a political meeting to indorse General Hancock as a candidate for the Presidency, held at Glen Cove, N. Y., September, 1880

MY FRIENDS:

It is old as Homer to invoke misfortunes upon evil-doers. As his verse expresses it, "That all the world may learn not to commit injustice." Thus it appears that even the pagan poet desired that the events of history should run in such order that they should recommend public morals. A momentous duty in that respect will devolve, this autumn, upon the voters in the United States, who are to choose as their President a successor to Rutherford B. Hayes. He and his cabinet and the one hundred thousand subordinate officeholders of his administration are actively engaged in partisan efforts to prolong their party tenure of power and to elect General Garfield President. Consider for a moment the full import of that fact. If President Hayes shall succeed in his efforts, will the good people of these States have declared their conscience in reference to the execrable fraud by which he and his party cheated themselves into power in 1876? Will that result teach the lesson "Not to commit injustice"? Or, rather, will not every fraud conspirator of them all interpret the result as a verdict of excuse and encouragement? Under the circumstances, would not the election of Garfield engrave on the scroll of our history a record that the majority of our nation does not condemn fraud? Our youth will so understand it; our adopted citizens will so understand it; the enemies of free institutions will exultingly so characterize it, and the humiliated friends of the Republic, with bowed heads, will acknowledge it. The unscrupulous political managers will be only too quick to take advantage of the lesson.

But, on the other hand, let the result be reversed, and Hancock be elected, then the case will present one feature which will be the chiefest and grandest result of the victory; it will be Homer's lesson. Every member of the falsifying returning boards, their coadjutant inspectors and their executive committees and visiting statesmen, their menacing military men, their pliant newspaper backers, their aliunde* Electoral Commission, and all the host of office-holding appointees who made themselves accessories to the fraud by seeking its booty and running after its spoils, will cower before the blast of popular indignation and feel their mark of infamy. Then, indeed, with self-respect regained, will the nation have trampled on the great election fraud. It will be an interesting sight, and instructive to watch that band of conspirators as they move off towards the habitation of the bats and unclean creatures that hide in the dusk. It must come sometime, and now is the best time, when they who saw the wrong shall behold the recompense. I expect it. Isaiah prophesied of the prospering wicked, "Their foot shall slide in due time." Then, the Republican party, which, as Governor Tilden well said, "Stifled its conscience," may find it quickened again. This question is not dragged in—it rises so high you cannot get out of sight of it. Among political questions it is Mont Blanc. General Garfield identified himself more than almost anybody else with the Presidential fraud. After the election, and when the result was known that Tilden was elected, Garfield went as a partisan to New Orleans. He joined hands with Madison Wells, who needed assistance. He helped work up a record to go before the Returning Board. The returns of one large parish, which were sufficient to decide the result, were in his hands, and finding that upon them the State Returning Board could not defeat Tilden, he helped in the work of getting

* "From another source."

the new and needed affidavits so that they would do. He first saw that the Democratic majority of West Feliciana Parish should be thrown out by the State Returning Board; then he took a seat on the Electoral Commission to decide that we could not look behind the act of that Returning Board, to expose the frauds which that Board and its assistants had worked up.

Do the cheated people understand the challenge implied in Garfield's nomination? What will they do about it? Here, now, I have suggested a reason for electing Hancock—the re-enthronement of public morality. But let us pass to others, which ought to be sufficient.

In 1868 General Hancock was in command of one of the military departments in the South, under what were styled the reconstruction laws. Soldier though he was, he, with exceptional moderation and wisdom, refused to set up the bayonet as king. He reinstated civil law as supreme, and did so with phrases so convincing that they turned again the current of public opinion into safe channels. It was a victory for the cause for which Gettysburg was fought and won. The country can never study too closely, or be too grateful for, the series of papers and orders issued by General Hancock at that period. He showed that he was thoroughly imbued with the spirit of American liberty and law, and that he was in advance of his eminent contemporaries in wise statesmanship. It is a good test of statesmanship in any man to learn his view of Hancock's policy. Would you believe it, if it had not been recently published, from records that, instead of sustaining Hancock, Garfield, being then in Congress, actually introduced and endeavored to secure the passage of a bill to discharge General Hancock from the military service? Garfield says he introduced the bill to show Hancock how completely he was in the hands of Garfield and his party, and to teach him (Hancock) "to keep his place"—that is, to compel Hancock to overturn all courts and civil laws and to wield the sword at the behest of the carpet-baggers. Note the honorable contrast: the soldier championing law and liberty, your boasted statesman forcing martial law and military rule. The shameful Garfield scheme was disgraceful in a legislator, and was an insult to every patriotic soldier in the army.

But we need not pause with these reasons for our Hancock advocacy. Let us take up another.   It is a great evil to foment sectional divisions in our politics, and to studiously keep them alive, as in Ireland, where they descend with the generations. But there never yet was a nation in which these divisions had taken root, which did not, from their dreadful evils, come to regret that they had not in time pursued the ways of peace and harmony. It is not that I plead for material prosperity—I would not put that first. I solemnly believe that, among its blessings, the political institutions of our Union are worth more than all these other things. Sectionalism is a stain and a strain upon our Government, and it is just as bad in one section as it is in another. It precludes healthy and wise law-making. Like an acid upon metal, it eats away patriotic sentiment. National interests are clouded by jealousies. And, my fellows citizens, rest assured that in the long run sectional indignities will not be one-sided. Whenever men are allowed to feel that government is identified with sectionalism, their love for it begins to die. Herein, then, because he typifies the idea of the supreme national authority and a consistent anti-sectional policy, we find new reason for electing Hancock.

But another presses for notice. It is as true as it is a source of satisfaction and pride, that the Southern Democrats have come to like, choose and support Hancock precisely for what he is, for what he did, and for what he represents as an Union soldier. *They* have come *to him*, not he to them. They say to him: "As the best and fullest representative of the Union soldiery, we enlist under your banner." What time in history, after such a war, was there ever such an incident, and could there ever be a people so unwise as not to welcome it?

And yet another reason for our organization presses upon my attention. General Hancock stands with his party, North and South, broadly and deeply resolved to maintain the Constitution as it is, with all its amendments, in letter and spirit. And right here arises occasion for the grand old Democracy to assert their traditional principles and apply them to the enfranchised colored people. The Democracy have always been the guardians of popular liberty and personal rights as paramount to all considerations of property. The individual voting franchise for the humblest and the poorest, unrestricted except for crime, is true Democracy. The universal distribution of that right is the best and the quickest educator towards good citizenship that has ever been conceived or tried. And, although immediately after the close of the war amid the complex and distracting affairs of the time, the subject has been neglected and the truth perverted, the time is at hand for the colored people to hear the fact. It is this:—that if ever their political rights be endangered, the Democrats, by the necessity and logic of their existence, will be found to be their first, their last and their staunchest allies. In the wisest sense, Democratic policy is in the interest of property, but in the great and perpetual struggle for liberty and the rights essential to its preservation, the Democracy must always be at one with the poor and the feeble, without regard to race, color or religion.

The temporary success of the Republican management to poison and alienate from the Democracy the minds of the colored citizens has well nigh run its course. Already large numbers of colored men are asserting their second emancipation and announcing their intention to vote for Hancock. The best information is that fully one-fourth of the colored voters in the United States will vote for Hancock. I congratulate and encourage them. They will find, in thus voting, an increase in their own self-respect, and in General Hancock's success a patriotic result which will fully satisfy them that they rendered service to their country.

When some one, as for instance, Secretary Sherman, insists that upon the election of a Republican President depends the maintenance of gold currency, I reply, all such assertions are silly shams. From the time when the Democratic party organized, it was, and it is, the only true "Hard money" party in the country. I remember when the Legal Tender Act was passed Governor Seymour, prompted by Democratic instinct for public faith, proposed that New York should continue to pay the interest on her State debt in gold, but the Republican legislature refused to acquiesce in the Governor's proposal, and in the name of New York practically repudiated an obligation which was honestly payable in gold only. If gold were in demand for export from this country under exigencies of trade, which may recur any year, the existing Republican financial legislation will be found to be totally inadequate to the emergency. Gold and greenbacks are exchangeable at par, only because there is no demand for gold for export. This country has never had a sound exchequer system except under Democratic auspices, and no intelligent business man should be deluded into withholding a vote from the Democratic candidate because of Mr. Sherman's wearisome platitudes.

Again, the Hancock campaign brings us face to face with principles vital to the American system. The divergent views in our politics have been, on the one hand, local self-government, trust in the people and rigid construction of the Constitution; and, on the other hand, a governmental scheme which is best defined by the term, "Centralization." The former is the theory represented by General Hancock and the latter is General Garfield's. I have no doubt which is the better for liberty and which the people will prefer. And the time has come when it is perilous to defer the return to the Democratic methods. During the long Republican rule the statute books have been filled with evil precedents. Whenever the Republicans undertook to legislate about a matter which in itself might be proper enough, their want of sympathy with the true principles of popular liberty would surely display itself. For instance, they could not legislate about elections without giving to deputy marshals arbitrary powers altogether variant from our entire judicial system and Bills of Rights. This tendency has become so engrafted upon the Republican mind that of itself it contributes a good ground for electing Hancock. Is it well to allow Congressmen to enact whatever in their partisan opinion is for the public welfare, or shall the people hold Congress to the express powers which have been granted in the great charter? The latter is the only sure anchor of liberty.

So it is in every aspect of our public affairs: because they have been going wrong, we want a change,—and Hancock.

❖

Another address made by Algernon Sydney Sullivan supporting General Winfield Scott Hancock, in his candidacy for the office of President of the United States, Brooklyn, N. Y., September 2, 1880

MY FRIENDS:

Unwonted intensity of feeling pervades the Democracy in regard to the Presidential election, and at your request I will state some reasons for that feeling. Irrational advocacy has hurt many a good cause, and mere hectic excitement is a dangerous substitute for words of truth and soberness. An hour of calm review of the case as it is now before the country befits every citizen.

First, then, I note an unalterable conviction in the minds of the majority that they have a grievous wrong to redress. In 1876 the Republican party cheated themselves into power. Theirs was a crafty, deliberate political crime, backed by hydra frauds, prompted by greed and cloaked in shameless hypocrisy. It was conceived after the election was closed, in which they had all the advantages of office and control of election machinery. They rioted in possession of unbounded power, the prestige of which was invoked by all their placemen. Swollen with pride, insolent and arrogant, their voices and corruption seamed the whole fabric of government. Men began to bow their heads with shame and sorrow as one disclosure followed another. The party, however, fronted public opinion and made desperate efforts, as they are now doing, to retain the offices. "That quail and manna should no longer rain," was a dread and a spur. To their amazement the people elected Samuel J. Tilden President, and the dismay of Belshazzar's feast fell upon them.

Among them sprung up quick plottings how to overthrow the ballot box. They said, "Wherefore, if not for such a time as this, did we make friends of the mammon of unrighteousness? Have we not carpet-bag returning boards?" In fine, the Republicans, as Governor Tilden well says, stifled their conscience and pirated the Presidency. The President thus intruded into the Chief Magistracy, every member of his Cabinet, the one hundred thousand officeholders of his administration and more than as many more hangers-on, are now actively engaged in partisan efforts to elect Garfield and prolong their party tenure of power. The situation forces the question to every voter: How will you declare your conscience with regard to this execrable public fraud? Now that appeals are being made to the business men of America, I would like to have them, and the reverend clergy also, answer these questions: Do you think any other consideration involved in the canvas as momentous as this? Ought that fraud to be condoned? Should it be left even doubtful whether there is a virtuous public opinion about it?

There is no mistaking how your vote will be regarded. Your sons, all the youth of the land, our adopted citizens, and the friends, as well as the enemies of free institutions abroad, will regard a vote for Garfield as a declaration by you that this political fraud can be excused. Consider well before you thus bow the knee to Baal. There can be no nobler trust than to assemble in grand inquest at the ballot box and rebuke such fearful guilt. Rest assured that every corrupt politician on all sides, every member of a falsifying returning board, and all their allies, including the accessories after the fact who accepted the spoils and plunder of office (which under other circumstances would have been honorable emolument) after the juggling award of the aliunde* electoral commission, will interpret your vote for the Republican candidate to mean that you set no value upon public morality. The reënthronement of morals is the animating purpose of the Democracy in their campaign for Hancock. By his election only can the old-time virtue and honor be restored in our national temples, and the retribution to evil doers teach to our time the Homeric lesson that "All men shall learn not to commit injustice."

I note again a special reason why the Democracy and independent voters are deeply roused upon this subject. The question forces itself to the front. Garfield's nomination is a direct challenge to the people in respect to it. He went to New Orleans immediately after the election. He joined hands with Madison Wells and the carpet-baggers. The returns of West Feliciana Parish were in his hands. It was a Democratic parish, and needs must be thrown out to secure an ostensible majority for Hayes. For that purpose the papers and documents furnished were insufficient. Consultations followed and Garfield took part therein. How was the case to be put in shape? An end was to be accomplished; what were the means? Garfield counselled as to the additional stock of affidavits. This is the record. The work was done. And now the returning board resolved that the votes should be thrown out, and then certified that the majority of the remaining votes were for Hayes. Sherman and Garfield hastened back to Washington. Garfield took a seat on the electoral commission, and then voted that you could not look behind the returns to expose the frauds upon which they had been procured. Tell me not that such is American honor, nor is it statesmanlike. All honor to patriotic Republicans like Charles Francis Adams, who proclaim their abhorrence of the infamy and of all who abetted it. Fellow citizens, you make no mistake when you give prominence to this subject as a holy trust; it elevates all who respond to it.

Another reason which justifies Democratic feeling and activity

* "From another source."

springs from the action of General Garfield and his party toward
General Hancock in 1868. I speak not of any mere personal
treatment but, as alone worthy of this occasion, of a matter
which involves sacred public principles. In 1868 Hancock was
placed in command of one of the military departments in the
South under the so-called reconstruction laws. The framers
of those laws had one paramount object—to use the South for
preserving their political power. The States, managed by military law, should elect Republican members of Congress, but had
no other political or civil rights. For rights are not such if
dependent upon the will of military power. The two cannot
coexist. Happily for this country and for the cause of constitutional liberty, Hancock appeared upon the scene. Soldier as he
was, he also understood the principles of free government and
he remembered the oath which he, with all officers, took to support the Constitution. Many members of Congress forgot their
oath. Hancock, with exceptional moderation and wisdom,
refused to exercise bayonet power in civil matters. He reinstated civil law as the only government, the military being subordinate. His statement of his reasons therefor was so convincing and so patriotic that it arrested public opinion and turned it
again into healthy channels. He won thereby his grandest
triumph in the same cause for which Gettysburg was fought and
won. Our country can never be too grateful for his example and
his precepts at that period. The Government was being blindly
pushed into a position absolutely destructive of our political
system. Hancock's hand saved us. It was not the South he
saved, it was the North; or, better, it was all alike.

Would you believe it, if it did not appear in public records,
that instead of sustaining Hancock's wise statesmanship, Garfield, being then in Congress, actually introduced and endeavored
to secure the passage of a bill to expel General Hancock from the
army? Garfield says he introduced the bill to show Hancock
how completely he was in the hands of Garfield's party and to
teach him "to keep his place"—that is, to compel Hancock to
overthrow all courts and civil laws, and to wield the sword at the

caprice of the carpet-baggers. Note the honorable contrast: the soldier championing law and liberty; your boasted statesman forcing martial law and military rule. The shameful Garfield scheme was a disgrace for a legislator and an insult to every patriotic soldier in the army.

But another reason for electing Hancock presses for notice. It is a fact, and a source of infinite satisfaction and pride, that the Southern Democrats have come to like, choose and support Hancock precisely for what he is, for what he did, and for what he represents, as a Union soldier. They have come to him, and not he to them. They say to him: "As the best and fullest representative of the Union soldiery, we enlist under your banner." What time in history, after such a war, was there ever such an incident, and could there ever be a people so unwise as not to welcome it?

But let me not fail to give due prominence to another most important feature involved in this canvass. His party, North and South, stands with General Hancock, resolved to maintain the Constitution, with all its amendments, in letter and spirit. Mark my prediction that in the future, as in the past, impatience with, and encroachments upon the Constitution must be expected from the opponents of the Democracy. Latitudinarian construction is as dangerous as nullification. Right here arises occasion for the grand old Democracy to apply their traditional principles on behalf of the enfranchised colored citizens. The Democracy has been preëminently the guardian of popular liberty and personal rights as paramount to all considerations of personal property. Unrestricted voting franchise for the humblest and poorest is true democracy. Conviction of felony is the only exception. The universal exercise of that right is the best and quickest educator toward good citizenship that has ever been conceived. Immediately after the close of the war the times were distracted and the truth perverted, but the colored people should now hear the fact. It is this, that if ever their political rights be endangered, the Democrats, by the logic of their existence, will prove to be their first, their latest and their staunchest allies. In the wisest sense, property interests are best subserved by Democratic policy. But in the perpetual struggle for liberty and the rights essential to its preservation, the Democracy must always be at one with the poor and the feeble, without regard to race, color, or religion. The temporary success of the Republican management to poison and alienate from the Democracy the minds of the colored citizens has well nigh run its course. Already large numbers of colored men are asserting their second emancipation and announcing their intention to vote for Hancock. The best information is that more than one fourth of the colored voters in the United States will vote for him. I congratulate and encourage them. They will find in thus voting an increase of their own self-respect and in General Hancock's success a patriotic result which will fully satisfy them that they have rendered service to their country. The natural political home of the colored men is in the Democratic party and the time is near when they will all realize it. It is one of the happy aspects of General Hancock's campaign that in a healthy, hearty way, all these questions are being placed in the forefront of discussion. I would like, if time allowed, to set forth the moral and patriotic advantages in Hancock's election toward an end of sectional divisions, in favor of the public credit, of honest money, hard money, and to expose the paltry misrepresentations against the Democracy as to repel debts, but I must finish by saying that the Hancock campaign brings us face to face with principles vital to the American system. The divergent views in our politics have been, on the one hand, local self-government, trust in the people, and rigid construction of the Constitution; and on the other hand, a Governmental scheme which is best defined by the term "Centralization." The former is the theory represented by General Hancock, and the latter is General Garfield's. I have no doubt which is the better for liberty and which the people will prefer. And the time has come when it is perilous to defer the return to the Democratic methods. During the long Republican rule the statute books have been filled with evil precedents. Whenever the Republicans undertook to legislate about a matter which in itself might be proper enough, their want of sympathy with the true principles of popular liberty would surely display itself. For instance, they could not legislate about elections without giving to deputy marshals arbitrary powers altogether variant from our entire judicial system and bills of rights. As Plunket once said to Parliament: "The vice in your laws changes wholesome nutriment into poison." This tendency has become so engrafted upon the Republican mind that of itself it contributes a good ground for electing Hancock. Is it well to allow Congressmen to enact whatever in their partisan opinion is for the public welfare, or shall the people hold Congress to the express powers which have been granted in the great charter? The latter is the only sure anchor of liberty.

So it is in every aspect of our public affairs: because they have been going wrong, we want a change,—and Hancock.

❖

An address made by Algernon Sydney Sullivan at a meeting to indorse General Winfield Scott Hancock, as a candidate for the office of President of the United States, Plainfield, N. J., September 23, 1880

FELLOW CITIZENS:

If I had not been told that I have also the honor of addressing a few of your Republican residents, I would have begun my address "Fellow Democrats"; but in the midst of all campaigns there is one thing greater than all partisanship—it is citizenship. In that spirit I shall endeavor, during the brief period I shall address you, to continue. There has been called to my mind by something your chairman said, an incident. It will be remembered that at one time during our struggle for liberty, General

Taylor and his little band were slowly and steadily advancing from point to point. As they advanced they erected behind them hospitals for their sick and dying. The gallant General was challenged to surrender, by the enemy—his reply was, "My wounded are behind me and I shall never pass them alive." In this campaign the Democracy occupy just such a position. They have their wounded behind them—a great wrong to redress. The wounds of the ballot box, that guardian of your interests and mine, must be healed; until then we will never give up. Four years ago the Republican party had already held power for sixteen years, and grown fat with plunder. Its members had become insolent and arrogant, and thought the federal offices should be handed down to their sons and other relations. At that time, when the air was full of stories of Babcock, and Belknap, and post-traderships, and whiskey rings, and Boss Shepard pavements, the people of the country came to the ballot box and recorded their decree that the administration should change hands and that Samuel J. Tilden was their choice for President. They recorded it by a popular majority of a quarter of a million and an electoral majority of twenty-seven. And the Republican party knows it! The judgment of the Almighty will come upon them with great shame! Our outraged ballot box is behind us, and we will never surrender until protection is accorded it. Some one says, "What has this to do with the present campaign?" Just this—the Republican party challenges us by nominating a man who not only was a member of this commission, but did more to work the plot into shape than any other one man. You remember four years ago, and that for weeks after the election all the newspapers and private telegrams stated that Louisiana had gone for Tilden as certainly as New York or New Jersey—and every one believed it. But the Republican Committee, at their headquarters in New York, began to plot and plan, and among other of the contrivances they conjured up, a number of "visiting statesman" were sent South by General Grant. One of those statesman—James A. Garfield—called upon that political saint,

Madison Wells, found out from him who were the members of the Returning Board and entered into the business of conferring with them. In the New Orleans Custom House, where the headquarters of the Board were situated, an inner room was secured by this same Garfield, where the returns were submitted to him and the affidavits set before him. He then saw that if the returns from West Feliciana and other parishes were accepted as received, Louisiana would be counted for Tilden. "Now, gentlemen," he said, "you want some affidavits of a certain kind." Witnesses were then brought to his inner room and conferred with him before being examined. After which, affidavits were made out and answers given merely to such questions as were drawn up by Mr. Garfield. (All this is a matter of record. I am not stating anything you cannot find contained in the examination.) Having got his affidavits in a shape to answer the purpose, Mr. Garfield returned to his seat in Congress. There he opposed a bill in relation to the matter that was presented. Why? Because it gave the electoral commission power to investigate the matter itself. We claim that those affidavits were lies. Seven voted "Aye, we will permit an examination, and if fraud is proven we will give the State to Tilden." Seven voted nay! There was one man then called upon to give the deciding vote. Remember who that man was! The man who arose to give that vote, and by it denied the right of the people to investigate fraud, was James A. Garfield. Why did he so vote? Because he was afraid to allow an examination of a plot of his own concoction.

Let us pass along to other considerations of great moment that justify our earnestness in this campaign. During the year of 1868 there was nominally a State government in the South— the people were subject to the will of the officers in command. These were ever willing to use their powers arbitrarily (always in favor of the carpet-bagger's demands) and to declare the bayonet supreme; in answer to appeals to shut the courts and suppress the newspaper that criticized. Such demands and appeals were made to General Winfield Scott Hancock, and it was given in that supreme moment by Providence, that there should be one wise man, one great soldier who would arise and dare to do right. He said, "I will not listen to any appeal to make the civil law subordinate to the military. You have your laws, the courts are open, the right of free speech is yours, and the bayonet is merely to protect such rights and privileges." You would like to have it said that everyone was pleased, but there was one in Congress who was not—that one was James A. Garfield. I do not wonder that you all hiss at the mention of his name. That action of his, in endeavoring to expel Hancock from the army, will one day be considered as infamous as the attempt of Benedict Arnold to betray his country. I say, as high as Mount Blanc raises itself above the hills of New Jersey, so Hancock's statesmanship rises above that of Garfield. We find Hancock standing by the constitution and enforcing its provisions—we find Garfield attacking him for so doing.

(Again the malcontent in the audience arose and with some difficulty stated that he was not satisfied with Mr. Ludlow's answer to his question,* and would like to have Mr. Sullivan's ideas relating to convict labor.)

I am not your candidate for governor (replied Mr. Sullivan); although I wish I were. But I have certain views on the question which I will express. I am one of those who believe always in making the convict work, but in such a way as will least compete with the honest workingman.

"The man who doesn't advocate that is a defeated man," said the questioner.

I do not care (continued the speaker); I would advocate it if I *were* a defeated man.

The Democratic party is the guardian of the rights of all, first, last and always. Its heritage and history is the recognition of the highest and the lowest. Though for a time, at the close of the war, the Republican party were able to poison the minds of our colored people with the belief that their enemies were

* Mr. Ludlow's address was made before Mr. Sullivan spoke at the same meeting.

the Democracy—yet I now know it to be a fact that one-third of the entire colored population, North and South, will of their own choice vote for Hancock. They say that we will overturn the prosperity of the country, and repudiate the Government bonds. Will a man burn down his house with his children in it? Two hundred and fifty millions of dollars are laid up in the savings banks of this country and by them invested in Government bonds. The owners of those savings are laboring people and Democrats! Trust us, then, to take care of our own, and conduct the affairs of the country as we always have, with justice and economy.

But, my friends, if I talked as long as your kind faces and attention encourages me to, I would talk until morning. So now I am going to propose three cheers for General Hancock, unless you start them yourselves.

(The building rang with hearty applause as the speaker retired, followed by cheers for Hancock, Sullivan and Ludlow.)

❖

One of the many speeches made in 1880 by Algernon Sydney Sullivan, who, in addressing these meetings of business men, urged their support for the proposed plan of holding a World's Fair in New York City

The exultation, the possible perfection and magnificence, of a great city enthroned by the sea constitute the trust imposed by their opportunity upon the citizens of New York. In due time her eminence shall overshadow all the grandeur of all imperial capitals known to history. How shall she attain it? I answer, by superadding to the enterprise and individual activities of her citizens a noble civic pride. The separate pursuit of their ventures by the multitude will surely lay up treasure in the

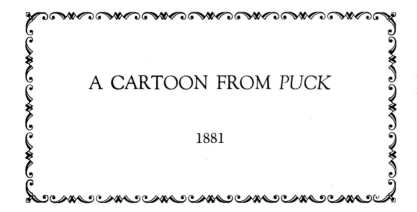

A CARTOON FROM *PUCK*

1881

THE proposed exhibition of 1883 was to have been in the nature of a World's Fair entitled the United States International Exhibition. It was to have been held at Inwood-on-Hudson, New York, in celebration of the one hundredth anniversary of the signing of the Treaty of Peace and the recognition of American Independence. The committee in charge included New York's most prominent bankers, merchants, professional men, and Government officials, a list of notables; and among the most active was Algernon Sullivan. This committee functioned under a National Charter from the Congress of the United States and one from the State of New York. The movement was considered of great importance to the development of the nation, but failed of its object through the apathy of the public,—the public of a city whose citizens, *en masse*, seem never to have been aroused to interest in such ventures. It was not through lack of confidence in the personnel of the committee but a passive unwillingness to interrupt their busy daily life, and a complete indifference to securing for the city enterprises of that nature.

The following editorial comment, February 16, 1881, appeared in *Puck* with the accompanying cartoon in which the head of the turtle pictures General U. S. Grant, late President of the United States and president of the committee. In front, on the turtle's back, is Algernon Sullivan. Below him and to the right are Morris K. Jesup, Russell Sage, and Mr. E. W. Stoughton.

"There is an E. C. of ours, a respected neighbor, who is forever crying out about the chief end of a Republican form of government being to preserve the 'untrammeled initiative' of the citizen. We have no objection to the preservation of the citizen's initiative in its most untrammeled condition; but what is to be done when the citizen has no initiative to trammel or to preserve untrammeled? The citizens of these United States are showing very little initiative in the matter of the 1883 Exhibition. With General Grant as the stay and stand-by of the whole commission, and with a large number of able gentlemen eloquently appealing to the public, the subscriptions are coming in very slowly. The amount asked for is not extravagant, yet the public does not step forward to subscribe it with any great show of spontaneous enthusiasm. Perhaps the best way, after all, would be to ask directly for aid from the national and the various state governments. If the Exhibition is a good thing for the country at large, this is the best and most dignified way of paying for it."

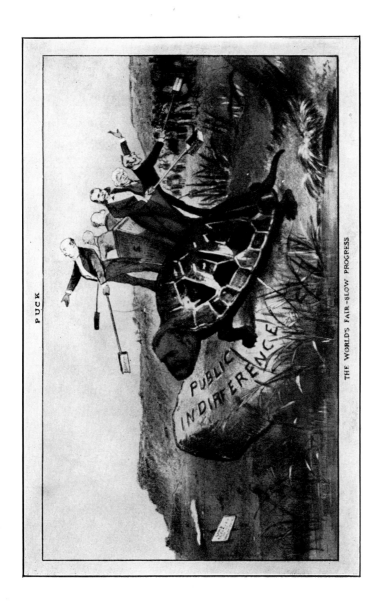

PUCK

THE WORLD'S FAIR—SLOW PROGRESS

coffers and wealth in the storehouse; but where shall appear the metropolitan glory? The name itself should have a lustre that belongs to itself and which like the day-star eclipses all the lesser lights. It is that public sentiment that has assembled here these hundreds of the men who are busy daily accumulating resources the right use of which shall help lift our beloved New York to its lofty plane now almost risen to view above the horizon. The practical consideration is, shall the World's Fair and Exposition on this island in 1883 be an exposition which shall not only be industrial, but shall collect the products of soil and mine, and all that ingenuity and taste have done to realize the beautiful, all that bears on the social problems of civilization, and all that will tend to bring into closer brotherhood of peace man with his fellows? About eight months ago a law was passed by Congress creating a commission which, acting under United States authority, was to arrange for and conduct our international exhibition in this city in 1883. A purpose so patriotic could not be entrusted to every community so fitly as to New York. General Grant will be called upon to open the exhibition not far from Harlem Plains. And right here let me say a commission, all to be chosen by stockholders, is an impossibility if the exhibition is to be international. An individual moneyed corporation can hold a fair, but the United States must appoint official commissioners, else they would not invite foreign governments to participate. Upon this point some misapprehension has existed, but reflection will correct that. The time is ample with the improved facilities we have in mechanics, with the experience derived from Philadelphia, and with the telegraph and telephone. With the aid already received and that which is promised, there can be no doubt of the entire success of the proposed exhibition.

❖

Address made by Algernon Sydney Sullivan at the presentation of
the Egyptian Obelisk from the Khedive of Egypt to the city
of New York, February 22, 1881

On behalf of the American Numismatic and Archaeological Society of New York, I have now to fulfil a commission, without which our proceedings should almost fail to express in rounded proportions the significance, the utility and the beauty of these stately ceremonies.   Yonder cuts the western sky, a memorial stone which has hitherto been a beacon under an eastern sky. While, as I speak, its shadow from the sinking sun moves towards us, it seems to people this museum, from the dim past of the Orient, with weird myths and mysterious and splendid legends.   That monolith was an emblem of Deity.   The kings and priests who set it up have been mummies for thirty centuries, and their sun-worship is giving place to the adoration of the *"Lux benigna et Divina"* of the true revelation.   Their monument has been moved to the new continent to be an ever-speaking witness to the continuity and unity of human thought. It is the fittest of all possible sentinels at the portal of our future great archaeological temple.

An appreciative token of the liberal financial donor, Mr. William H. Vanderbilt and of the skilful and indefatigable engineer, Lieutenant-Commander H. H. Gorringe, U. S. N., to whose mediary agency we owe this souvenir of Egyptian methods has been stamped upon medals to commemorate this occasion medalically, artistically and historically.   The first impressions from the die, in silver, in the name of the distinguished society already named, and in view of this assembly, I now deliver to Mr. Vanderbilt and to Lieutenant-Commander Gorringe, whose great services to the cause of art and historic enlightenment are hereby recognized by all the educational circles of New York and America.

But there remains the closing and not the least important feature in the design of this celebration.   I turn to the gallery above us, and I see one hundred faces of so many bright boys of

New York who represent the one hundred thousand children who crowd her public schools.

My lads, you are welcome participants in our ceremonies. It is, perhaps, the first time in the history of New York that the children have been formally given a station in great public movements, but I hope it will not be so hereafter. We wish you to grow up with the feeling that the monuments, the museums, the schools, the libraries, the statues, the public institutions, the churches, the parks, and all the agencies that look to the improvement and the refinement and the health of the people, to the honor and virtue and morals of the city, to its public spirit and its civic pride, to its good repute and its magnificence, are a trust which you are soon to assume. They are now to influence and educate you, and we beg you to cherish them continuously. Let your book-studies be associated with all these sentiments. Meditate upon them with love. Determine to take a part in the community for its good, and that New York shall be better for your having lived in it. Revere such benefactors of mankind as dear old Peter Cooper, and ever remember that "A good name is better than great riches."

In the hope that this day shall be a great teaching day to all the children of New York, and lift them forward on an ascending plane, I address you as the representative of all of them. I also present to each of you a medal, which, as a talisman, shall ever remind you of the beauty and duty of good citizenship. The motto upon the medal is taken from a Latin poet, and is "*Discipulus est priori, posterior dies,*" and it may be translated, "Today must learn from yesterday." I entreat you to observe in your lives the lessons, the wisdom and the examples of experience.

You will have little difficulty in interpreting the artistic language of your medals. In the field the obelisk is seen, a little towards the right on the medal; in the background, the sun is represented rising over the sea, being an allegory recalling the ancient association of the obelisk with the worship of the sun and also representing a part of the arms of the State of New York. In the lower field of the medal are represented the shields of the United States and of the city of New York, grouped; that of the United States being surmounted by the American eagle, and that of New York, resting on the scroll bearing the word, "Excelsior." These two shields, entwined and grouped with laurel, are meant to represent the recipients of the gift from Egypt, forming in all, a trio emblematic of the East and West. An inner border, ornamented with stars, representing the States of the Union, separates somewhat the legend from the subject, and on the ground of the outer circle, on which the motto is placed, a garland of Lotus flowers, cut in low relief, under the lettering, will appropriately recall the souvenir of Egypt. The reverse of the medal tells the story of the monolith:

Presented to the

UNITED STATES

by

Ismail, Khedive of Egypt,

1881.

Quarried at Syene

And erected at Heliopolis by

Thothmes III.

Reërected at Alexandria

under Augustus.

Removed to New York

through the liberality of

W. H. Vanderbilt,

By the skill of

Lieut.-Comm. H. H. Gorringe, U. S. N.

❖

An address delivered by Algernon Sydney Sullivan at the Shakespeare-Poe Festival and Benefit Entertainment at the Academy of Music, New York City, April 23, 1881

LADIES AND GENTLEMEN:

There is no name in poetry with which to conjure like that of Shakespeare. On his birthday each hour seems to bear a winged censer, which kindles before the poet's shrine that is lodged in every breast. It awakens the fancy, so that the horizon of life becomes a gold-embroidered mist; and borne in on all the winds come echoes, as from Apollo's nine-stringed shell. Old beliefs revive, and all the forces and objects and aspects of nature, and all its mysteries and enchantments, are once again personified. Beneath this spell, what votive offering in Shakespeare-worship can be more fitting than to honor, as we do tonight, in an unpretentious, though sympathetic spirit, the memory of one who was the greatest among our early American authors? We have, perhaps in a somewhat reckless fashion, named this entertainment the Shakespeare-Poe Festival; yet we may hope that, in bringing these two names together, we are offering to neither an injustice and to both a respectful and affectionate homage. Our practical motive, as you know, is to gain an amount of money which shall be used to purchase an enduring memorial to Edgar Allan Poe, and which shall be placed in one of the corners of the Metropolitan Museum of Art. That corner, if our hopes be fulfilled, shall be known as the Poets' Corner; and all of our brave, true and favorite poets should look forward to having their names inscribed there, whither, in time to come, the living minstrels as pilgrims shall wander, and where their heads shall bow, their eyes shall moisten and their hearts glow with unseen fires. When death takes from us a true poet, it is our right and our duty to illustrate in some sweet and heartfelt manner our love for him and our respect for his memory. All the great peoples have honored their poets; all the great nations are greatest in their singers. We may forget the history of the Elizabethan age, but when shall Shakespeare be forgotten?

The public of New York have often been accused of indifference and neglect towards their poets, and it is said that our society is too materialistic to value them and to remember them. A festival like this goes far to disprove the accusation. At any rate, it is a beginning in the right direction, and however short it may fall of an ideal literary festival, its effect will be, I am sure, to bring the public and their poets into more tender and more cordial relations. It is a bond of union, a common ground of appreciation, a suggestion to the generation growing up, and which is represented so gratefully and graciously in this entertainment. American literature is on the threshold of its glory. It is you, and especially those of you who have youth and aspiration in your hearts, to whom the future of our literature looks for its support and its reward. In honoring Poe you are honoring all the men and women who are working for the intellectual renown of our country, or who have done aught to build up that renown. In honoring him, moreover, you show your admiration for what is more rare, most noble, most lasting of all human things—genius. Of his life I will here say little. Too much, considering its sometimes unkind and unforgiving spirit, already has been written about that. I would reproach myself, however, if I omitted to express, briefly and simply, one thought in that connection. When we pass beyond the line of his one infirmity and fault, we find ourselves in the presence of a man of clean ideas. This is a fair judgment on a review of all the facts. Poe was not an immoral man; he was not a libertine; he was not a malignant man. There is not an impure, an unchaste or an impious line from his pen. There is not an instance where he excused vice or masked it in deceiving beauty. Poe's was a sad and sombre life—a flower that faded too early, a splendid day-dawn that darkened too soon into night. But his genius was left to us, a heritage that will always be precious. He was, perhaps, greater as a prose author than as a poet. Not because his poetic gift was less remarkable than his other extraordinary gifts, but because his finest song remained unsung. The music in his soul was hardly voiced, yet its few notes are clear and dominant. The subtle and original melody of his verse—a melody which is akin to some of Shelley's delicate and irregular rhythm—its imaginative and dream-like loveliness, its deep indenture of sorrow and despair, its mingling of the unreal, the mysterious and the human,—all this appealed in the beginning, and has continued to appeal, to the ears of men; and the slight bulk of the poet's work has been accepted reverentially, not only as the fruit of his genius, but as an indication of its possibilities. There is visible, through his whole endeavor, continual advance towards the spirit of absolute beauty and of the highest truth, but the unrest and disappointment of his honest yearnings were not ended when his lyre was broken. To the last, the murmur that ran through his life song was his well remembered refrain:

> Is all that we see, or seem,
> But a dream within a dream?

I need say no more. In the name of the ladies and gentlemen who compose the committee, I thank you for your presence. I feel that you sympathize with the purpose which animates them, and I feel, also, that our living American poets, the veterans who have won their fame and the young singers whose eyes are set upon the promising future, are in accord with us all.

❖

John W. Foster, ex-Minister to Russia, delivered before the Young Men's Hebrew Association in February, 1882, a lecture, " The Czar and His People." In proposing a vote of thanks to Mr. Foster, Algernon Sydney Sullivan said:

Mr. President:

History seems to delight in contrasts, and I can recall very few more picturesque and suggestive than those which passed before our imagination as we listened to the graceful and happy lecture of ex-Minister Foster. Direct your thoughts for a moment to a point within the Arctic Circle at the mouth of the River Lena, to which those phantom warriors who guard the coveted secrets of the North Pole have driven back our adventurous sailors sick and sore. Russia pities and comforts them, and we thank her for it tonight. Now look at another scene. Great Atlantic ships, tossed by wintry storms, land in America. We have tidings in advance of their coming, and we meet them at the shore. Who are there that crowd the decks? Ah! They are Russians and surely we will hospitably shelter them. We ask, were you driven by stress and fury of inclement latitudes and seasons? Humanity and Religion, bow your heads at the answer! Patriarchs and mothers in Israel, leading children and children's children, "Weeping as they go up," ascend our shores, to which an evil spirit of intolerance in the breast of so-called Christian neighbors and Christian rulers has driven them. America's response is: "Shelter, home, freedom, liberty of conscience you shall have. These we give to you, as the good angel showed 'A well of water' to Hagar." Let us all learn anew and in a broader sense than ever before the lesson of charity and toleration, not in any spirit of vituperation towards Russia. On behalf of the audience and of the benevolent cause which he has so efficiently served by his presence this evening, and in the name of the Young Men's Hebrew Association, I move a vote of thanks to John W. Foster, ex-Minister of the United States to Mexico and to Russia, for his interesting and scholarly lecture upon "The Czar and His People."

❖

*At a fair held by St. Lawrence's Church in New York City, May,
1882, Algernon Sydney Sullivan was awarded the prize in a
popularity contest.   It was a handsome cane provided by the
Governor of the State.   Mr. Sullivan's reply to the presentation
of the cane by Judge Brady follows:*

It is in no spirit of self-complacency that I take pleasure in
this gift.   Each of my competitors knows that I know he would
have won the cane, if extraordinary merit, or good looks, had
influenced the votes.   At any rate we are all friends, and in any
real-life struggles will be glad to give to each other the salutations
and hand-grasps of sincere friendship.   Indeed, I would not be
surprised if the candidates for governor of the State of New York,
next fall, shall be two of my late rivals, Secretary Folger and
Congressman Flower.   Either of them will be a good governor,
and I think I will vote for both of them.   I generously stand aside
for them, content with the greater honors awarded here tonight.

By his opinion on the case before him, Judge Brady has, just
now, more than ever shown himself to be a good judge.   He has
been so discreet, so liberal, so courteous and so full of humor,
that each party thinks judgment has been rendered in his favor,
and we will long remember his graceful speech.

But some one asked me yesterday, "Who was St. Lawrence?"
And that set me a-thinking how, by familiarity in a great city
like ours, we cease to note the lessons which show themselves in
monuments and names, all about us.   Surely it must be from
some enduring and very powerful impression that in England
two hundred and fifty Protestant churches are dedicated in
honor of St. Lawrence and that there is scarcely a city or town
in all Christendom that does not contain a Catholic Church
and altar dedicated to his honor.   Do you remember his legend?
I will not apologize for quoting his splendid story even amid
these festivities, although the reverend clergy present could do
it so much better.

A young and pious priest, who walked meekly and blamelessly
before God, he was made arch-deacon by Sixtus II, Bishop of

Rome, the twenty-fourth in succession from St. Peter, and who had in his care the treasures of the Church. Sixtus being denounced as a Christian to the Prefect of Rome was sentenced to death. Laurentius, the deacon, in great affliction, clung to his friend and pastor, saying: "Whither goest thou, O my father, without thy son and servant? Am I found unworthy to pour out my blood with thine in testimony to the truth of Christ?" But the Bishop replied: "I do not leave thee, my son; in three days thou shalt follow after me, and thy battle shall be harder than mine; for I am old and weak and my course shall soon be finished; but thy torments will be longer and more severe, and thy triumph the greater. Grieve not; Lawrence the Levite shall follow Sixtus the Priest," Thus he comforted the young man, and, moreover, commanded him to take all the possessions of the Church and distribute them to the poor. Sixtus was quickly put to death, and Lawrence took the money and treasures of the Church, and walked through all the city of Rome, seeking out the poor and the sick, the naked and the hungry. From house to house he went, consoling the persecuted, dispensing alms, and performing works of charity and humility. Being required to tell the Prefect where the Church treasures were concealed, he gathered together the sick and the poor, to whom he had dispensed alms, and said: "Behold, here are the treasures of Christ's Church." Thinking he was mocked, the Prefect, in a great rage, commanded that Lawrence should be taken by night to the baths of Olympias, near the villa of Sallust, the historian, there to be stretched on a sort of bed formed of iron bars in the manner of a gridiron, and a fire to be lighted beneath, which should gradually consume his body to ashes. The executioners did as they were commanded, and the victim, never swerving from his faith in our blessed Lord, was roasted alive. Lifting his dying eyes, he exclaimed: "I thank thee, O my God and Saviour, that I have been found worthy to enter into Thy beatitude!" And his pure and invincible spirit fled to Heaven. His words are reëchoing through all the ages.

Does someone ask why I repeat this story tonight, amid the

busy whirl of New York? I will answer. I wish all the traditions of holy living and self-denying Christians, in every age, to
be brought more into the light, that they may preach. I would
not have, and there shall not be, if Christians of all denomina-
tions will awake, an "eclipse of faith."

I would adopt the thought of Dr. Arnold, of Rugby, who says
that we do not consider the excellence of this martyr-spirit half
enough. The contemplation of suffering for Christ's sake is a
thing most needful for us, in this day, from whose daily life suffering seems so far removed. If you listen to the grand hymns of
the far-off, early ages, and follow them flowing like a river
through the history of the Church, receiving tributary streams
from the heavenly meditations of believers, you will see that
among the sacred memories which the Church has garnered, none
are more radiant and fragrant than He who redeemed the world
by His precious blood, and is adored by angels, apostles, prophets
and martyrs. Whenever has been sung the "*Te Deum lauda-
mus*," no versicle therein has been more precious than "*Te
martyrum candidatus laudat exercitus*"—"The noble army of
martyrs praise thee."

In one sense the world will never grow old, and like a little
child must ever be learning the simple lesson, "For duty's
sake, come weal or come woe."

❖

*Algernon Sydney Sullivan's reply to the toast, "Non Nobis Nati
Solum," at the Annual Banquet of the New York Chamber of
Commerce, May 9, 1882*

MR. PRESIDENT AND GENTLEMEN:

That motto has been already sufficiently translated by the
graceful, happy and appropriate speeches that you have listened

to. The toast is at once recognized as the motto upon the seal of the first mercantile society in America, the Chamber of Commerce of New York. One hundred and twelve years have passed since His Majesty, George the Third, granted your existing charter to certain of "his loving subjects," and authorized them to have a corporate seal, and the same to alter, change, break and make new at their pleasure. The purpose of the association was stated to be, "To promote by just and lawful ways" such measures as will tend to promote and extend "just and lawful commerce." (Cheers.) Thus, justice and law were printed on each of your doorposts. Your seal was prepared in 1770, under directions of Theophylact Bache, the Treasurer of the Chamber. It was engraved in London, and brought to New York on Saturday evening, April 11, 1772, on board the ship *Duchess of Gordon*, eight weeks out from London. It has never been broken or changed, and just as it was made I now hold and exhibit it to, you. (Applause.)

It may interest younger members to have a brief description and history of the seal.

It is known in the numismatic scale as size 46, and the legend reading, "The seal," etc., surrounds a field with a figure of Mercury winged, holding in his left hand a caduceus. On medals this is a symbol of good conduct, peace and prosperity. The right hand of the figure supports a shield, with the arms of New Netherlands resting on a bale of merchandise marked "G. B." The emblems to the left are barrels, an anchor, cannon and a beaver, typical of commerce. The barrel marked "N. A. Flaxseed," is significant. A horn of plenty is in the lower part of the field. A ship under full sail is seen, as also the rising sun. The exergue, "*Non Nobis Nati Solum*," is a quotation from Cicero.

By resolution, it was made the duty of the president for the time being to keep this seal in his possession. At the close of the War of Independence, Mr. Isaac Low, the seventh president of the association, was among those who withdrew from the city and made his residence in England. Some years thereafter a gentleman interested in the affairs of this country, looking over a miscellaneous collection of articles in a London curiosity shop, discovered among them this signet of your Chamber of Commerce. He purchased it, and with true public spirit restored it to its present proper ownership. Probably it was an inadvertence on the part of Mr. Low to take it with him to England, and there is no clue to the mystery how it came to the London shop.

But now a word as to the significance of this motto. No doubt the circumstances of the period influenced the selection. The public mind was under great excitement. The controversies between the Colonies and the Parliament had been violent. The British Stamp Act had been answered, so far as New York was concerned, at a general meeting of her merchants, by the adoption of a non-importation agreement until the act should be repealed. So throughout the preliminary struggle, the merchants of this city, without regard to disastrous consequences, took the patriotic side. But it is their preëminent distinction that they always sought a Congress, wishing to make common cause with all the Colonies, and looking to a union. The Stamp Act was repealed, but then came the duty on teas. New York merchants again renewed their non-importation agreement. The city then had 20,000 inhabitants, and an ocean commerce of 600 entrances and clearances annually; and her merchants were ready to sacrifice trade rather than abandon a right. It has been said, that which a man desires in his youth, he hath in his old age. At the origin of all institutions, there is some impulse which marks and develops all their future. The starting point of the Chamber of Commerce, translating its motto to one word, was *Justice*. (Cheers.) Not, "Every man for himself;" not, "All is fair in trade;" not, "My neighbor's necessity is my opportunity;" but commerce and exchange which go hand in hand with all that is large-minded and honorable, and generous and well-wishing, and helpful among mankind. (Applause.)

The lesson has not been in vain. From the beginning our merchants have prospered, but always by fair trade and just dealing, and liberally do they dispense it for the benefit and refinement of their fellow men, not only at home but throughout the globe. The motto of the Chamber of Commerce of New York is but a practical paraphrase of the second great commandment, given from the lips of Him who spake, as never man spake, "Thou shalt love thy neighbor as thyself."—"*Non Nobis Nati Solum.*"

❖

An address delivered by Algernon Sydney Sullivan at the banquet of the semi-Centennial Convention of the Alpha Delta Phi Fraternity, New York, May 18, 1882, in reply to the toast, "The Past of Alpha Delta Phi"

For his own sake and for yours, brother Alpha Deltas, Professor Dwight's absence is to be regretted. He is such a conspicuous part of the past of our Fraternity, that, at best, I can be but a poor substitute. I cannot, on this summons, chronicle the incidents in our history, but as I listened to the sketch of the founder of the Society, as it was read just now by Brother Whiting, the life and character of Alpha Delta Phi, as a whole, rose in distinct image before me. Its genesis in the heart of a noble, scholarly, Christian gentleman, with associates of like quality, moulded its entire future. Our thoughts have run backwards, —the long path displaying everywhere the verisimilitude of its opening. The case is like that of the peasant whose story, by an old writer, I will quote, and whose home was at the foot of the Alps. It was in the charming age when men's imagination deified the forces and harmonies of nature, and every locality was the dwelling-place of a god or a goddess. A mountain brook fertilized our peasant's garden. He piously adored the naiad who fed the stream, and who increased its quantity and its coolness as the summer's heat increased. A fancy struck him that he would go and discover the place where she concealed her inexhaustible urn. He began to follow upward the track of the rivulet. Every step in the ascent revealed to him new and interesting objects near and far. He passed the line of snow, and even there the Alpine harebell bloomed at his feet. He proceeded in hopes of reaching the blessed abode where the gods preside over the destiny of the world, and at last he arrived at the foot of a glacier. Where now was his beneficent naiad? Was his divinity but a mass of ice? Was this the inanimate source of blessing to his sweet home and his tranquil valley? We can answer for him. In all the revolving seasons, the fleecy clouds and the stormy tempests have piled their treasures of dew and snow upon the mountain. The sun lifted the ocean's vapors, the viewless winds bore them landward, and they crystallized on ever-rising pinnacles until they propped the incumbent skies. In due season, resolved by the sun, the imprisoned waters returning to the basis of the sea enrich the peasant's garden, and diffuse abundance in a thousand different channels. In all these various movements, the law which controls them, and the wisdom, are something more than the majesty of nature. It is the providence of the God of the universe. Our Alpha Delta Phi brotherhood, in all its past, has felt the impulse of the Christian faith and the Christian character of the men who laid its foundations. As the sky over our heads this night shows the constellated beauty of the star and the crescent, above the font of our Society's baptism was the Star of Bethlehem, in the faith of its earliest members.

In these days of infidelity and agnostic philosophies, I do not feel that I transgress the limits of propriety, even on a collegian's festival night, when I thus recall the seal and impress of religious belief which was put upon us, for all time.

So, may the dear old Society continue, clear, pure, fed from the upper heights, imparting honor and happiness to all within its influence, like the meadow brook,

Which gently kisseth every sedge
It meeteth in its pilgrimage.

❖

*An address delivered by Algernon Sydney Sullivan at the laying
of the corner stone of the New York Produce Exchange, June
6, 1882. Mr. Sullivan spoke extemporaneously at these
ceremonies, at less than an hour's notice, replacing the orator
of day, the Hon. William M. Evarts*

MR. PRESIDENT AND MERCHANTS OF NEW YORK:

The true orator of the hour is this corner stone of polished
granite, solid, square, and level, typifying the foundation principles upon which commercial business must rest. It has been
well laid. The auspices have all been favorable. See how the
splendor of a New York noon-day sun pours lustre upon it!
The fair hands of your wives and daughters have decked it
with a coronet of June roses. Patriotic songs, sung by yourselves, made music as it was lifted into its final resting-place
of use and honor. And then, as became the merchants of a
Christian community, the man of prayer was called upon to lead
us all in prayer to Him, without whose blessing nothing can
prosper. I rejoiced to witness this, especially in these days,
when many are apprehensive that unbelief may remove from
the hearts of the sons of those who settled and built up New
York, the grand old faith in the true and living Corner Stone,
who abideth forever. (Applause.)

And now, how shall I put in a few brief sentences the thoughts
which this scene, these rising walls and columns, force upon me?
Standing upon this New England granite, and looking around,
I do not see you only. What attendants are these, whose majestic presence fills with dignity your opening halls? Yonder
stands the figure of Agriculture. The dew of morning sparkles
in her hair and the crimson of setting suns has dyed her robes.
The beauty of health and benevolence glows in her countenance.
Her right hand holds the sickle and her arms are filled with the
bounty of rich harvests. The plough, the reaper, and all the
implements of husbandry support her pedestal. Oh, vision
fair! You carry our thoughts far afield, over the bosom of kind

mother earth, teeming with grasses, grains, and fruits, to make strong and glad the hearts of her children.

Above us the sky is rainbowed with the flags of all nations, and beneath their canopy behold another stately image smiling amid these ceremonies. It is Commerce, diademed with gems from land and sea. Hail and welcome, benignant guardian of tranquillity and intercourse among the nations! This Exchange shall ever be one of the noblest shrines to your honor! Grouped around these, I behold the genius of Navigation and of Manufactures, and of every Guild of Toil and Labor which bring wealth. I see the symbols which typify the spirit of justice and friendship, to govern intercourse and exchange all over the world. That spirit you recognize as present, and its hand is clasped by every man of you, while I speak.

A corner stone, as its name implies, is not merely to support one wall, but to unite, while it supports, two walls. I discern in this the sentiment of concord and harmony between all exchanges and branches of industry. You illustrate it now, by inviting as your guests, representatives from all the exchanges in the city. To you have also come, with compliments and good wishes, delegates from the great mercantile centers of Europe. You have also gathered to your company, to share in your not unbecoming pride, representatives of the Arts and Sciences, in many branches. This is well. The structure which is to crown these foundations will mark an epoch in the advance of architecture in our beloved city. New York should have no honors so costly, but that she will lay them at the feet of architects who will build the city up to the finest conceptions of use and beauty.

Concluding this address, and these ceremonies, let me impress upon you that the merchant—not the mere shopkeeper, not the mere tradesman—but the merchant of New York, in the real dignity of that term, is never fitly engaged in his vocation unless he carries his thoughts and love of his city beyond the passing wants of his mercantile exchanges; and unless he remembers to carry, hand in hand with the prosperity of merchandising, all that relates to the education, to the religion, to the refinement and beautifying of Manhattan Island, the matchless—of New York, the bejewelled commercial queen of the world, as she is destined to be.

❖

Address of Algernon Sydney Sullivan at a philanthropic meeting in behalf of the Presbyterian Hospital, 1882

None of you can feel more than I that words enough have been said,—apt, beautiful, impressive, and certainly words that will be very lasting in the memory and in the hearts of every one who is here. All that I will add, in response to the very courteous invitation to which I respond, will be that which has been suggested by the words or allusions of my predecessors.

There came to my mind, when Dr. Hall * referred to that intensely interesting episode in European History, the rise of the Nihilist party, and culminated in his allusion to that tragedy which probably startled the Christian world as greatly as anything that has occurred in our times (the assassination of the Emperor of Russia by the Anarchists), and when he drew aside the curtain to show us what he thought was the prevailing state of mind and religion in Russia,—there came to my mind, as sometimes does the rain from rent clouds, one of the memories which constitute a charming treasury of knowledge with regard to the men who are doing sweet work in this world of ours,—the memory of one who is a Russian. I do not know whether any of you have had the pleasure of reading the essays or prose poems of that Russian, Turgenev. A little sketch came to my mind, when Dr. Hall was uttering his golden words, as somehow fitly

* The Rev. Dr. John Hall, member of the Board of Trustees of the Presbyterian Hospital.

expressing the dominant idea which surrounds this institution today:

"I went out walking, and a figure met me, an early old man; poverty and sickness had made him look very wretched and very repulsive; his eyes were inflamed, his clothing was rough, his skin was made loathsome by the marks of disease; he whined and asked me for alms. I felt in my pocket and I found that I had brought no money, and I had neither watch nor handkerchief nor anything to give him; while I looked and was embarrassed, the hand (and as I believe, the faith hand) was still extended to me and to my attention; and when I found I had nothing for him I reached out and grasped his hands and I said: 'Don't blame me, brother, I have brought nothing with me.'

"The blood-shot eyes were lifted to me, and at the same time I felt the clasp of his chilled hands; the color came into the blue lips of the sick beggar, and responded to the extended hand and to the apology which ended with the word brother, and he said, 'This, too, is a gift; I thank you for this, brother.'"

And Turgenev says: "I laid down that hand and felt that I, too, had received a gift from *my* brother." It is that idea which seemed to be echoing round the words of Dr. Hall as he uttered them today.

Who is it that gets the gift on this day, in this institution? My friends, it is not the poor patients alone. That is not in the order of Providence; and that blessed God whose purpose it is that there shall come the realization of the ideals of life, and who has permitted that men shall be his co-workers, has also arranged it so and planned it so and intended it so that disinterested and enlightened service of our fellow men is the way towards developing that spirituality and that refinement and that idealization of life which is yet to grow and to grow, until all humanity shall have had that advancement of uplifting which it is the purpose of God to give to his race whom he has planted upon this earth. I rejoice when I am to share in ceremonies like this; when it happens as it did today, that the first word which broke upon our ear, as we stilled ourselves when the man of prayer arose to open the exercises, was "Our Father." That is the lesson that has been taught by these reverend gentlemen as they have said it so beautifully and so aptly. It is the lesson of an occasion like this, and it is all about us in these halls and these walls and these grounds.

We have said today that the sweetness and the beauty and the glory and the happiness of life is just in proportion to that sentiment of universal brotherhood which enters deeper and deeper among the throbbing hearts of all mankind. The common fatherhood implies the common brotherhood; and as that exercises itself, it builds, it enlarges, it purifies, it beautifies, it sweetens life and makes this influence for us who are here or us who go away. Only in like work and under like sermons and occasions can we find an influence which is as sweet as that of the setting sun that comes through these stained windows into this chapel today.

My friends, the occasion has been made very auspicious; it has been made so interesting by the record of progress and of growth, by the announcement of the increase of friends who support it and who actively sympathize with it. It has been made so interesting by the wonderful record of its success, working out the design of its founders; it has been made interesting to those, who, like myself, for the first time have walked through the beautiful and well-arranged and well-furnished private and public rooms, dormitories and halls. It has been made impressive as illustrating what science and beneficence can do; it has been crowned now by such a radiance that we today, straining the imagination, can almost hear in the working, the spirit of the blessed Master and of the Great Physician; we can see, in imagination in the perspective of the ages, the times when the sick of all kinds flocked in to him who was the head of the church, that he might heal them. To this extent, the example of the Lord is being followed by those who come after him and would be like him.

As that thought has been forced upon me today by these addresses, I love to think of what is to be the result. What men and women may hope for as they cultivate this movement and those exercises which spiritualize life, spiritualize their souls, less and less encumbering their hearts with the rust and the dust and the selfishness of this world; and, in becoming more and more spiritualized, ever growing toward that state of purity which, under the promises of the gospel, is open to all who believe in it.

As we draw to the close of these exercises, may we not fairly ask the men of the world, such as am I, covered with its dust, yes, and stained with its dust, for a moment at least, to think of that blessing which is promised to those who develop the spiritual nature and the purity of heart which they are encouraged to believe is required of them and is promised to them? May we not at least ask them to think, in common with the suffering who fill the hospitals, the maimed and the blind and the deaf and the dumb? And may we not, with profit, dwell upon that chief of blessings in the wonderful promises of the Lord upon the Mount, where, after pledging his blessings to the meek and to the merciful, he promises to the pure in heart that they shall see God.

We are in the house of prayer; we are in the house sacred and dedicated to his name, and adjacent to the hospital. Our thoughts have been necessarily carried along until we can do nothing except to make the occasion as it were, a religious and joyous service.

❖

An address delivered by Algernon Sydney Sullivan before the American Numismatic and Archaeological Society, Quarter Centennial Meeting, March 20, 1883

A quarter of a century is a short period, contrasted with the centuries familiar to the archaeologist, yet it is not without some pride that we pause at a twenty-fifth anniversary, to look over the years which have passed since thirteen residents of New York

founded this Association. Many individuals in the city were
learned as antiquarians, and many, as amateurs, had rich cabinets of coins and medals. One gentleman, distinguished as a
classic scholar, had and still owns a cabinet filled with medallic
treasures, which for size and variety of subjects ranks among the
best of known private collections; you readily understand I
allude to our esteemed President, Professor Charles E. Anthon.
I trust that some liberal citizen will secure for our public institution that cabinet upon which Professor Anthon has bestowed so
much time and cultivated taste. If to our own accumulation of
three thousand valuable coins and medals, with our library of
about two thousand volumes of bound books and pamphlets,
were super-added the Anthon Collection, New York would have,
as it ought to have, a numismatic museum, the best in the
United States. What friend of education and art will, by making the endowment secure, add his name to the roll of honor of
New York's generous sons?

The founders recognized that it was only by association that
the study of Numismatics could be efficiently fostered, and a
cabinet formed which would really serve the purposes of History
and Art. Private collections are soon lost or scattered; besides,
the usefulness of a medallic collection is much in proportion to
its completeness and the consecutive order in its specimens. As
an agent to accomplish these conditions, a permanent corporation is indispensable.

Finding that the Association interested many who were not
members, and that its library and cabinet were enlarging, the
members caused the institution to be incorporated. This was in
the closing year of our Civil War; since that date coins and medals and books of great value have been presented to us. They
have been obtained in a quiet way, without endowment or large
gifts; enough has been done to put the success of the institution
beyond question, and to show that it has the growing confidence
of the public, as a trustee to preserve these contributions to a
great Museum of Archaeology and Numismatics. At first it
was not contemplated that the archaeological work in this

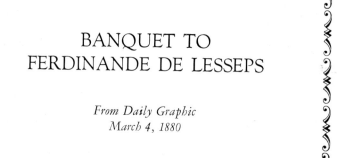

BANQUET TO
FERDINANDE DE LESSEPS

From Daily Graphic
March 4, 1880

THE Banquet to Ferdinande de Lesseps, eminent engineer of the Suez Canal, was given on Monday, March 1, 1880, at old Delmonico's in New York City. The sketch by the special artist of the *Daily Graphic* appeared in their issue of March 4th. At the speakers' table, not far from the guest of honor, the Reverend Dr. Bellows stands speaking. At his right is the venerable Peter Cooper, and farther along are General Schofield and the Reverend Dr. Richard S. Storrs.

At the extreme left Algernon Sydney Sullivan may be seen standing leading the applause, and around him a group of New York's distinguished citizens. Mr. Sullivan was a prominent and active member of the Committee of Arrangements.

NEW YORK CITY—BANQUET TO FERDINAND DE LESSEPS AT DELMONICO'S LAST MONDAY NIGHT.

FROM A SKETCH BY OUR SPECIAL ARTIST.

Society should be as prominent as that in Numismatics, yet both were distinctly conjoined, and hereafter increased attention must be given to Archaeology. We have in our possession much interesting material in that line, and through other channels New York continually receives rich archaic dowry.

We find in the Metropolitan Museum in New York the coins of Philip and Alexander of Macedon; the vases, the engraved gems and stones, and the myriad relics impress the imagination with a strangely combined feeling of curiosity and reverence. I felt that all the old yesterdays were in reanimated movement about me, when, in looking over the Museum cabinets, I saw the official seal of Thothmes III, the Egyptian King who captured Cyprus three thousand three hundred years ago; and then, lifting my eyes, I saw between me and the sinking sun that obelisk of incalculable value in its relation to Archaeology in New York, and the gift of which should preserve the name of William H. Vanderbilt in honor, as long as bronze and granite shall last.

Let us not permit this topic to pass without an expression of the lively interest which our Society takes in the archaeological researches now in progress on both hemispheres,—those under the direction of that accomplished French savant, M. Désiré Charnay in Yucatan; in those at Assis under the auspices of the Archaeological Institute of America, of which Professor Charles Eliot Norton is President; and those resulting in the splendid discoveries by Mr. Henry Schliemann on the site which I believe to be the very site of the very Troy of Homer. I am not of that school whose critical skepticism has found voice in the phrase, Homer's Troy was but a city built in the ethereal region of his fancy. I believe the true Ilium to have been unearthed in the hill of Hissarlik, ground which the Greeks have neglected to search during more than fifteen centuries.

The present is an auspicious time for our Society to carry into practical form the suggestions outlined on a former occasion by our President, proposing the organization of the members under sections, each devoting itself to special departments in the general field of labor which the Society has undertaken. They

are substantially as follows: Section A, devoted to Numismatics;
Section B, to that of Archaeology, including all branches of research into the life of past ages in the old world; Section C, to be
employed with the aboriginal antiquities of America; Section
D, to be related to the home or local antiquarianism of our
beloved city of New York. A committee should be appointed
at once to prepare details for thus developing and prosecuting
our scientific labors. Specialization in this form promises great
results. The field of American Archaeology and that sub-
department of it to be prosecuted within the immediate limits of
New York are the most inviting.

The opportunities of this anniversary would be neglected if
we did not recall the important historical celebrations which
have revived national sentiment, and which as a centennial
series will soon complete themselves, in relation to the events of
largest moment in the formation period of our government.
Perhaps that which will most strike the imagination is the approaching public ceremony in this city, intended to mark the
centennial of the evacuation of New York by British troops at
the close of the War of Independence. Our Society should be
an active participant in the celebration, and through its agency
a suitable medal should be prepared as the most durable form of
recording the event which is to be commemorated, and of the
spirit and purposes of the commemoration, which themselves
will become historic facts of importance. Let the officers of the
Society be directed to confer on this subject with the state and
city authorities, and with the various civic bodies which will
determine the character and features of the memorial.

*Address made by Algernon Sydney Sullivan at the opening of the
New York Produce Exchange in 1884*

Fine in architecture and colossal in proportions, sprung from
massive corner stone ribbed with iron and walled with bricks
burned in the hottest kilns, opening windows to every sky, and,
like a beetling cliff commanding the eye of the homebound mar-
iner, Oh, tower-crowned Trade Hall! Thou standest imperial
and complete. Look from thy parapets down the bay where
three arms of the ocean meet, and listen to the swash of their
flood-tides. They come in with the swelling pomp of all their
waters and toss their waves as if with glee for the great argosies
which thou wilt entrust to them tomorrow.

Look again, but this time, westward, across a fruitful continent. The leaves fresh in spring-life and all the blades bow their
heads toward the east in anticipation of their Harvest Home next
autumn, here beneath the gorgeous skylight.

For good or for ill, thou art a temple or a Stygian cave. Art
thou a temple where thoughts shall grow grand? What altar
hast thou set up and with what light wilt thou kindle its fires?
Worship thou wilt have. Shall it exalt the nature or leave it
"subdued to what it works in, like the dyer's hand"? What
shall be thy matin songs and thy vespers? What?

Loves thou wilt have, hopes thou wilt have; fears, plans, successes, failures; successes and failures not to end within thine
own confines but which will send their throbs of joy or sorrow as
wide as humanity.

Guests thou must have, guests born of the day or guests born
of the night. It is the law universal, and this very May day
thou must choose of what thou wilt be the tabernacle. No man
liveth for himself, and no institution exists for itself alone.

May I, closing these dedicatory ceremonies, be thy herald, and
summon some of the guests whom thou wouldst bid to thy birth
feast, and constrain to stay with thy sons to the end?

Approach then, first, ye who come through the double-leaved
doors of memory. Welcome! Shades of dear companions with

whom these merchants had sweet fellowship in the brave days of the Old Exchange. Your work well done, but strong no longer to bear the burden and heat of the day, you passed over the silent river. Some in youth, some in middle life, some struggling until life's winter frosted your locks and life's cares furrowed your cheeks; but with truth and honor as the staff of your right hand and of your left, one evening you said, "Good night," and never came again to say, "Good morning."

Hail! Old comrades, in these moistened eyes, perceive thy welcome and that each tear is bright with a love-lit smile. Revisit this scene from year to year as ye do this day, that thy names may be a bond upon thy successors for all that makes a perfect manhood. We have not forgotten thy widows nor thy orphaned children.

And next I summon a goodly company, Spirit of Truth, that bond without which society itself cannot exist, come thou with all thy train of open and ingenuous life, with courage and enterprise and faith in mankind and love of manly methods, and contempt for meanness, and desire for a well-rounded, well-balanced, beautiful life; come, with reverence for law, not as a hated command but as being true liberty,—law as having its home in the bosom of God and whose voice is the harmony of the world.

And thou, Spirit of Charity, come; with a mind that is always a cheerful thanksgiving and not a nest of grudges against fortune, with thy forbearance with infirmities, with kind construction and lenient judgment, with helpfulness in the day of difficulty, a hand to raise the fallen and to strengthen the weak, with every gentleness of life and every grace of manner; with feeling to judge oneself with severity and all others with allowance.

And come, too, Spirit of Moderation and Sobriety—prudence of living and love of simplicity, hatred of idle show and of all deceit; come, Love of Knowledge—liberality to all the arts and sciences; come, Genius of Hospitality—international welcome and fraternity with the nations; come the sentiment that opportunity begets obligation; come, Contempt for Mammon; come spirit that subdues the soul to an ever-present sense of responsibility to the sovereignty of conscience and that relates man to Him that sitteth upon the throne of eternity. And oh! In thy loveliest form, come, Gentle Spirit, teaching that the counting room and the Exchange, after all, are secondary in value to the hearthstone and the rooftree, the sweet, sweet home that enshrines child and wife and the mother quite fair enough to love and almost divine enough to worship. To you, ye bright host thus summoned, in the high hour of this your visitation, I consecrate this building. The rustling of your wings and the trailing of your garments lift our souls to the sphere of your upper dwelling places!

This occasion should not end without a word to correct a prevalent error as to education. Too often the term is exclusively appropriated to the study and acquirements belonging to the academy. Some one has well said that to the observing man, the activities and communications of New York life make it a university. The legitimate training of a merchant's life is precisely in the habit of clear perception and expression, exactitude as to fact, distinguishing the essential from the accidental, and a strictly logical method of reasoning to conclusions and generalizations. It is academic training. From first to last the merchant's work is mind work. Here, then, is a department of our great City University, and in the characteristics here to be developed we have a right to look for results of a liberal education. It is our own American Emerson who writes: "All departments of life at the present day—Trade, Politics, Letters, Science or Religion—seem to feel and labor to express the identity of their law. They translate, each into a new language, the sense of the other."

They each express in word and act, in aim and results, that which belongs to their individual genius. That expression is Art, perpetually struggling to form itself in beauty, truth and goodness. And never yet was anything seen so beautiful or so artistic as a beautiful life.

* * * * *

Allusion has been made to the circumstances under which the corner stone of this temple was laid. Have you ever thought that there were some who were present at the laying of that corner stone full of pride and hope, who are not here today to witness the placing of the final crown, which was prefigured by that graceful and beautiful gift from your wives, and sisters, and sweethearts, with which the corner stone was laid? They are gone, and yet the thing and the lesson to be remembered, impressed as it has been by nearly every speaker today, is that there is to be another life, an Exchange within the Temple itself, and that never is to die. Let us remember that the old are the young, and the absent are the present, and that it is in every respect an Exchange founded on that true corner stone that abideth forever.

❖

Address made by Algernon Sydney Sullivan at a Memorial Meeting for Charles O'Conor, one of New York City's most eminent members of the legal profession, whose death occurred May 12, 1884.

Several years ago, in association with a number of professional brethren, I took an active part in causing to be made a portrait bust, in marble, of Charles O'Conor. It was finished by Mr. Wilson Macdonald, a sculptor of this city, and then, at a regular session, we presented it to the Supreme Court of this city, to be preserved in public view in the Court House.

The presentation ceremonies were simple, but the tone of the addresses from the Bar and the Bench expressed the utmost regard and veneration for our much loved leader.

Soon afterwards Judge Leonard sent for me and showed me a letter just received from Mr. O'Conor, wherein he referred to the testimonial, and with modesty disclaimed any merit of such a tribute which, nevertheless, was very gratifying to him. But he also said that as his career at the Bar was not closed and he might yet be engaged in professional contests in the Court, he felt it to be more delicate to withdraw the bust from the courtroom until the close of his life, suggesting that, by some mishap, the sentiment of the Bar might undergo some change.

On the contrary, since then the fabric of his great character has knit itself more and more solidly, and day by day it has lifted itself into a nobler grandeur. Bring forth, therefore, once again, the marble presentment of the face, every line and feature of which tells of thought, study, reflection, earnestness, uncompromising integrity and courage!

Mutely eloquent, let it speak to us, suggesting what a sacred trust is that of a Counsellor of a Court! Let it tell us that the ministration of an advocate is to aid the Court to preserve the law and justice! Let it be a present inspiration to magnanimous purposes and a solemn sense of duty to dominate all other considerations within these walls!

His was no story of misspent talents or of an ineffectual life. He exemplified that it is practicable to unite judicial thought with the argumentative brief of an advocate, and in both respects to keep within the field of sound jurisprudence.

Neither should we forget the force and vitality of his character which impelled him to activity in affairs to the last hours of his life, reminding us of the tribute to the greatest of the Romans, *Nil actum reputans, dum quid remanet agendum.*

❖

An address delivered by Algernon Sydney Sullivan from the steps of the United States Sub-Treasury building in Wall Street, during the Cleveland-Blaine Presidential Campaign of 1884

FELLOW CITIZENS:

We are here to testify that one thing is more important than party, and that is the honor of the American people and of their political system. We are an assembly of those who remember

Washington's warning against excessive party spirit. It is as if Washington called this meeting to order and presided over its deliberations. One of the strongest inducements for me to be here is that I may pronounce a grateful tribute to the legions of independent Republicans who have led the grand revolt in favor of reform. They have won a great triumph already. Actual success is about to follow their efforts and Cleveland will be elected. But that much-to-be-desired event is not the chief glory of this campaign. I am here to rejoice in the revival of a better political faith, an emancipation from a thralldom which was strangling our political manhood. The example has been met by a response from the Democracy for whom I speak, and today they are inspired with a more liberal, a less partisan, a loftier public spirit, as they move in one rank with the Independent Republicans. I see a quickening of the public moral sentiment and an elevation of the standard of public service. Revolt against old parties and abandonment of them were the gates through which the Republican party was formed. In order to follow old principles of conscience they threw off old allegiance to become Republicans, and by the same token they now march out. (Cheers.)

This occasion would lose one of its useful and fitting features if we did not pay this tribute as patriotic citizens and acknowledge the value to our country of this bright example. But the practical question is, what ground is there for the growing opposition to Mr. Blaine's election? The first answer is, we have his own record when he held one great office. In that office he exhibited the practices of a man whose inclinations led him to be corrupt. His former office was one of enormous power. Under the rules of the House of Representatives, its Speaker, who appoints the committees and decides the points of order at critical moments, has more influence upon the legislation of the country than perhaps even the President of the United States. He unites judicial, legislative and executive duties. He should be clear-minded and clean-handed, esteeming his office as a solemn trust, never to be dealt with as his personal property, for his individual gain. He should no more defile it than the priest should desecrate the altar. The majesty of the people, the public welfare and public justice should be enthroned in the Speaker's chair. (Cheers.)

Now, my indictment against James G. Blaine is that, when Speaker, he traded for an interest in a railroad and offered as a consideration for that interest, in part at least, the benefit which he had rendered to the railroad in his post as legislator and Speaker. Mr. Blaine's correspondence with Fisher discloses his humiliating barter and how he thereupon got an interest in the railroad. This would have been shameful even if the railroad were not one that derived benefit from Congressional legislation, and even if he had not added his assurance that he would not be a deadhead in the enterprise if he embarked in it. It all implied a promise of legislative service if any were needed. I single this only as one example, because one color stains alike each of the many official and public acts for which Mr. Blaine is justly arraigned. Have we even yet realized what Mr. Blaine thus carried into the shambles? The robes of office were not his property. The title, the dignity, the power were the people's. He was their instrument. It was trust property which he was guiltily using. Mr. Blaine knew his was a guilty service, for he denied it, and did not expect that Mulligan would expose it. We have here his standard of virtue in public office. If he was such a Speaker what would he be as President? (Renewed cheering.)

Wall Street is an excellent tribunal to try this question. Faithful trustees alone give Wall Street its power. Once lower the standard of honor and truth on this street and the gold and the bonds will all be taken away. Security and confidence command the gold. Who in Wall Street would feel safe as to his money held on trust if his trustee having once done what he called a favor to a borrower began to dicker for a share in the borrower's business, which it was evident was to continue to be that of a borrower? Would not his promise not to be a deadhead mean, "Come to the bank whenever you wish to borrow; I make your interest mine also?"

My second indictment against Mr. Blaine is that his success, as the record now stands, would operate to corrupt the moral judgment of the country. Under party whip all distinction between wrong and right would have been brushed out as of little moment. If we accept the claim of Mr. Blaine that there is nothing in the series of his acts disclosed in the Mulligan and Fisher correspondence that is inconsistent with the highest notions of integrity and honor, we must prepare to revise all our standard codes of morals. For myself, and I believe also for you, I denounce Mr. Blaine's plea in the words of the old prophet, Isaiah, the son of Amoz: "Woe unto them that call evil good, and good evil; that put darkness for light and light for darkness; woe unto them which justify the wicked for reward." It is time that more consideration should be given to this peril to our ideas of public virtue. (A voice, "That's true," and cheers.)

Again I indict Mr. Blaine for this, that his own speeches and public letters have brought his character as a man of truth into widespread distrust. It is needless for me to say more on this topic than to point to the painful proof furnished in the daily papers, simply by collating Mr. Blaine's own words.

Again my indictment gathers its counts, that Mr. Blaine furnished evidence when Secretary of State that he was not competent to take care of the nation's honor abroad. He lacked courage and wisdom. He permitted Earl Granville to refuse his demand for information of the particular charges against American citizens then under arrest on suspicion only. He did not even insist upon a speedy trial. At the same time his diplomacy in the Chile matter was bullying and deceitful when it should have been open and friendly; it was based on false notions of international law, and, above all, it was stained with signs of private money interest. The United States were humiliated by Mr. Blaine in foreign matters as they never were before. (Cheers.)

Again, I see a prospect that if Mr. Blaine should be elected the White House would be a modern cave of wreckers. We cannot hear of a single man who in all the years of loose administration has grown rich in monopolies and schemes for private gain at public expense who has not enlisted under Mr. Blaine's banner. We distrust him for the friends he has made. We consider such broad aspects of the canvass as these because practically there is no issue between the parties on economic questions save one. Governor Cleveland and his party, the people, insist that right now excessive taxation must stop. No more taxes must be levied than shall suffice to economically administer the Government. Nearly one hundred million dollars per annum can be saved to the people.

Governor Cleveland, as President, will save it. Let us enable him to do it. I conclude by saying that, in my opinion, his election will be the beginning of better days for the Republic. Old-time, rugged honesty will control his administration. Simple style of living will follow extravagance which has debauched the morals of a set who have too long been a governing class. The qualities of Washington, good sense, firm and sound judgment, with official integrity free of suspicion, will insure to President Cleveland the respect of the people, and to the people once more their own self-respect. (Loud cheers.)

❖

Honors to Sir Moses Montefiore, 1884

To the Editor of The Evening Post:

SIR: I hope the Christian churches in New York will not forget kindly greetings to our Jewish brethren while they celebrate the one hundredth birthday of Sir Moses Montefiore. His life has been one philanthropic act, and he has been devout in his worship of the God of his Bible.

In the cause of peace and of justice to the poor and the oppressed he has been a bold and wise counsellor of kings. The service he has done to ameliorate the condition of his own race cannot be overestimated, and he has done more than any other man to take away the barrier of prejudice between the Jew and the Christian. The Christian believes that Old Testament promises lead to New Testament conclusions, but that does not furnish the least ground for that reprehensible prejudice which too long obtained.

The character of the grand old Israelite in London wins to him the veneration of all without regard to creed. "Thou, God of the spirits of all flesh, didst prosper his desire to magnify Thy law, and make it honorable."

His example has kindled the emulation of many, and the tribute of Lamartine to Fenelon—"It was his privilege to elevate others to his own standard, and to inspire as well as to perform noble actions"—applies to him.

(Signed)   ALGERNON S. SULLIVAN.

New York, October 24.

❖

An address made by Algernon Sydney Sullivan who represented the American Numismatic and Archaeological Society at the presentation of the Evacuation Day Medal, February 21, 1885

On the eve of another of our national holidays, recalling the name and fame of Washington, it is our pleasant task to crown the Centennial Celebration of the Evacuation of Our City by the British at the close of the War of the Revolution. That celebration will long be remembered for its popular enthusiasm, for its civic and military pageant, for the brilliant oration of Mr. George William Curtis, and for the unveiling in Wall Street of the statue of Washington, on the site where he took his inauguration oath as President of the United States. Your committee realized that the occasion had claims to be perpetuated by every resource known to art, and very properly their thoughts recurred to the

Historic Medal as that which has vindicated its claim to be the most enduring memorial of History. The American Numismatic and Archaeological Society felt honored by having committed to it the selection of a design and inscription and the supervision of the execution of such a medal. With a solicitude that comprehended fidelity to the facts of history, the claims of art and the sentiment of civic pride which had prompted the Centennial Celebration, the Society undertook the task. They determined that the design should be in spirit and in execution distinctively American, and after taking pains to secure sketches and drawings from many competitors, by the advice of some of our most distinguished artists they awarded the prize for the design which upon the whole was best, to our fellow townsman, Mr. Charles Osborne. The matter of cutting the dies was intrusted to probably the most distinguished artist in that field—Mrs. Leah Ahlborn.

The great value which will attach to our medal will not be that it records dates but that it records the patriotic remembrances and recognition by our people of the events that preceded them by a hundred years. It is that expression that gave eloquence to the celebration and which will give significance to the memorial of it. You have upon this bronze recorded that a hundred years have not dimmed, but, on the contrary, have brightened the popular glory of Washington; that the fortitude of the soldiers of the Revolution is remembered as the price of an independence which has brought a century of peace and prosperity; that the political scheme which was the logical outcome of the Revolution is daily vindicating its claim upon the intelligence of the world as being the wisest and most beneficent that has yet been known in history. Whoever in future ages shall see this medal will read in it, as upon a tablet of the American heart, that at the end of the first century of the practical establishment of American independence the citizens of the metropolis, without regard to party, could put no measure upon their enthusiasm as they rejoiced in the courage and the political wisdom of their ancestors who had brought into existence our happy Republic.

In the celebration of that Centennial the people of the United States have renewed their fealty to the principles of constitutional government, and have, with an emphasis which attracts the attention of the world, said to all mankind, "The growing experience of each of the hundred years of the past century starts us into the first of a new century with an abiding confidence that the true principles of government for the happiness and prosperity of a people we have found to be those upon which our State and Federal Governments have been constructed."

❖

An address delivered by Algernon Sydney Sullivan at the unveiling of a memorial bust of Edgar Allan Poe at the Metropolitan Museum of Art, May 5, 1885

LADIES AND GENTLEMEN:

My part in these ceremonies is an introductory statement of what has been done, and of the sentiment it embodies.

A sculptured memorial of Edgar Allan Poe has been designed and finished by an American artist, Mr. Richard Henry Park. The trustees of the Metropolitan Museum of Art have consented to receive and preserve it. And now, under auspices of a national enthusiasm, it will be unveiled to public view.

As the curtains fall away from it, we will then realize that it has brought into this museum something in addition to itself. With its entrance, a portion of this hall has been transformed into a shrine, a shrine of intellectual worship; and, setting it up, we have founded here the American Poets' Memorial Corner, we have dedicated our American Pantheon.

These things have been directly brought about by members of theatric profession. First suggested by Mr. Edwin Booth, they received prompt sympathy and generous aid from Mr. Lester Wallack, Mr. Steele Mackaye, Mr. Joseph Jefferson, Mr.

John McCullough, Mr. William Florence, Mr. John Gilbert, Signor Salvini, Miss Agnes Ethel, Miss Mary Anderson, Miss Clara Morris, and many other actors of distinction; and from Mr. A. M. Palmer, Mr. M. H. Mallory, Mr. Henry E. Abbey, and other prominent managers of theaters. Ladies in the circles of New York society brought their approval and efficient help. Men of letters, themselves favorite poets, like Mr. Edmund C. Stedman and Mr. William Winter, led in cheer and assistance from that class. A graceful gift from Mr. Poe's friends and admirers at the University of Virginia was not the least valued of the resources upon which the work progressed. The press of this city has been most liberal in its support of the actors in their undertaking. And all have been reënforced, and our endeavor carried to the point of success, by the sympathy which has throbbed through the great heart of the people.

The more immediate motive that prompted these expressions was a deep and personal sympathy between the stage and the literature of America, especially the literature of its poetry. To interpret poetry, as the highest union of nature with thought, into living expression, is the actor's art. The poet, on the other hand, is the wizard, who, with creative touch, makes the actor-artist realize a new consciousness. Their two souls become one.

But it was not alone this general feeling that led to the event of this day. It was felt that our literature has developed such growth and character that America should significantly review and mark it.

And, finally, the actors realized that the true estimate of Poe's genius as a poet, and of his personal fame, must be on a plane immensely above and beyond that upon which it was placed by his earlier biographers and critics.

This tribute has the force of a judgment of reversal. It gives the palm, with all that means, to him who merits it.

Nay, more, it is a confession and a revelation of our later thought, that Poe's genius was a lighted torch, gleaming farther than the frustate searcher could securely go himself, into the mystery and the pathos of being.

Baffled, sorrowing soul that he was, "The flush of squandered fires" left the all-encompassing mystery less hidden, and less unknown, for those who come after him.

Because of him, the way of the searcher is less

> . . . like the crumbled stair
> That winds and winds about a ruin'd tower,
> And leads no-whither.

And now, in the name of American literature, in the name of the American drama, in the name of American art, in the name of poetry, the ideal beauty of all letters and of all art, I consecrate yonder alcove "The Poets' Corner."

❖

An address delivered by Algernon Sydney Sullivan at the opening of the New York Mercantile Exchange, April 6, 1886

MR. PRESIDENT AND GENTLEMEN:

I look at this volume containing your charter and the regulations of the Exchange, and I find much that is interesting, and but one thing to criticise: You run in the teeth of the old proverb, which tells us not to put all the eggs in one basket. Think of the national egg product being marketed here. A member of the Produce Exchange called my attention to it; in envy of your growth, he is whispering dolefully of eggs and breakage. He says that your enterprise is chiefly to build telegraph lines to the poultry yards of the country, and telephone lines to every nest, so that the cackling will tell you each morning whether to bear or bull the market.

The spirit of trade can make chicken music tolerable, although it was so hateful to Carlyle; you remember that he growled that he could not write because of his neighbor's hens. He said,

"They will not hatch in quiet, nor let me." I read with interest in your classification that you put new-laid eggs in one grade and fresh eggs lower. New Yorkers understand that. We have long known that time is the essence of a contract for a fresh egg. But enough of pleasantry.

You have most fitly opened these ceremonies by the address of President Urner. You begin today a new epoch in your history. The field of trade to which you devote yourselves becomes more distinct as a department of commerce in New York. The system, regulation and concentration of action and capital resulting from this solid organization will give order and fixedness to trade in the valuable products which are dealt in here. You establish a center of sound business methods; here will be unvarying standards of quality; here will be regularity as to credits and inflexible definitions and terms of trade; here will be increased facility for shipments, economies in expense, a balance tending to keep the supply equal to the demand. Standards of trade will be kept up to a mark of ideal honor; and mutual confidence, the very sheet-anchor of commerce, will be greatly advanced.

The history of Trade Exchanges, of which your President has made a study, should be preserved as a valuable part of your records. Let me follow with a few more suggestions prompted by his address.

You are incorporated by the laws of New York; you live by law, and through law, and you should be constant in your fealty to law. Your relations to the public, and distinctively to the State, which arise from your acceptance of your charter, are a theme well worth an address. A charter is simply one law of the State; the entire body of laws is to promote the public welfare. Each incorporation is a grant by the State as a public trust for a public use. This should never be lost sight of. A creature of the law, it should be remembered that its by-laws should be for the promotion of justice. A corporation like this is in some sense a coördinate branch of the Legislature and of the Courts of Justice. You have not combined merely to make this a shop for traffic; you are, and I am glad to see that you distinctly avow that you are, a public body. You add dignity to this occasion by a patriotic display. The nation's flag is spread all over your walls; and it was another happy thought to display there also the coat of arms and the great seal of each of the old thirteen American Colonies. It belongs to public bodies to keep alive the memories which turn to the beginnings of our nation. It is instructive to look yonder at the symbols which recall the days when the foundations of our Government were laid in the Declaration of Independence. Your act is a confession that its principles have been the life-blood of all our institutions, and have made ours the happiest and most prosperous of people.

Every day public opinion, that silent but powerful legislation, becomes more potent. It is due in a great degree to the increase of organized bodies like this. Men are more and more drawn away from private places of business, and they form opinion by consultation; they express it in union. Our great trade halls in the cities have become to a large degree the real centers of public opinion. Every question that can affect the public welfare must here be considered and passed in judgment.

For instance, at the present moment throughout the country we are having a serious agitation in reference to the labor question. It is not necessarily a ground for alarm; but if, under unwise leadership, it adopt the erroneous views of the communists, it is full of public danger. Therefore this Exchange promptly reviews the principles involved. Public order and business prosperity go hand in hand. Let the New York workingmen form associations to promote their common welfare; they have the right to do so, and in many ways they can, by combination, benefit themselves; but in view of some declarations made in the name of labor by wicked men, it is time for us here to say, not as enemies of the workingmen, but in the interest of the great brotherhood of American citizenship: "Brother, we, whose line of business and work is as important for the honor and prosperity of the land as yours can be, call your attention in a friendly way, but in an earnest and in a determined way, to the great American truth and doctrine: that while all men have the right to the pursuit of happiness and prosperity in this land, yet the fundamental principle of success and prosperity is that no man and no association of men can be above the law of the land."

Do I say that in a spirit of unfriendliness? No. I say it as I would say it to you, gentlemen, my neighbors and friends, if I saw you embarking in some course that might bring you across the track of the people's law; I should warn you and say: "You are by your mistaken course ensuring the failure of so much of your cause as has merit in it." There never can be any cause in America so good or so urgent that it may be safely bought at the price of the overthrow of the law as it has been established by the legal representatives of the people of the State and of the Union.

Again, recent events in New York illustrate the constant need of attention to our public affairs by members of Exchanges of honest merchants, like this. The reputation of New York has been seriously hurt by the scandal in reference to the Broadway railroad. Now if there be any instance of public wrong and of shameless perversion of public trusts by servants of the people of New York, whose fault, Mr. President and members of the New York Mercantile Exchange,—whose fault is it? Will you tell me that, if the great body of men in New York making up the membership of the Exchanges in all the different departments of trade, if they who have no interest in politics except to see that righteous laws be passed and that they shall be administered and enforced by good men in a righteous way, would forego the blindness of party zeal and mere political partisanship, would exercise the voting franchise on the principle of public citizenship and public duty, would they not prevent such shameless wrongs as those which are now reported, and which mantle our cheeks with blushes for the good name of our city? Is not most of the blame for these great political evils, and such like misfortunes, upon us, because you and men like you, and I, and men like me, forget the higher obligations required by good citizenship? Good citizenship ought to be the ultimate result of every school in this country; and there is no school, no college, no university, that does

more to educate men in New York than the business of being a
merchant.   I do not refer to being a mere shopkeeper, but I say
a merchant.   What is he?   He must be a man of the strongest
and closest observation; a man of trained memory; a man knowing the connection between causes and effects, and how to trace
them; a man of the widest information, learned in the subject
matters of his trade; knowing the conditions of the law of their
production; knowing the commercial laws of his State and of his
country; knowing the facts that influence supply and demand.
He must study climate, geography; he must study languages,
customs, the law of transportation; he must be a man of correspondence and a man of opinions; he must be a man so trained
as to have his faculties always at his command; and crowning all
that, he must be educated to the fact that there is not a law that
does not begin with the fear of the holy God.   He must be a man
who is honest, not because it is the best policy, but a man who is
honest because everything inconsistent with honesty is bad commerce, and because it is as much at war with the law of a true
merchant's existence to be dishonest, as it is with the law of
heaven itself.

Members of such a school, what a reproach it will be upon
every one of you if that school does not bring out men imbued
with the principles of citizenship.

Let us remember that there is no progress in humanity, there
is no endurance for our State, that separates itself from good
laws and good government.   There is no point in New York
where it is more important to cultivate this sentiment of public
obligation, than on the floor of this Exchange.   It is destined to
last as long as New York itself shall last.   Your agency is the
agency that distributes commercially many of the most important
and valuable products of our land; and the aggregate of value of
the commercial transactions in the products of the dairy, of the
poultry yard, in cut and salted meats, in dried and fresh fruits
and canned goods, far exceeds in volume and value the entire
value of the cotton crop of the United States, or of the products
of the mines of the United States.   And after the ceremonies of

this day the community will realize more than ever the vast field of usefulness that is open to you.

When I look again at the emblems of the original thirteen States displayed before us, it calls up more vividly the relations between the material prosperity of the people, and the establishment of sound principles of law. Immediately west of New York is a group of five great States, from which so much of your traffic comes. Nothing in history more illustrates the principle which we are considering. Those States were formed out of what was called the old Northwest Territory, which once belonged to the State of Virginia. But immediately after the close of the Revolutionary War, and when the Union, deeply involved in debt, had no public territory, some of the Eastern States were jealous of Virginia, because of this immense domain. But those were days when men were patriotic unselfishly. Virginia passed an Act in 1784, by which she ceded to the Union that territory which now constitutes the States of Ohio, Indiana, Illinois, Michigan, and Wisconsin. But as conditions of that cession, it was required that there should never be within that territory any slavery; that there should be always provision made for the establishment and maintenance of public schools; that there should always be maintained liberty of conscience, and freedom in worship and in matters of religion according to the dictates of conscience of every individual. And they crowned it all by the protest that this action was for the good of the Union. Congress in 1787 passed their ordinance that out of that territory thus baptised—baptised for freedom, baptised for public education, baptised for freedom of conscience, baptised with the spirit of love for the Union and law—five States should be ultimately created, in the constitution of each of which should be incorporated the fundamental principles of Virginia's grant.

What a lesson does that give to us, Mr. President and gentlemen; calling upon us, as our day shall be, to provide for sound politics based on pure and good principles. Look at them today; what magnificent States those five are! I do not believe that on the face of the earth there is an equal number of people to the population of those five States, who are so universally prosperous, so universally happy, so generally virtuous and patriotic, and where there are less to be seen of the extremes of poverty and the extremes of wealth. The people were trained from their birth, drawing it in from the breast of their mothers, in fidelity to good public citizenship. They are an example to the world; they are like the prophets of old, set apart.

And now, gentlemen, I believe that this Exchange is the very youngest of the great Exchanges of the City of New York. I understand that it was organized under its first name in 1873. You are entitled to be congratulated by your guests upon the perfection of your Exchange Building. Your guests on this platform have come from the different Exchanges; the Produce Exchange is represented; the Cotton Exchange, the Metal Exchange, the Maritime Exchange, are all here by their representatives. And I am glad to see a representative, Mr. Townsend, from the Maritime Association; it may be one of the duties in forming public opinion, imposed upon this Exchange, to answer the question, "What can we do to enlarge the mercantile marine of the United States?" If so, there will be no duty which will be more entitled to your attention than that. For, while the American plowman moves the ground for the sake of its products, American merchants should ever keep in mind as a field of American enterprise the domain of the seas, from which at present we reap comparatively nothing. I hope this Exchange will not fail, when public opinion is to be directed in that respect, as to what ought to be done by Congress to encourage, promote and reëstablish that marine which once covered the sea with outgoing ships, and brought them back laden, like the golden argosies of old, to pour their wealth into the treasure house of the City of New York.

I congratulate you especially upon the principle of mercantile accuracy and fidelity as illustrated in the erection of this building. Your Building Committee report today that they have completed the house and paid it up at a cost less than the original estimates. As a citizen of New York, I wish that our public buildings and our great public works, as for instance the new Croton Aqueduct, could be entrusted, not to politicians or political appointees, but to Building Committees appointed from this Exchange and from the other mercantile exchanges.

In conclusion, gentlemen, let me ask, what will you give to the City and State of New York in acknowledgment of your obligation that you are creatures of law? That is the standing interrogation mark which I hope will be before your eyes as long as this shall be the scene of your mercantile activity.

❖

Address delivered by Algernon Sydney Sullivan indorsing the nomination of Abram S. Hewitt for Mayor of the City of New York, Tammany Hall, November 20, 1886

FELLOW DEMOCRATS:

This is not the first nor the hundredth time that I have had the pleasure of meeting my fellow citizens in this historic hall, but I may say that never in my experience here has there been an expression or an act which more deeply moved my heart and commended itself on grounds of high public duty to my judgment than the nomination which has just been made, and which designated that Abram S. Hewitt should be transferred from one field of public duty to another, and than which there is none more honorable in the public service in the United States. To be the mayor of the city of New York by the chosen suffrages of the good people of New York is an honor which any man may be proud of. And one reason why I am glad to stand here and indorse the nomination is that Mr. Hewitt is a man who, in whatever position he is, believes in the maxim that the public office is a public trust. The last time that I stood on a platform advocating Democratic principles before an election I was on the same platform with Mr. Hewitt, with Governor Dorsheimer and many others on the day when that mighty host of Democrats and independent citizens, Tammany Hall and the others, marched around the city bearing the banner of Grover Cleveland. I believe that Abram S. Hewitt's nomination will command the confidence, the respect of the good people and of the Democracy of the city just as Grover Cleveland's nomination did.

I congratulate the convention, I congratulate the president that it has been his good office to preside here when one of the great merchants of the city, one of the great manufacturers, one of the great legislators, a self-made man, the friend of good, honest clean government, has been put forward by Tammany Hall on the part of the party. I take it for granted that Mr. Hewitt, as a public spirited man, will accept the nomination for the honor and duty it puts upon him.

❖

A brief address made by Algernon Sydney Sullivan at the Democratic Club in New York City on Andrew Jackson's Birthday Anniversary, January 8, 1887

To me, nothing in respect of General Jackson is so remarkable as this: It is years since he died, and yet, he is just as much a living force as ever. In fact, his personality is so real that he is constantly thought of by us all as an actually living man. It is difficult to explain, but we may easily recall some facts that throw some light upon it.

First, his individuality and personal independence were exceptional among all our historic characters. He was a party man, believed in the general principles of the party to which he adhered, but he never was, and in the nature of the case it was not possible for him to be, a mere partisan. Individual judgment became independent judgment. Rightly estimated, Jackson's character and life are a brilliant plea for independence in politics.

The lesson is a good one for these times, and for all parties.

Second, he was unselfish. His heart was a warm and sympathetic one and its tendrils went out to all humanity. Democracy to him was another form of the golden rule: Love thy neighbor as thyself.

A sincere desire for the good of his fellow men was a sentiment which became a reason for his intellect. He based conclusions for public policy upon that sentiment with entire conviction that it was the greatest wisdom. That made his public character simple and honest, straightforward and bold. The eye that was in his heart was single, and the whole body of his public life was therefore full of light. The heart, which warmed to the many, found that the hearts of the many opened in love to him as to a guest whose place remains filled by his shadow even when he has died.

Third, he inspired absolute confidence in his fidelity to his trust. Who ever dreamed of questioning it?

Such a man, even should we differ with him on some questions, becomes the embodiment of the best thoughts and feelings of his party.

It may not be amiss to draw here a happy comparison. In my view, the essential and better Jacksonian ideal is realized again in Grover Cleveland.

I like his individuality, I like his independence, I like his courage, I like his abstention from extreme partisanship; I like his simplicity and frugality of life, I like his sympathy with the common every-day people and with their needs as affected by the government; I like his faithful keeping of his pledges to the people who elected him, I like his consistency with his Chicago platform, I like his honest support of the principles and practice of reform in the Civil Service. I like his fair consideration of and regard for the opinions of independent public-minded citizens of all and every party, Republican or any other, be they called

Mugwumps or by any other name. And so long as he abideth firm on his present and past record I am, on Jacksonian principles, for Grover Cleveland against all comers.

❖

Notes from which Algernon Sydney Sullivan made an address to the Young Men's Club of Harlem on the Fourth of July, 1887, the one hundred and eleventh anniversary of the Declaration of Independence

Your celebration of the one hundred and eleventh anniversary of the Declaration of Independence most fittingly winds up with my toast, "Our Reunited Country."

For, first, the Declaration was made by "The Representatives of the United States of America, in General Congress assembled."

Second, it was made "In the name and by the authority of the good People of the Colonies" and in their name was solemnly published and declared.

Third, the representatives of the United States and of the "Good People," for the support of this Declaration, "Mutually pledged to each other their lives, their Fortunes, and their Sacred Honour."

This Charter of Liberty was so broad, so comprehensive of human rights, so expressive of common American sentiment, that union of Americans was inseparable from it.

United opinion demanded a united Declaration.

Fourth, in its turn, it proved itself to be so perfect an ideal for the body politic, that it was an irresistible power pointing to perfect national union of the States.

If then it was the voice of united Colonies, if it was proclaimed by them, if it was proclaimed to them and for them—then in the Sacred name of the Fathers, let it ever be celebrated by and for and in the name of a United Country.

But my toast goes further, and speaks of a reunited country. Thank God for that! The blessings of a restored Union are too numerous for mention now, but this occasion requires that I emphasize one of them.

American ideas of liberty are far in advance of any practical presentation of civil rights which the world has yet known.

They are not only our heritage of enjoyment, but they are a sacred trust to be preserved by us, and to be worthily exemplified and commended to the nations. No man liveth unto himself, and no nation liveth to itself alone. Opportunity begets responsibility. We are to be propagandists of the gospel of human rights and progress.

And nothing is clearer than that we would fail in this honorable privilege and precious obligation, if the States became severed.

Our influence would be paralyzed. The foes of Liberty would wag their heads in triumph at our lapse into discordant fragments, a prey to all the jealousies, burdens, and ambitions which sacrifice freedom.

Are we then a reunited people? The reunion that I speak of means a union of hearts, "Where every man, at the call of the law, would fly to the standard of the law, and would meet invasions of the public order as his own personal concern."

While we assemble here, an eloquent and pathetic response comes to us from the battlefield of Gettysburg. Let us review that wonderful spectacle in the history of nations that is transpiring on Cemetery Ridge today.

Amid tens of thousands of interested spectators, there are lines of veteran soldiers with different uniforms.

We soon see that they are only the few survivors of once well-filled regimental ranks, and that they are the very men who met in battle twenty-four years ago, in the decisive battle of the Civil War, and in the most brilliant and gallant hand-to-hand struggle that soldiers ever saw. The occasion is the dedication of a Soldiers Monument by the victors.

These victors invite, as their honored guests, the remnant

surviving of the renowned Pickett's Brigade whose charge was repulsed; and these repulsed soldiers come.

The sun never looked down upon a reunion which reflected more honor upon a people than this. All carry the same flag; all are devoted to the honor and glory of one country.

And more than all the victors are they who say to their one-time foes, come here, ye also, and erect your monument to your fallen heroes, and let the passions of fraternal strife die out of sight as the blood of friends and foes have been absorbed from view by the sands beneath our feet.

Oh! My Countrymen, you have done a patriotic duty well to-day, here in Harlem, in response to the act of the veterans of Gettsyburg.

I rejoice to think that the number of those who would fan into flame the embers of sectional hate, who would in the words of the President *traffic* in it, is comparatively small.

The people, in mass, are in harmony once more: harmony that has no ranklings, no envyings, no disposition to wound and sting by humiliating reproaches.

The glories of the future are looked to. American destiny allures the heart of the people, and nothing in the past hinders the most perfect union between the sections.

Let me assure you, I can speak advisedly as to the feeling of the South.

Every step which the North has made towards them in the path of reunion has been responded to by two or many times two steps for fraternal union on their part. And the day will come when on History's page will be written all the causes of the Civil War, all the devotion, the patriotic fervor, the self-sacrifice, the gallantry, the courage, and the results of the war; and amid the splendid tributes on many pages the glory will at last be seen in the rainbow over-arching them all, on which will be inscribed, "Conflicts of Civil War ended in perfect reconciliation; disunion was followed by a perfect reunion. *Esto Perpetua.*"

❖

*An address made by Algernon Sydney Sullivan, delegate from the
Miami University Chapter, at the banquet of the Semi-Cen-
tennial Celebration of Amherst Chapter, Alpha Delta Phi
Fraternity, June 28, 1887*
The Chivalry of Alpha Delta Phi

MR. PRESIDENT AND GENTLEMEN:

After the splendor of oratory which has shone upon us today, I
can almost imagine that the real purpose of the Amherst Chapter
on this occasion was not to celebrate its fiftieth anniversary, but
to exhibit to the world that, although its matchless trinity of
orators has been broken by the translation of Henry Ward
Beecher and Roswell D. Hitchcock, it still remains true that the
brightest star and the fairest flower in the field of American
eloquence still abides in the possession of the Amherst Chapter.
Dr. Storrs gave the key to all the thought that must continue to
the end of the celebration and the festivities, placed upon it by
the inexorable law, his own conception of what it is to be an
Alpha Delta Phi.

My toast, as I look at it, seems to me to be a little too heroic,
and yet the very circumstances which the speaker mentioned—
my knowledge of the foundation, although not contemporary
with it, of the first child of Alpha Delta Phi in the organization
of the Hamilton Chapter and my acquaintance with the brothers
whose names have been mentioned—make it necessary that I
should at once accept the term, "The Chivalry of the Alpha
Delta Phi," in a sense that was made obvious today. Taking it
to mean that faith which knights to knighthood bore, how at
once our hearts come in sympathy with it as a proper toast somewhere in the order of proceedings this evening! Faith, inspiration, aspiration, duty, high endeavor and high achievement, if,
indeed, it be the right thing to say in the presence of an intelligent company like this that there is not high achievement except
with high endeavor. Certainly it is not true that there is high
achievement without high endeavor when we are considering the
subject on the plane of action which ought to be above all.

Tracing the succession of thought that occurred to me on the acceptance I give to the term "Chivalry," it occurred to me when thinking a few moments ago of the approach of the summons to respond to this toast, what a kinship there is, what a potent action there is in all ideal plans. The ideal of knighthood I have sketched, but how true it is that all ideal paths move nearly in parallel lines in this respect of the advance of thought along a line that is not only forward but is always upward, until it will bring us to just that plane which I have defined.

Now, gentlemen, it is true that I come as a delegate from one of the Western chapters of this Fraternity, and come under circumstances and with reminiscences that make it peculiarly interesting to me if, for a moment, I can hope to make it interesting to you. You will bear in mind—and I indulge in the reference to it the more readily because it has not yet been referred to—that our society, its character and its qualities, had the personal characteristics that belonged to our founder, Samuel Eells. He wrote no creed; there is no constitution which was to be subscribed to. There were no pledges. No man can find any writing from him or contemporary with him, giving that law which every member of the Fraternity realizes and feels to be impressed upon him, and yet he knows that it is absolutely true that Samuel Eells's character, Samuel Eells's methods, Samuel Eells's aims, his intentions, his purposes, his efforts, his whole being, gave at once, when he formed this society and when he formed the chapter in which I had the honor to be initiated—to it, and to its members, the impress of his own character, of his own feelings. It has abided until today, it has culminated in an assembly here in these classic grounds, a convention representative of all that is strong, active, noble, elevating, influential, beautiful in the life that is the expression of American thought and American ideas and American purposes.

I remember when I left my little village home in Indiana and moved to Oxford, Ohio, to attend the Miami University. Immediately on my arrival the subject of discussion, as usual when any new class arrived, was with regard to the societies connected with the college. First and foremost was always mentioned the name of the little society Alpha Delta Phi. Mr. Eells had then died, but the coterie personally selected by him still continued in existence, and I soon learned, when I had the honor of being requested to become a member of the society, that the entire membership looked to Samuel Eells with a sentiment that was akin to devotion. He seemed to make such an impression, not only upon members of the society but upon the college, that there was no more honored name than that of Samuel Eells. And I may be permitted here to say that in that college, which could fairly be described as being almost a frontier college, there was gathered a body of the members of the Alpha Delta Phi, who, with one exception, the speaker, have gone out into life and have continued to live shining lives, and who do so at this very hour. I only wish some of this company whom I could name on that list, instead of myself, as the representatives and delegates from that first-born chapter of Alpha Delta Phi, were here to speak for it and duly represent it. I remember when, after leaving college to study law, selecting Cincinnati for my home, I entered there again into active fraternal intercourse with the men who had learned to know Mr. Eells during the four years that remained to him of his life after he went to Cincinnati for the purpose of making it his home.

I may be permitted to recall again what is mentioned in our book of authority and records, that, as Brother Salmon P. Chase loved to say privately and at all times, Samuel Eells displayed, as the founder of Alpha Delta Phi, his character as a Christian. I have heard Governor Chase, again and again, speak in terms of almost idolizing fondness of his youthful partner, who died so soon after the opening of his career in Cincinnati.

Now, gentlemen, this matter of the chivalry of a society means, necessarily, a great deal when there is a convention at the end of fifty years of the existence of any chapter or of any order, in this, that the history of the society has already made itself—in its past and for the future as well. This society is today and will be just that which it has lived up to and lived out in its fifty years, and I ask you if it be not fairly true that there has been a vital force impressed upon it?

In its nearly twenty chapters there has come to be a uniformity in the high standard, as Samuel Eells intended it, of morals, of character, as being preferable to mere intellectual culture or the accumulation of knowledge. He himself has said that this character development of the entire man in his manhood, moral, social, as well as intellectual, was the purpose and aim that he had in assembling kindred spirits and in founding this organization. Has it not come to be true of the organization? I ask you to turn your thoughts back for a brief ten hours from the moment when I am speaking, and I ask you had it been otherwise than I have supposed, could it have been possible that Dr. Storrs, in coming to make this semi-centennial oration, could have felt that the occasion, the audience, the Fraternity about him, was of itself the occasion and the impulse of that masterly and beautiful review and study, the educative effect of history in an academic course and in the course of formation of character— character that was to be in sympathy, wholly, with the law and the example which he put forward almost unintentionally and irresistibly as the sum of human character as developed in realization of the law of Him who spake as man never spake. It came from him as the expression of his own conception that that which he knew would alone meet the requirement and expectation of a convention of the sons of Alpha Delta Phi. It constitutes, in my mind, the best of all testimonials as to the history and the nature and the essential quality of the association.

Now, gentlemen, it is very easy for us to say this in general, but there is not a day nor an hour in which there is not, in the call directly presented to every such association and to every individual of it, a call for the manifestation of the sentiments and principles which constitute the foundation and keystone of our order. I never thought of it more than I did in an incident which occurred to me during the day. I stood, on a stormy and dark night only a week or two ago, on the heights above Hoboken. It

Drawing by W. E. Mears

THE MAIN BUILDING AND THE CAMPUS OF MIAMI UNIVERSITY AT OXFORD, OHIO, IN 1844

Sketched from an old wood cut, by permission of the University

happened that I was detained down there by a storm; when the storm had passed I went to the brink of the hill and there I had that exciting and beautiful view, the like of which is to be found in few countries, for it is not often that there is a great city near which there is a high beetling cliff as a point of outlook. As I stood there watching the lights that mark the homes and move-ments of nearly three million people, extending almost from my feet eastward and southward for nearly a score of miles, not a man was discernible, not a sound from their existence was heard, and yet I could feel that I was on the shore of this sea of humanity—all in its entirety, moved by the same hopes and the same plans. And following some of these moving lights my eye was arrested by one which fixed and held my attention, and in a moment my fancy reminded me of what it was. I could not see what was beneath it, but I knew that, raised and pointing far into the upper air, it was the blazing beacon upheld by the hand of the Statue of Liberty. There it was! And so it is that over every community there is, to the eye that will look for it, some beacon and some signal that will be a pointer and a monitor to tell its purpose. It relates to and calls out the proper sentiments and the sense of duty towards one's fellow man. I could not see that figure, but I knew it was there. I knew what that beacon told. I knew that it reminded me of the fraternity between fraternal nations. I knew that it reminded me of the guardian-ship and great trusts that were put upon the people of the city of New York. I knew that it reminded me of the hearty sym-pathies of all the world towards America. I could but then, as I do now, feel an unuttered prayer: Oh, ye gods of the winds, touch lightly that central herald in our harbor! Oh, ye mists that come in from the ocean, string and gem it so that it will shine like diamonds in the morning sun, but never hide it from the faithful sons of Alpha Delta Phi, who gather in such an increasing colony in the cities about that harbor! Let it be for ages that it, too, shall stand there as a consecration of the chivalrous sentiments, the freedom and the spirit of evangelism and good citizenship, to all that are within its reach. So it will be, and so it is, and so I can speak not only for the Western representation of the Alpha Delta Phi, but for the entire Fraternity. To the voice of chivalry calling from that statue they respond by recognizing the duties, the claims of manhood and good citizenship.

So it will ever be, my brothers. I never realized it so fully as now, when I see the magnetic attraction that has assembled this rare convention, and I am only glad that it is recognized, that it is more than a mere mechanical line of beauty for the sons of Alpha Delta Phi, and that there is that spirit of gallantry and courage of truth, of high endeavor, to which, without great extravagance, the term "Chivalry" can be applied.

❖

The address delivered by Algernon Sydney Sullivan at the First Annual Dinner of the New York Southern Society, February 22, 1887

Only seventeen years have elapsed since the close of the Franco-Prussian War. Yet this very hour the world trembles at the din of preparations for renewed war, and at the prospect of these great and neighboring nations, in almost savage hate, springing again to mutual slaughter. Let us at home ponder and rejoice over a contrasted picture. It is twenty-two years since war ended between the Union and the Confederacy, and now we have perfect peace. Indeed, there is almost rivalry in a common patriotic enthusiasm between these recent foes. Even the ashes from once-glowing embers have been scattered by the merciful winds, and we find not a spark of burnings or hate. On the contrary, all camps and all hills and valleys send up the song in unison. Tonight it centers at Mount Vernon's hallowed tomb and echoes across the continent:

Our country! 'Tis of thee,
Sweet land of liberty,
   Of thee we sing;
Land where our fathers died!
Land of the Pilgrim's pride!
From every mountain side
   Let freedom ring.

Under these happy auspices we meet, with the spirit and the
hopes of the New South, to keep our Memorial Day.

We meet as the Southern Society of New York. We are not
only in it, but we are of it in deed and in very spirit.

Together with New Yorkers we turn our thoughts to the shining moments in the nation's history, and, among its shining men,
preëminently to Washington, whom time and comparison do
not rob of a ray. (Applause.)

As we ask our compatriots to unite with us in appropriate
tributes, we signify the spirit which animates the Society. It
is fellowship in thought and sympathy with all others in New
York who would make this City of Cities a shrine for the excellent in all things.

Will they honor the nation's heroes, "our loftier brothers,"—
we will honor them, too. (Applause.)

Have they projects, by popular education, to develop the mind
and refine the character,—we will support them. (Applause.)

Will they make efforts to purify politics and the public service,—we will unite in those efforts. (Applause.)

Have they enterprises to enlarge commerce and the industrial
arts,—we also will engage with them. (Applause.)

Do they undertake plans to ameliorate the pains and cares of
humanity,—we will coöperate. (Applause.)

Will they bind respect for law and order, and all the obligations of good citizenship about their necks,—we ask leave to enlist with them in the ranks. (Applause.)

Do they hold the sentiment that in our country each section
exists for all sections and every section for each,—we respond
with a deep sense of its obligation on ourselves. (Applause.)

Would they care for and uphold those of our fellow citizens, without distinction of race, whose lot is affected by any burdens of the past,—the members of this Society represent those who have feeling and purpose to follow duty along that upward path. (Applause.)

Will they stand by an indissoluble Union of indestructible States, in a spirit of justice and friendship, in the spirit of Washington,—they will ever find in this Society a faithful, a courageous, and an honorable ally. (Long continued applause.)

❖

Address of Algernon Sydney Sullivan, on May 12, 1887, who as President of the New York Southern Society proposed that the Society erect an historical tablet to mark the place of General Washington's departure by boat for Annapolis where he was to tender to Congress his resignation as Commander-in-Chief of the Continental armies

I ask your indulgence while I make a short address in reference to the special subject which is to be laid before you for your action this evening.

Washington's Birthday has been accepted as the date of our Annual Dinner Reunion,—and it is now proposed that we also use the next anniversary to mark with a suitable tablet a locality in this city which has great historical interest. It relates to the period next following the evacuation of New York by the British troops.

General Washington, when disbanding the army under proclamation of Congress, a few weeks before, at Newburgh, retained a small force until the peace establishment could be organized. On the 25th of November, 1783, at the head of his troops and of the civil authorities of the State, he made formal entry into this city. It was the scene of great public festivity.

But amid it all, Washington was preparing to lay down his military character, and he determined to go without delay to Annapolis, where Congress was assembling, to resign to them his commission.

Before divesting himself of supreme command, the time had come when he was to bid a final adieu to his comrades in arms. That affecting interview took place in New York. We propose to erect a memorial tablet in bronze at the very spot where the farewell took place.

I will not repeat the story of it in my language, but will give the account in the words of the great Chief Justice John Marshall:

> At noon, on the 4th of December, the principal officers of the army assembled at Fraunces Tavern, soon after which their beloved companion entered the room. His emotions were too strong to be concealed. Filling a glass, he turned to the men and said: With a heart full of love and gratitude, I now take leave of you; I most devoutly wish that your latter days may be as prosperous and happy as your former ones have been glorious and honorable. Having drunk, he added: I cannot come to each of you to take my leave, but shall be obliged to you if each of you will come and take me by the hand.
>
> General Knox, being nearest, turned to him. Incapable of utterance, Washington grasped his hand and embraced him. In the same affectionate manner he took leave of each succeeding officer.
>
> In every eye was the tear of dignified sensibility; and not a word was articulated to interrupt the magestic silence and the tenderness of the scene.
>
> Leaving the room, he passed through the corps of light infantry, and walked to White Hall, where a barge waited to convey him to Powles' Hook. The whole company followed in mute and solemn procession, with dejected countenances, testifying feelings of delicious melancholy which no language can describe.
>
> Having entered the barge, he turned to the company, and waving his hat bade them a silent adieu. They paid him the same affectionate compliment, and after the barge had left them returned in the same solemn manner to the place where they had assembled.

The White Hall, mentioned here, stood on the battery where the barge office is now; and the point from which Washington

entered his barge is the same from which the boat starts hourly
with excursionists to the Statue of Liberty.

With permission of the United States Government and of the
City of New York, we will set up there a large bronze tablet on
which shall be, substantially, the following inscription:

> Here, at the White Hall, General Washington took barge on the
> fourth day of December, 1783, after His Farewell to His Officers.
> Erected by the New York Southern Society, in behalf of the citi-
> zens of New York.
> February 22, 1888.

In a broad civic spirit, we will invite to participate with us
in our public ceremonies—The Public Authorities; the Society
of the Sons of the American Revolution; the Society of the Cincinnati; the Grand Army of the Republic; the Chamber of Commerce of New York, with which, in fact, the idea of this tablet
originated; the New York Historical Society; the Numismatic
and Archaeological Society; the New England Society; the Ohio
Society; the St. Nicholas, the St. Andrew's and St. George's, and
the oldest of them all, I believe, the Friendly Sons of Good St.
Patrick.

And above all, we will invite delegations from the public
schools in the down-town wards, so that the children of our
beloved city may learn to know and cherish the patriotic memories which associate themselves with many localities in the city.

Knowing as I do, that this Society is imbued with strong public
and patriotic spirit, and resolved to do all it can to promote
the honor, the prosperity and the beauty of the city of New
York, I heartily commend this undertaking to you.

I am also in full sympathy with two other resolutions which
will be offered this evening.

One of them, directing our Committee to confer with the Commissioners of Parks in the city in reference to erecting suitable
monuments or tablets on the site of the battle of Harlem Plains.

The other is a response to a movement under the auspices of
the Chamber of Commerce, to have a national celebration in

New York in 1889, on the 30th of April, the centennial of the inauguration of Washington as first President of the United States. Our century of free government by the people may well be celebrated with rejoicings beyond all royal jubilees.

❖

Address made by Algernon Sydney Sullivan at the meeting of the Bar of the City of New York in memory of Mr. Francis N. Bangs, 1887

One and all of us seem to have had but a single thought as the first impression on this occasion, and it has been to remind us how true it is that at high noon our own shadow comes back most closely to us and clings to our feet. And it is when the sun is at its zenith and the man most erect that he and his shadow most nearly become one.

The impression of last Monday, when most of us attended the funeral of Mr. Bangs at his old home, still lasts with me in respect to the impression that was made by the ritual of the Church as we there heard it, and which had two effects, one of which was saddening on that morning, and another which presents itself to us at this hour. Those of you who were there will remember that the lawyers gathered in Mr. Bangs' library were engaged in conversation, telling reminiscences of their friend, and that once in a while, the door opening, there floated in the sounds of the busy street of New York. There was enough of it to be distinctly audible, so much so, that without anyone knowing just when it began there was a little notice from one to another and a hushing, and there came to the consciousness of every one that was there a low, solemn monotone of musical speech reciting this wonderful old liturgy of the Church. It floated in like a sigh or a sob so that people had to strain to hear it, and yet everybody distinctly understood that amidst the noise of the life of that day it was to remind us of the old monody that has run through life forever—"Ashes to ashes, dust to dust."

It was saddening that morning, it was subduing; but to the minds that had a full conception of that ritual it was necessary that that meeting should be followed by just such a meeting as this. For all the truth there is in that glorious old selection, the truth is only half stated when at the funeral, at either side of the bier, we say ashes to ashes. The fullness of the truth, as has been said here today, is only when the rest is said, ashes, and ashes only, to ashes; and there was that about Mr. Bangs which we know was not laid away with his dust—there was something more. It is here expressed by the fact that this court room is crowded by those to whom Mr. Bangs is unseen and unheard, but not unremembered, not unlamented; the memory of him was not laid in the dust; the example, the teaching, the lessons of his life, those are not with that which was laid away by symbol as dust to dust.

And, Mr. President, there is one other observation which I would regret not to repeat here, even though I see the rays of the sun rising on the walls as he sinks in the West. I wish that every member of the Bar who ever knew Mr. Bangs during the last few busy and most trying years of his life and had seen that weary marking of his features by his toilsome and arduous labors, had done as I did—taken one farewell look at him as his face was exposed before being covered for burial. Those of you who saw it will attest that what I say is true; that this was one of those instances where the kindly hand of death, relieving his body and mind from the wear and anxiety and troubles of his laborious life, had permitted his face to assume an expression of kindliness and a sense of repose and calmness which those who had not seen him, but had heard his friends describe him, would expect his face to present. It was a face that, even dead, spoke more of the heart of Francis Bangs, and the general dominant and prevailing character of his mind, than I have seen his living face wear for the last ten years. It was the face of a generous man; it was the face of a man who had sunk really to rest. And there occurred to me then the lines from one of our American poets as fitting expressly just such a case as this of our friend whose death ended, as one and all of the speakers have said, a struggling battle with life, and ended just when he would be supposed to be likely to continue his voyage. But with him, it seemed to me after looking at that face that it was the entering of a haven of rest. May I try to repeat the lines?

In contemplating such a death, this poet said:

> And now it is over,—over,
> And now it is over at last.
> Down sail! The sheathed anchor uncover!
> Life, like a tempest of ocean,
> Hath out-blown its uttermost blast.
> There's still a faint sobbing,—seaward,
> But the calm of the tide deepens leeward,
> And behold!
> Like the welcome of heart-pulses
> Throbbed through the river,
> Those lights, in the harbor at last,
> In the Heavenly Harbor, at last.

❖

Address delivered by Algernon Sydney Sullivan at the laying of the corner stone of the Consolidated Stock and Petroleum Exchange, New York City, September 8, 1887

No exchange is well founded unless it grows out of the wants, and is dedicated to the uses, of wholesome and legitimate business.

What, then, are the significance and interest of this occasion?

You intend to trade here in one natural product, and in public securities, but also and chiefly in stocks.

Your building is one more monument to make the amazing increase of corporations, in number and variety and in the magnitude of their properties.

It also calls attention to the growing tendency of the industrial world to substitute corporate for individual proprietorship.

Reflecting men anxiously ponder over the problem, what is to be the outcome of this movement which appears as if it will put all business, perhaps even yet, the agricultural interests, in the hands of corporations?

In addition to the special charters which each State and Territory in the Union is granting, it has provided facilities for incorporation under general laws. The States appear to be rivals which can contrive the most easy and liberal laws for this purpose.

The effect is visible in many ways. It is practically nullifying some of the maxims which our forefathers deemed essential to the existence of our political policy. The laws against primogeniture and entail, the laws against perpetuity of trusts, the laws declaring void all grants which suspend the alienability of property for a term longer than two or three lives in being, and the policy adverse to unlimited accumulations in one proprietorship are practically becoming of no effect. Corporations live indefinitely long, without change of tenure, and without that distribution of estates which our ancestors thought was desirable as often as the death of every individual. Money and power swell in the possession of corporations, as accumulating snows at the North Pole raise mountain tops to cloud land.

The statutes of the several States are all dissimilar as to the organization and management of corporations, as to the safeguards provided in behalf of those who deal with them, and the remedies for mismanagement, yet the investments in them grow visibly larger every day.

It is said by some careful statisticians that the railroad companies own one-fourth of the property in this country, and when you add to this the property owned by insurance, banking,

Algernon Sydney Sullivan in 1853

manufacturing, mining, telegraph, canal, gas, water, street car, steamboat and other companies, we cannot greatly err when we estimate that nearly one-half the wealth of the country is owned by corporations. An able writer on this subject, Mr. Richard T. Ely, from whom I almost copy these statements, sanctions the opinion, also that the wealth of corporations in the United States increases three or four times as rapidly as that of private concerns.

There may well, then, be called into existence many new exchanges, like this, to facilitate dealing in the shares of these proprietary companies.

Indeed, there does not seem any other method for the dealings, so safe and so expeditious as through stock exchanges. Take, for example, your own by-laws in regard to listing stocks to be dealt in.

You cause the company's title to its property to be examined, and also the legality of the certificate of incorporation and of the issue of the stock.

By facilitating quick transfers of stock you make certificates which represent one-half the values of property in the country almost equivalent to money for active use.

As you are an association to promote and regulate the traffic in shares of this character and value, it would seem to be your bounden duty to study the peculiarities of corporate laws and their defects, and to suggest remedies.

The diversity among the various State laws causes confusion, uncertainty and loss in many ways. Corporation securities would be safer and more negotiable if there were a uniform law for incorporations throughout the Union.

I venture to suggest that you recommend it. It may be that a partial remedy for existing evils could be effected by a convention of delegates from the various States, which would agree upon and recommend a uniform law to be adopted by each State. This method has been resorted to recently, in this city, in regard to the laws regulating the requisition for and the rendition of fugitives from justice.

But it may also be a still better consideration whether the magnitude of the interest involved does not warrant Congress to pass a general law providing for the creation of corporations throughout the country, with uniformity as to power, rules, liability and publicity. In my opinion Congress has the power under the Constitution for such legislation, in cases where the business of the corporation is commerce among the several states, and it would be as wise to exercise it as it was to pass a Bankrupt Law, the Interstate Commerce Law and the National Banking Law.

I wish time justified me in enlarging upon the benefits which would result to the property and business of the country from such a uniform law, putting safeguards around "Share Certificates," this new representative of one-half of the property of the people.

There is one other most important subject which is well worth consideration today by a great and progressive exchange like the Consolidated.

Certain combinations, called "Trusts," are rapidly coming into existence. Their plan is to get control of all corporations which are engaged in some one department of industry. By bringing them under one general controlling superior they pervert management of these corporations from the hands to which the law committed them.

The corporation is an artificial person created by public law. The first implication of its duty is to serve public use and to harmonize with public policy. That is the law of its being.

I ask today, can a corporation which has become a slave of a "Trust" in order that it may thus combine with other corporations, and smother competition which has been deemed essential to the public good, justify itself, if the Attorney-General, on behalf of the people, shall petition in due form of law, to annul its charter for misuse? I believe not. The first principles of the charter were abandoned, and its public purposes perverted when it joined "The Combine." In fact, by that confederacy, it agreed to submit the management of its affairs to outside parties, that is, to the confederate companies under the "Trust," instead of retaining it in the board of directors elected from its own stockholders. In form it observes the law, in spirit it stamps upon, and violates it.

The result must be injurious, because the principle is bad. Its first purpose is monopoly, pure, simple and thorough.

Its methods tempt and must lead to the ruin of every individual who would compete.

It facilitates and therefore generally leads to a swindle of the public. In practice it has generally been carried out on a basis of exaggerated capitalization, upon which a monopoly can forcibly collect a dividend.

It enables false values to be imposed upon a public dealing in the trust certificates, because its records are secret, and the State cannot (as is claimed, although a doubtful ground I think) demand publicity, and exercise a visitorial power, as it does in the case of corporations.

In short, in trade and commerce and in all industrial economies, this new creation is not an agent for sound, wholesome, just and honest business. It is the cuckoo egg in the commercial nest and must be cracked. It is the device of ingenious wits to circumvent the law, by getting control in unapproachable hands, of the corporations which are the creatures of the law.

That which I appeal to you to do is to set your face and lift up your voice against this dangerous contrivance, and insist that laws shall be passed, if that be found the only way of effecting it, to vacate these trusts, or to bring them under fixed and wholesome regulation.

A great public Stock Exchange must not be recreant to its duty to the public, by silently conniving at agencies and methods which menace fairness and equality among individual citizens, and above all, which lift up impious hands against the Law, which, to an American, should be as sacred as was the Ark of the Covenant to the armies of Israel.

❖

Tributes and
Memorial Notices

*I*T would be impossible to convey adequately the affection, the admiration and the respect in which Algernon Sydney Sullivan was held without quoting those spontaneous expressions of sorrow which flowed so freely from the pens of so many after his death. Obviously, however, it is also impossible to include some two thousand testimonials which are available.

That this volume may lose nothing from its completeness and secure the interest and corroboration contained in obituaries, testimonials and resolutions, a representative selection has been made for reproduction here.

A. M. H.

THE ALGERNON S. SULLIVAN
MEMORIAL COMMITTEE
1890

Hon. Noah Davis
President
2 Wall Street

William L. Trenholm
Chairman Finance Committee
160 Broadway

Walter L. McCorkle
Secretary
3 Broad Street

George C. Barrett	Thomas L. James
George F. Baker	Eugene Kelly
Albert Bierstadt	John J. Knox
Calvin S. Brice	Joseph Laroque
Cornelius N. Bliss	Seth Low
James C. Carter	George DeForest Lord
Grover Cleveland	William B. Leonard
Henry Clews	Henry G. Marquand
Andrew Carnegie	Cyrus H. McCormick
John D. Crimmins	William Moir
John C. Calhoun	Peter B. Olney
Frederic R. Coudert	A. E. Orr
Edward Cooper	Joseph J. O'Donohue
William Nelson Cromwell	Willis S. Paine
Joseph H. Decker	Edward Patterson
Theodore W. Dwight	Rev. Francis M. Patton
Benjamin F. Dunning	Theodore H. Price
Julien T. Davies	Rt. Rev. Henry C. Potter
Andrew G. Dickinson	Gen. Horace Porter
Chauncey M. Depew	O. B. Potter
Rev. Dr. Charles F. Deems	Henry Parish
Franklin Edson	Wheeler H. Peckham
Roswell P. Flower	Roswell G. Rolston
Dr. Matthew D. Field	W. L. Strong
John H. Flagler	Alvan S. Southworth
Hugh J. Grant	John Stevens
Elbridge T. Gerry	J. Edward Simmons
Dr. Norvin Green	Jesse Seligman
W. S. Gurnee	Samuel Sloan
Henry Hentz	Wager Swayne
Rev. Richard D. Harlan	Rev. Dr. William Taylor
Rev. Edward Everett Hale	S. V. White
Rev. Dr. John Hall	William C. Whitney
Robert L. Hewitt	John H. Watson
Wilson G. Hunt	Charles G. Wilson
Abram S. Hewitt	Erastus Wiman
George Inness	Stephen A. Walker

MEMORIAL MEETING OF THE SOUTHERN SOCIETY OF THE CITY OF NEW YORK

Held at the Brunswick on the evening of December 13, 1887, to adopt resolutions regarding the death of the late President, Hon. Algernon S. Sullivan.   Jno. C. Calhoun, Esq., in the chair

THE REV. DR. DEEMS opened the meeting with the following prayer:

Almighty God, our Heavenly Father, we worship and adore thee.   If thou wert only Almighty God, what would our worship be to thee,—the worship of us men, mortal, perishing before the moth, our breath and our nostrils, what would our worship,—the worship of us sinful men,—all sinners,—be to thee?   But oh, Almighty God!   Thou art our Heavenly Father, and we are thy children, and though we have been disobedient sons and have been wayward, like as a father pitieth his children so hast thou pitied us, for thou knowest our frame, and thou rememberest that we are dust.

We bow ourselves before thee most humbly, seeking penitently to be forgiven of our sins, and in this mortal life to be prepared for that immortal estate which thou hast for thy children.

O Father!   Thou hast the keys of life and of death.   Thou openest and no man shutteth; thou shutteth, and no man openeth.   Thou callest thy children together upon earth, and then thou callest them away.   And so hast thou, from our circle, called one of thy sons, so much better than we, one of our beloved brothers,—a real brother, a brother in times of adversity, —and thou hast called him to the heavenly home.

We pray God that we men, diligent in business, fervent in spirit, may be serving God in our several callings and pursuits, in a simple, honest, child-like manner, so that when the Father shall call us, each one of us may go to join our brothers who have fought the battle to its close and are called to the eternal victory.

Send down, we beseech thee, O Lord God, the benediction of thy heavenly grace upon our society, that in all the things we purpose to do we may please God and love one another with a manly friendship, constantly bearing one another's burdens, and so fulfilling the law of Christ. We pray, O God, that there may be added to our numbers men whose vigor of intellect, and whose cleanliness of hands, and whose purity of heart, and loftiness of life, may increase in us the reverence for all Godly and goodly things.

We bow our hearts before God, asking for the divine sympathy for the bereaved family of our brother, that they may not sorrow as those who have no hope, seeing that he himself died with the hope of that blessed immortality which Christ died to purchase for us all. Bless us in all our intercourse, guide us in all our ways, and bring us to join the general assembly of the first born, and to be added to the number of those who have been made perfect, even just men upon earth.

Grant unto us in this present world, we beseech thee, a knowledge of thy truth, and in the world to come life everlasting.

Our Father who art in heaven, hallowed be thy name. Thy kingdom come, thy will be done on earth as it is in heaven. Give us this day our daily bread, and forgive us our trespasses as we forgive those who trespass against us. Lead us not into temptation, but deliver us from evil, for thine is the kingdom, and the power, and the glory forever and ever. Amen.

And now, may the peace which passeth all understanding keep your hearts and minds in the knowledge and love of God and of his Son, Jesus Christ our Lord, and the blessing of God Almighty, the Father, Son and Holy Ghost, abide with us evermore.

The Vice-President, Hon. Jno. C. Calhoun, said:

Gentlemen:

In response to a sentiment shared by all of us, this meeting has been called for the purpose of paying a proper tribute to the memory of our late President, the Honorable Algernon S. Sullivan. His loss to the Society cannot be estimated. Ever vigilant of its interest and welfare, he had always in view the one object which we all so much desire—its success.

As soon as his death was announced your Executive Committee met, appointed twenty-five members of this Society as a committee to attend his funeral, and took every step in their power to convey to his family your profound sympathy and to pay to the distinguished dead every mark of respect.

No word of praise can warm the heart now stilled in death, but we have felt that you would desire formally but lovingly to place upon the records of our Society such resolutions as might be dictated alike by our affection for the man and our admiration for his exalted character.

Mr. Sullivan was indeed a remarkable man. Possessed of extraordinary ability and great strength of will he fought his way to the first rank in his profession; genial, gentle, dignified, and courteous, he became one of the most prominent figures in the social life of this great city where gather the brightest, the most cultured and distinguished people of the entire country; brilliant, gifted by nature with the voice, the sentiments, the graces of the orator, he won a lasting reputation as a brilliant public speaker; generous and open-hearted, his purse, his advice, his services and his sympathies were ever at the command of the poor and the suffering; public-spirited and patriotic, he was the leader in many societies and in many works of charity. His tongue and his pen, his time and his brain, he freely gave to the service of mankind. No narrow spirit ruled his actions. In every sphere of life, in public and in private, he was always the liberal, broad, high-minded Christian gentleman. Few men had so many friends; no one ever possessed greater power of attracting to himself at once those with whom he was thrown. His ability, culture, taste and "silver-tongued" oratory, combined with his affection for our society and his great desire to promote its interest, make his loss peculiarly great to us. Vacant forever must be his place among us.

Your Executive Committee has appointed a Committee on Resolutions, of which Gen. Roger A. Pryor is Chairman. ROGER A. PRYOR said:

Mr. Chairman and Gentlemen:

I am instructed by the Committee to propose this resolution for your adoption:

"*Resolved,* That in the character of our late President, Algernon S. Sullivan, the members of the Southern Society recognize all the qualities that give dignity and worth to human nature: That in his relations with us he ever exhibited himself as the true gentleman, the wise counsellor and the faithful friend; that the impression of his virtues will abide with us as an incentive and guide to noble conduct; and that we lament his death with the sincere sorrow of tenderly attached and deeply affected hearts."

The resolution I submit presents a fitting tribute to the memory of our departed associate, and gives appropriate expression to our sense of the bereavement which afflicts us.

If, in its celestial abode, the spirit of our brother be cognizant of transactions on this sublunary sphere, he will accept your offering as not the least of the rewards of a well-spent life. I cannot but imagine that, among the felicities of Heaven, a principal joy reserved for the good is afforded by the recognition and remembrance on earth of the virtues they exhibited in their mortal career.

Of the virtues that entitle to affection and esteem, Mr. Sullivan's character was a conspicuous illustration. That bland and beaming countenance, which conciliated at once the regard of casual acquaintance, was but the revelation of a spirit instinct and overflowing with every gentle and kindly feeling. The amenity of manner which distinguished him as the urbane and affable gentleman was not the formal civility of the courtier, but was rather the involuntary and unconscious effusion of a heart throbbing in responsive sympathy with all human gladness and sorrow. In requital of a kindliness so universally diffused and engagingly manifest, Mr. Sullivan enjoyed the respect and good will of the community in a measure rarely accorded to any man in the rivalries of this strenuous existence. His popularity was proverbial. But the character of Mr. Sullivan was not mere surface and semblance. Its substance was of genuine though unobtrusive worth. No man was ever a more faithful and steadfast friend. From the eminence to which his abilities and virtues had enabled him to attain at the Bar and in society, he eagerly stooped to lend a helping hand to the unfortunate and forlorn; and many are the hearts that mourn, in his death, the loss of their best benefactor.

Entrusted as lawyer with the custody and protection of interests which men most prize, he betrayed none, whether from indifference or sinister motive, but devoted himself to the cause of his clients with a zeal and fidelity that made him an honor to the profession.

While engrossed by the anxieties and labor of the most exacting of vocations, he neglected not the least of the duties of citizenship or society; and whether the occasion requiring his activity was a political exigency, or an interest of religion, or an appeal of charity, or a social pastime, he was ever ready to contribute his sagacious counsel, and his eloquent voice, and his quickening sympathies, and his genial and gracious presence, to the welfare and delight of his fellow men.

And yet, with all this kindness of nature, and gentleness of address, and suavity of speech, Mr. Sullivan was not a weak or irresolute character; but when principle or punctilio prompted he would resist a wrong or resent an affront with the most daring and inflexible courage.

Of his virtues in the dearer and more intimate relations of life —of his indulgent tenderness as father, of his chivalric devotion as husband—of the unclouded and hallowed happiness which the never failing clemency and serenity and cheerfulness of his spirit diffused in the retirement of domestic seclusion, I cannot speak without invading the sanctities of home, and opening afresh the wounds which time and oblivion alone can assuage.

To the members of this Society especially, the death of Mr. Sullivan is a most afflictive bereavement. As individuals, they were attached to him by the tenderest ties of affection; and as he was yet in the meridian of life, they anticipated many years of happiness with him in the interchange of the grateful offices of friendship. We do not accuse the dispensations of Providence, but we cannot but lament the blow that so suddenly and grievously smites us. To us in our corporate capacity, the death of Mr. Sullivan is, indeed, an irreparable loss. After many ineffectual endeavors by others, he at last collected together the scattered sons of the South here resident; by his tolerance and tact reconciled their divergent interests; by his equable temper moderated the vehemence of their nature; and united them firmly and fraternally in the association over which he presided with such inimitable grace and dignity.

He is gone: but the remembrance of his virtues will animate us to a noble emulation; the image of his benignant presence, like a ray left by the departed luminary, will gild any cloud that may darken our horizon; and the recollection of his counsels and his example will inspire his successors to preserve our Society in its pristine strength and prosperity.

The permanent institution of the Southern Society will be the fittest monument to Algernon S. Sullivan.

MR. HUGH R. GARDEN, in seconding the resolution, said:

Mr. President:

If more positive proof than the mere presence of this assemblage was required, that the good which men do lives after them, it would be found in the eloquent words which have fallen from the lips of the distinguished brother who has preceded me.

"The good which men do lives after them."

It rarely falls to the lot of man to so compass the battle of life that, after threescore years of arduous service, he may lay aside his armor, untouched by a single shaft of envy, hatred or malice, and come to his rest, not only with the record of a life well spent, but with every page of that record stamped with the good will and affection of his fellow men.   The memory of such a man are we honored in commemorating tonight.

Surely that was an admirable character which could make, and retain, and leave behind, so marked an impression; and, if that be true, as men and brethren, we dignify ourselves in realizing its influence and in bearing testimony to its excellence.

Of all the qualities of head and heart which unite to form a man, those are always the most attractive and the most enduring in their effect on human action, which develop the arts of graciousness and conciliation; arts by which men are drawn together and endeared to one another; under which virtue grows by communication; and from which, as illustrated in the life and character of our departed friend, there springs that noblest of all human impulses, the pleasure which waits on Charity.

CHARLES G. WILSON, ESQ., President of Consolidated Exchange, then said:

Mr. Chairman and Gentlemen:

I esteem it a privilege of the highest order to be enabled to second the resolution just presented, and in doing so I feel satisfied that I voice the sentiment of one and all of the members of the New York Southern Society.

It has been my good fortune during the past four years to have been brought in almost daily contact with Mr. Sullivan, and I feel that I, that we, have lost a dear and faithful friend, an honest, upright and able adviser.

It was my privilege to be with him while he was engaged in the trial of a cause during the three days immediately preceding his last illness, and more than ever I felt the power of his persuasive eloquence.

As a private citizen, public official and professional man he adorned his every station, his voice was ever strong in the right and his arm ever lifted in defence of the oppressed.

A man whose many virtues, public and private, endeared him

to the people of this city, and closed his day of life with a glorious sunset. (Applause.)

MR. ANSON MALTBY also seconded the resolutions:

I am glad we have assembled to do merited honor to our late President. I am glad of the opportunity of paying tribute of affectionate remembrance to my friend.

A total stranger arriving in this great city of ours and strolling about through this stony labyrinth of stately structures is sure to feel overpowered with the sense of utter loneliness, helplessness and homelessness.

Such a feeling would seem more natural in the explorer of deserted cities like Pompeii or Petra, where not a soul has lived these hundreds of years; where the latchstrings that hung from hospitable doors crumbled long ago into the dust that blows hither and yon with every wind.

But particularly to the Southerners, coming as many did soon after the war, from countrysides, where they were known and welcomed on every hand, to this teeming city filled with thousands of people lately opposed to them in deadly strife, and now all absorbed and eager about their own affairs, and few of them even realizing the newcomers' existence; to such men under such circumstances the lonely, homeless, helpless feeling came with added force. Their individuality seemed sunk into nothingness. They were but grains of sand among thousands of others upon the strand.

How grateful, then, to this class of men, and to many others as well, was the cordial welcome to his adopted city, readily extended to them by Mr. Sullivan. Of southern antecedents and connections coming here just before the outburst of our great war; with his great warm heart throbbing in sympathy for the sufferings of the South he was prompt to aid by advice, by sacrifice of time and labor all those who needed. It was fitting then that we should have in remembrance of these things put him at the head of our Society, whose duty it is to welcome the strange southerner to our city and make it for him a home.

Of handsome countenance, graceful bearing and considerable courtesy, with a fine vocabulary and happy phraseology, he needed but his great sympathy with humanity and enthusiasm for carrying out all good aims to make him what he was—a natural orator.

It was this sympathy and enthusiasm of his that made him so ready an orator.

I think it was when the corner stone of the Produce Exchange in this city was laid that, on an hour's notice, he delivered the principal address—a capital oration.

As an advocate before jury and court, in addition to his eloquence and grace of diction, his great fairness and candor of manner and of thinking made him powerful.

As a counsel his extensive learning, his wide experience of men and his ability to put himself in the place of his adversary, of the judge, of the jury, and so judge of the probable reception and adjudication of a case made him a strong arm to lean upon.

As a prosecuting officer I know that in him justice was tempered with mercy. As an elder brother in the law, I and many another younger lawyer are under great obligations to him for his unselfish counsel and aid during the earlier years of our professional life.

To how many of the weak and suffering has he in many ways brought succor! I remember how years ago, in the evening when his own work was done and his not too strong frame required rest, his house was frequented by persons in distress, who needed counsel and there received it without price.

In religion, in politics, in thought, and feeling, his catholicity was apparent throughout. His prejudices seemed to be held in check by his candid appreciation of the causes bringing about the mental results shown in the diverse opinions of others.

The curtain hangs undrawn by me over his home of singular felicity.

It seems to me that the tone that can be found throughout his whole life is that of charity—of charity as the word should have been translated from the Greek—of love, of love for his fellow men.

How appropriate, then, to the character of our departed friend, are these fine lines of Leigh Hunt:

> Abou Ben Adhem (may his tribe increase)
> Awoke one night from a deep dream of peace,
> And saw within the moonlight of his room,
> Making it rich and like a lily in bloom,
> An angel writing in a book of gold.
> Exceeding peace had made Ben Adhem bold,
> And to the presence in the room he said:
> "What writest thou?" The vision raised its head,
> And with a look made all of sweet accord
> Answered, "the names of those who love the Lord."
> "And is mine one?" asked Abou.—"Nay, not so,"
> Replied the angel. Abou spake more low
> But cheerily still and said: "I pray thee, then,
> Write me as one that loves his fellow men."
> The angel wrote and vanished. The next night
> It came again with a great wakening light,
> And showed the names whom love of God had blest,
> And lo! Ben Adhem's name led all the rest.

HON. J. FAIRFAX McLAUGHLIN addressed the meeting as follows:

Mr. Vice-President and Gentlemen:

The resolutions and touching tributes which we have heard in memory of our deceased President admonish me that I may expect to add but little to the deep voice of sorrow which wells up from all hearts this evening. A long and most intimate acquaintance with Mr. Algernon S. Sullivan afforded to me exceptional opportunities to admire, as though written in illuminated letters, the character of him whose loss taxes the resources of all our wit and words and accents of tribulation. But if perchance I may have seen during my long acquaintance with Mr. Sullivan some new view of that inner life to lay as a message before you, my rising to add another second to the resolutions may be like the lapidary when he handles a diamond, and shifts his position in order to behold the gem at some new angle of coincidence, and from some new vantage ground of observation.

When the great soldier passes away, his countrymen delight to recall his brilliant exploits and achievements in war. Not less worthy of admiration is that man, nor less willing his countrymen to bestow the laurel wreath upon him who has won his way to the front by civic virtues, who, by his strong arm and stronger heart and head, clears a space about him in the walks of peace, and who, when he is no more, and dust to dust returneth— *et in pulverem reverteris*—leaves behind him the priceless heritage of a good name whose memory shall not perish from the earth forever.

As a lawyer, as a citizen, and as an ornament of the social life of New York, the departed President of this young and vigorous Society, long ago took rank among the magnates of the city.

Mr. Sullivan's father, who was a Virginian and a warm personal friend of President Monroe, emigrated in the early part of this century to the Western Reserve. The son was born in Indiana, received an excellent education, practised law successfully in Cincinnati, and nearly thirty years ago took up his residence in the City of New York, where, after a long career of ceaseless activity and enviable walk in life, he has at last laid down his head on the pillow of religious hope, and "sleeps the sleep," as we reverently trust, "of the just made perfect."

Soon after Mr. Sullivan came to live in this city, he organized the movement for the removal of the remains of President Monroe, his father's old friend, from New York to the bosom of his own Mother State, and on the 5th of July, 1858, the bones of James Monroe, having been borne back amid the profound respect of a whole nation to the land of Washington, Jefferson, Madison, Marshall and Lee, were lowered at their final interment in the beautiful Holywood Cemetery, at Richmond, Virginia.

Mr. Sullivan devoted all his energies to the law, and never failed to impress his learning and logical acumen upon the Court *in banc,* where the abstruse principles of the profession alone count.

His talents were both powerful from nature, and not meanly cultivated in letters, and especially in the science of the law. Before juries, where the eloquence of the heart has larger play, he was a ready, effective and eloquent advocate, and won high reputation for forensic powers among the foremost members of an exceptionally brilliant bar.

About a week before his failing health confined Mr. Sullivan to his residence, I visited his office on business, and had a long and pleasant conversation with the deceased. Little did I dream that it was to be my last interview with my friend. Many of you, gentlemen, no doubt have been there, and can recall the busy scene which it presented of a great lawyer's office life. I spoke to him of his engrossing cares. "Yes," he said, "but I can assure you that I compose twenty, thirty, yes forty causes of strife and discord where I now try one case." No lawyer that ever lived could wish for a nobler epitaph than those simple words express, and yet certain it is that this lawyer whom we now mourn, not only made his profession with my Lord Coke "the perfection of reason," but with Howard the great philanthropist, a road through the higher humanities of life, and a "circumnavigation of charity" among his fellow men.

But, gentlemen, it was as a citizen of the world at large that Mr. Sullivan was on very many accounts one of the most memorable men of his time. Public spirit, the life of patriotism, the soul of commonwealth was never dormant in his bosom, but burned there in a steady flame. Duty, which Robert E. Lee in a letter to one of his sons declared to be "the sublimest word in the English language," was the polar star in Algernon S. Sullivan's life. Thus I have seen him emerge on a sudden from a stormy political meeting, where the passions of men were lashed into wild excitement, and enter forthwith into a refined and exclusive circle of ladies and gentlemen, where the courtly manners and fascinating graces which so distinguished him everywhere were brought into instant play. I heard him, for he insisted on

Drawing by W. E. Mears

THE HOME OF ALGERNON SYDNEY SULLIVAN AT SIXTEEN
WEST ELEVENTH STREET, NEW YORK CITY
Still owned and occupied by his widow

my going with him on that never to be forgotten occasion, address that circle with all the ease and elegance of Chesterfield, or rather he addressed the leading personage in the room, bore a message to him, took one back from him most impressively delivered, returned to the meeting to announce it, and once more Algernon S. Sullivan was the strong, aggressive, masculine, rough and ready orator in the Commune, quelling the passions of the multitude, and winning them over to harmony and peace. The occasion to which I refer was the night of the presidential election of 1876, when the largest meeting I have attended, even in this city of monster meetings, sent Mr. Sullivan to wait on Mr. Tilden to take counsel with that distinguished statesman in a moment of supreme national peril. In less discreet hands a crisis might have been precipitated, consequences of which no man could foresee. But Mr. Sullivan, responding to the earnest appeal of Mr. Tilden, poured oil on the troubled waters, and New York, which seemed that night to be rocked in the throes of a rising revolution, was restored to its wonted calm.

But to this Society of Southern men resident in the City of New York, the loss of Algernon S. Sullivan is peculiarly an affliction. He loved the South, her people, her home life, her plantation manners, where more high-bred courtesy "than ever taxed the lips of ancient story" was enshrined as if in its favorite abode. One day while Mr. Sullivan was dining with a number of Southern friends, the returning prosperity of the South was adverted to, when immediately his eyes kindled and he repeated with indescribable pathos that verse from one of William Gilmore Simms' songs:

> Oh, the South, the Sunny, Sunny South,
> Land of true feeling, land forever mine,
> I drink the kisses of her rosy mouth,
> And my heart swells as from a draft of wine.

Came you from the shores of the Potomac, or the land of the Everglades, from the Gulf Stream or the Rio Grande, you had a welcoming friend in Algernon S. Sullivan, whenever and as often as ever you came to New York. He bade you welcome with that voice of melodious accent, which went straight to all hearts and riveted them to him with hoops of steel.

If at his departure from this life, Mr. Sullivan had only been the learned and successful lawyer that he was, the champion of the down-trodden, the promoter and almoner of public and private charities, the lover and patron of music, painting and the drama, the centre of a very great and astonishing variety of agreeable societies, many of which, the mainspring gone, may become dissipated by his death; even then this favorite son of New York, this Maecenas-like patron of Art and of all her joyous sisters, would have challenged the admiration of this great City of New York, and his name and his deeds would be recorded among the chosen ones in her annals. But when to his talents and his versatility, which rose to the level of genius, are added the virtues of this man, the warmth of his heart, the sweetness of his temper—that combination of almost perfect character, not perfect, for none is perfect—and no poet "in the highest heaven of invention" has ever adequately portrayed a perfect character —the measure of our loss may be gauged—the cause of our sorrow may be understood. But *vixit*, he is gone. "May flights of Angels sing him to his rest."

Mr. Hugh L. Cole said:

Mr. President:

I do not rise to pronounce a eulogy, because even if the hour were not so late it would be impossible for me to add to the eloquent remarks which so many of our fellow members have already addressed to you upon this mournful subject. I therefore only arise to make what may be called an apology. I found upon my table yesterday a notification that I had been honored by being appointed by the Vice-President a member of the committee of twenty-five to whom was entrusted the duty of attending the funeral of our late departed President. I was in the South at the time, and consequently knew only of the death of Mr. Sullivan from the notice that I saw printed in the daily papers.

I opened the *New York Sun* at my old home in North Carolina, and found there an admirable woodcut of his beloved face, and I said to myself: "There! Sullivan has done another good thing, and the city is ringing with it!" And looking farther down the column I was shocked by the announcement of his death.

There are few men in this community for whom I had a greater affection, and not one for whose character I had a greater respect.

The very first case that I had, I believe, after I came to New York, came to me in this wise: An old clergyman from Mobile, whence I had just come, found a young Southern man, who had gone wrong in a very peculiar way, in the Tombs. He had embezzled some money, and, singularly enough, had spent almost all of it for the Sunday School, and in doing all sorts of religious work. And this old clergyman came to me about the matter. I knew nothing in the world about criminal law, especially as practiced in the State of New York, and I asked Mr. Sullivan to help me. The young man turned over to us all the property that he had left, and instructed us to take out our fees, and turn the balance over to his late employers. We did what we could for him and got a small sentence, the best we could do, and I said to Mr. Sullivan: "What shall we do with this property?" "Why, we will turn it over to the employers, of course; neither one of us wants it." This was my first experience with him, and he worked on the case as if he were going to get an enormous fee and an immense amount of honor—all for love of this Southern man, and love of humanity generally.

And so, all through my acquaintance, his singleness of purpose, and his gentle Christian life was a model to every man with whom he came in contact.

As I said at the outset, I do not mean to drift into a eulogy, but I could not help saying to you, and to the members of the Society, how deeply I regretted that I was not here to pay that tribute to his worth which my appointment upon that committee would have enabled me to do had I been in the city.

The resolution was then submitted to the members of the Society and was adopted by a unanimous vote.

DR. J. H. PARKER then offered the following resolution:

"*Resolved*, That a copy of the above resolution, and a copy of the remarks in reference thereto be furnished to the family of Mr. Sullivan."

Which was also adopted by a unanimous vote.

DR. NORVIN GREEN said:

I rise to make a motion which I think due to the respect we bear to the deceased, and I wish I could lay one small flower on his bier, or contribute one line of praise worth aught as a tribute to his memory.

I have known our deceased President for a great while. I knew his father, in Madison, Indiana, who, after he had withdrawn from the bench of one of the superior courts, was my counsel in a case I had there. He was a man universally beloved, who respected the simple Christian life and character, who died lamented by the whole community. The son followed the example of the father.

I assume that he was not a man rich in this world's goods, but he had a wealth of brilliant intellect and of nobility of character that money cannot purchase, and that nothing but death can take away. He was always ready to contribute his valuable time and his brilliant talent to every cause of deliverance and every undertaking of patriotism.

It is a pity that such men should die,—it is a calamity that they should die,—it is a public calamity that they should be stricken down in the very strength of their manhood, and in the highest pinnacle of their usefulness.

As it is not fitting that the kindly feeling and profitable impression made by these remarks should be diverted to any business purpose, I move that, as a further tribute, we do now adjourn.

The motion was seconded, and carried.

Adjourned.

FROM THE MEMORIAL ISSUED BY THE AMERICAN BAR ASSOCIATION IN JANUARY, 1888

"Mr. Sullivan was distinctively a lawyer, by heritage from his eminent father, by a natural judicial cast of mind, by a cultivated and liberal legal education. His other accomplishments and works, distinguished and varied as they were, were only secondary to his profession. The law was his life work and his life love as well. Not a lawyer in the commonplace acceptation, he was a legal guide, practical, wise, judicial, with exquisite tact, with infinite patience, with a sense of equity almost intuitive. Adversary and client alike felt the power of his lucid, conscientious, wise advice. His natural talents and his attainments especially fitted him for the *nisi prius* practice, and he was recognized as one of the strongest, readiest, and most successful jury lawyers at the Bar. His learning and tastes were so varied, however, that he was equally accomplished in the conduct of the practical and daily duties of his profession. For thirty years in the city of his adoption, and for ten years in the State of his early labors, he was a working lawyer, and it was in this aspect that he most loved to be regarded. The law was a great mother to him, and he studied its philosophy, he pictured its principles with such love, wisdom, and fairness that no lawyer envied the preëminent rank which he attained and so easily held. It is fair to say that no lawyer, however great his fame, was regarded by the Bench with greater confidence and esteem. The Bench itself was not more sensitive than he to its dignity and honor. His life, his virtues, his judicial quality, unwavering honesty, and legal acumen led all judges to receive his words almost as those of a friend of the court—not merely as those of an advocate. No lawyer equaled him in the affection and admiration of the Bar. No other lawyer occupied so peculiarly interesting a place in their hearts. He was ever the obliging friend, the fair adversary, or the alert coadjutor. While other great names may claim equality with his in the ranks of the profession, among the judiciary, in the councils of the Nation, it is only laying upon his bier the laurel of justice to say that no lawyer of his day attained so high a place in all these fields of activity.   A great lawyer, a wise counselor, a charming and convincing orator, a statesman wise in council and fearless in declaration, a philanthropist in the broadest sense of the word, active (but as a recreation only) in matters of literature, art, music, and the lighter graces of life, his talents, virtues, and accomplishments made his life one beautiful and instructive to contemplate and glorious to emulate."

❖

A COMMEMORATIVE SKETCH BY WILLIAM WINTER

It is a significant fact with reference to the character of Algernon S. Sullivan that, even by those who knew him only at a distance, he is remembered first with love and then with admiration.   He possessed in unusual measure the capacity to inspire affection.   This result was due in part to personal charm and in part to the influence of his great humanity.   His aspect was that of an almost austere natural dignity, but also it was that of exquisite gentleness and benevolence.   He had intuitive knowledge of the good qualities in the character of every person with whom he came in contact.   His mental vision was so broad that he could see all around every object at which he looked. Life in his eyes was a great drama, in which every man and woman has to play a part; and his sense of the relation of persons and things was unerring in its keenness and truth.   Although his heart was warm, his judgment was always devoid of passion. He was aware of the infirmities of human nature.   He never wished to relinquish any one as hopelessly wrong and bad.   No one could pass beyond the pale of his charity.   He always saw the redeeming trait and the extenuating circumstance.   He understood the condition and the feelings of all classes of persons. He met the world with sympathy.   He recognized merits before he looked at faults, and as his spirit was manifestly pure and perfectly sincere, his conduct straightforward, his manner gentle, and his industry incessant in doing good, he naturally called forth the good qualities of those who came within the scope of his influence. His courtesy was intuitive, and neither care, worry, haste, responsibility, nor pain could make him unmindful or neglectful of the consideration rightfully due to every human creature. If ever man acted upon Hamlet's precept, "Use them after your own honor and dignity," Mr. Sullivan was that man. Such a nature could not fail to be loved, and as this lovable temperament was associated with mental qualities equally valuable and brilliant, he was in a kindred way respected and admired. His learning was varied and exact. His eloquence was natural, fluent, sweet, persuasive, often impassioned, always guided by pure taste, harmonious with reason, and directed upon noble objects. His veneration for the law and his high sense of moral responsibility invested his manner with a peculiar grace of splendid distinction; and this combined with accuracy of legal knowledge, lucidity of statement, felicity of illustration, and copiousness of vocabulary made him one of the most impressive orators of the American Bar. In literature he had ample resources, a light and gracious touch, and the rare faculty of taste. His political creed was the honor of American citizenship and the welfare of his fellowmen, and perhaps the essential principle of his public life may be best expressed in his own memorable declaration that "*No man can truly serve his country to the best of his power who has not in his mind all the time a service still higher than that of his country.*"

❖

EXTRACT FROM THE NEW YORK *EVANGELIST* OF DECEMBER 30, 1888, BY REV. RICHARD D. HARLAN

His was the tribe of God Almighty's gentlemen.—*Dryden.*

It is now many months since Mr. Sullivan fell asleep, and these simple lines of tribute to his memory may seem all too tardy, as indeed they are. But the vacancy he left in numerous enterprises which had for their object the helping and ennobling and beautifying of the common life of the metropolis, and the aching void in the lives of many men and women over the land whom he had linked to himself in closest friendship, would give a responsive audience at any time to one who would speak of him.

Immediately after his death the secular journals had much to say from their standpoint, by way of praise of his career and work. But for the honor of Jesus Christ, such a man should not drop out of the ranks of the Church Militant without some public attention being called to his life and influence from a religious point of view; and although there are many who would be far better qualified to tell of his worth, yet as the minister of that venerable Church of which he was a devoted and consistent member, a strong pillar, and a shining ornament, I feel constrained to take this opportunity of putting on record some impressions of the man as many saw him.

In the warfare waged by the King's army against the wickedness of this world there is need for all kinds of service and all types of Christians. We are very apt in these days of multiform ecclesiastical machinery and activities, to accord the chief honor only to those men, laymen as well as ministers, who give most of the energies of their life to the *direct* work of Christianizing their fellow-men. The current standards of religious "usefulness" are so cast-iron and conventional that we often fail to recognize the distinguished and incalculable services rendered to that cause, which is so dear to the heart of Christ and of His people, in another part of the field of battle—in that part which is popularly known as "the world." This service is rendered by an entirely different type of disciple, by men who are not conspicuously identified in the mind of the general public with religious work, who, on the contrary, are mainly distinguished in purely secular circles; *but who exhibit in these worldly spheres the spirit of Christ and of our holy religion.* It is well that all disciples are not of the one type, and we cannot be too thankful for the existence of Christian men and women of the world, whose main efforts seem to be, and indeed are, in the world, but the true source of whose life is "hid with Christ in God." Such a man was Algernon Sydney Sullivan; and if there are any distinctions in the Church Triumphant, such as hold among men, we reverently believe that in the Great Captain's welcome, "Well done, good and faithful servant," this disciple has received an heavenly knighthood as a reward for his great services on the earthly field of battle.

What the trenchant Dryden satirically wrote of one of the characters in his "Absalom and Achitophel," could be said in sober earnestness of this chivalrous servant of Christ: "His was the tribe of God Almighty's gentlemen." It is too risky an experiment to try to enumerate the marks of a gentleman. One thing is certain: it is not a question of blood, or even of manners, much less of money. We can all recognize the gentleman, even although it may be difficult to define him. Now there are many earnest, good Christians in the world, and the tribe of true gentlemen is not without its representatives in every land; but if we use terms discriminatingly, the combination of the two in their highest forms is not an every-day thing. Not many in any one community deserve to be admitted into the number of the Christian Immortals, that "tribe of God Almighty's gentlemen"; but, beyond dispute, here was a man who could be truly called, *par excellence,* a Christian gentleman. As a distinguished metropolitan preacher wrote of him shortly after his death:

He was a true man, combining in himself the highest qualities both of the Christian and the gentleman; and though mingling much both in society and in public affairs, still bearing himself in both without fear and without reproach. He carried his Christian principles into his daily life thoroughly, and yet not in such a manner as to provoke either the sneer of the scoffer or the antagonism of the ungodly. *He compelled all to respect both his Christianity and himself.*

This is high praise, and yet it does not over-estimate his influence from a religious standpoint.

Now it would not be becoming in a minister of the Gospel to say a word derogatory of the efforts of those zealous and sincere men, to whom many in the Church would give the distinctive title of "Christian workers." But there is great need at this time that men pay earnest heed to the New Testament truth, often lost sight of, that all work, all business, the pursuit of the ordinary callings of life, even the fulfillment of the round of social duties, if done in the spirit of Christ, is Christian work. The Church of this age seems bitten with the idea that Martha is the highest type of Christian character; that a man must be full of bustling activity, busy about many things in Church work, if he would be a fruitful disciple. Professor Henry Drummond has done one great service for modern English Christendom in re-calling attention to the laws of growth in grace. He has re-minded us that we do not attain the highest levels of Christian living by striving after outward activity, but simply by fulfilling the conditions of growth in the personal religious life, and so growing after the pattern of Christ. Now a man may be the most active of Christians, as the phrase goes, and yet fall far short of the highest spiritual attainments. On the other hand, here is another man who is put by God in a conspicuous place in the world; a man whose life is providentially so filled to over-flowing with what seems purely secular that there is little oppor-tunity left for "Christian work," so-called; and yet such a man may, as did Mr. Sullivan, render yeoman service to the Great Master by doing this divinely given work in an upright, dutiful, honest-hearted fashion, "walking in the fear of the Lord," with love to his fellow-men, and striving in all things to have the mind of Christ. It is encouraging that in the Apostolic list there is no such fruit as "usefulness"; it is, "love, joy, peace, long suffering, gentleness, goodness, meekness, brotherly kindness, charity."

And these fair flowers of Christian character may be seen far up amid the Alpine snows of politics and public affairs and society, just as well as down in those valleys of distinctively Christian work, in which place, alone, some of us are often tempted to look for the sweet influences of religion. To the deeply devout man there is no such distinction as between secular and religious life, just as there is none between profane and sacred history. As all history is but the unfolding of the grand purposes of the Eternal, which take within their sweep all the currents of politics, of commerce, and even of war; so all careers are, or may be, a ministry, an heavenly calling. We may do the work given us to do in a Christ-like spirit, and so fulfill the law of Christ. Such a life was Mr. Sullivan's, and it is refreshing and instructive to contemplate it, because of the very environment in which it was cast.

It is not the purpose of this modest article to make any sketch of his life or attempt any analysis of his intellectual gifts, but simply to recall to those who knew him a few of the traits of his loving and lovable character, in order to show how beautifully he exhibited the spirit of our holy religion. Whatever would be named as the dominant elements of Mr. Sullivan's nature by those who stood in the innermost circle of intimates, there were two features in his character which are especially recalled by the mass of his friends, perhaps because they were the very links by which he bound them to himself, and in each do we see the mind of Christ.

The first of these qualities was that spirit of helpfulness with which he moved through life. Some one said of him: "He always *reached out both hands* to his fellow-man." It is a pleasing and life-like portrait. His large heart beat for humankind. He felt the sorrows and troubles and difficulties of others as if they were his own, and he gave freely of his time, his money, and, what was best of all, himself to their easement. He always espoused the cause of the weak, the oppressed, and the friendless, and chivalrously threw himself, like a modern Christian knight, into every scheme for the helping and uplifting of men which came to his attention. This disposition revealed itself very early in his life, and he was but filling his natural place when, as a mere youth, the people of Cincinnati, where he was then residing, sent him to New York to join in that welcome to these shores which was given by the country to Louis Kossuth and his fellow-exiles, and to invite him to partake of the whole-souled hospitality of their Western city. Among other things which he said upon that memorable occasion, he maintained that "the government that intermeddles to assist one nation to oppress another is as much the enemy of liberty and happiness as the pirate on the high seas. Every man's hand and every nation's hand should be against her, and there should be no sanctuary of precedent or policy whither she could fly for safety." In these words the youthful orator struck the keynote to which his whole nature responded, and to which his whole life kept true. His quick sympathies always went out with a prodigal generosity to all that were down-trodden in any way, and especially to those who were striving to push their way upward. This spirit of helpfulness appeared in a most attractive form in the affectionate interest he always took in the success of the young men of his acquaintance. Many a young man, coming as a stranger to this great city, found that a letter of introduction to Mr. Sullivan was not only the "Open Sesame" to the hospitality of his charming home and to numberless other courtesies, but also to opportunity and success in business; for he went out of his way to put such strangers into a position where they could help themselves. What one young man recently said is true of many others in New York: "No small part of my success is due to the good words and kind offices of Mr. Sullivan at the outset of my career." It is no wonder that so many of them loved him as a father, and to this day mourn his departure with a deep sense of personal bereavement. It was in these unselfish ways that he tied men to himself, so that his associates found it hard ever to feel envy for his achievements; while his friends always took a kind of affectionate pride in any success that he won.

The other shining characteristic of the man, which struck all who met him, was a combination of real sweetness of disposition

and gentle courtliness of manner. As a young woman once said
of him, "He was sweet to the very core."   And that chivalrous
bearing and winning grace which was so admired was not the
thin veneer of the mere courtier, but was a natural expression, so
graceful because so genuine, of a heart-born kindliness and
thoughtfulness of others.   An intimate associate has offered this
significant tribute to his memory—significant because the action
which he mentions is so slight and yet so constant that it was as
true and natural a manifestation of Mr. Sullivan's real character
as bubbling waters speak forth the cool depths of a spring: "His
greeting to the messenger boy in his office was as courteous and
thoughtful and as considerate as to the most distinguished citizen
of our city."   And he went on to say that during five years of
most intimate association with him he never heard a harsh, unkind, inconsiderate, or intemperate word pass his lips.   Those
who knew Mr. Sullivan will recognize the photographic truthfulness of this strong statement; and it is a very impressive one
when we stop to think how often, in the fierce round of daily
business, that mask of conscious effort after good deeds and kind
words, which is worn to a greater or less extent by all men, is put
aside, and the real man underneath makes himself known.   In
this connection I should like to put on record the testimony of a
good woman, who for sixteen years has been a faithful helper in
his household; it is a telling tribute to the abiding gentleness of
his character, because so many good men seem to feel themselves
privileged, in the unguarded privacy of their own homes, occasionally to relax their self-control.   She says that in all those
years she "*never once heard Mr. Sullivan's voice raised in anger or
irritation.*"   It seemed never to change from the key of kindness
and good cheer.   Although capable of a righteous indignation,
which was at times terrific, mere anger rarely had any lodgment
in his breast.   Many of his friends can recollect trying circumstances in which most men would have shown great temper, but
under which Mr. Sullivan accepted the situation with an un-
ruffled sweetness of spirit which won the admiration even of
those who differed from him. He loved peace, and studied

always how to win it. He never used his gifted tongue to greater effect than in quelling passion and in explaining away differences. He loved always to find the common ground on which men could stand and work together. There was no bitterness or suspiciousness in his nature. He believed in God; he believed also in man. Bacon's words are singularly fitting to Mr. Sullivan: "He moved in charity, rested in Providence, and turned upon the poles of truth." His character had in it that which turned evil into good.

These two special characteristics, which have been recalled to those who remember Mr. Sullivan, both belong to that part of human nature which in the popular psychology is called "the heart." Now Mr. Sullivan had great intellectual gifts and attainments, but that which makes so many men mourn his departure with a sense of personal loss were those qualities which came from the heart and which spoke to the heart. His own tribute to the character of the late Chief-Justice Church is exactly descriptive of a leading feature of his own:

Heart-wisdom is the lily-white chaplet which I would lay to-day by the opening grave of Sandford E. Church. Heart-wisdom! It is a heavenly gift, that seems to lead its happy possessor intuitively into the paths of truth. When Moses unfolded the economy of the Jewish State, it was revealed to him that for certain duties and services "wise-hearted" men should be designated. The phrase presents to the mind images of simplicity, purity of intention, directness of motive, unselfishness, and, above all, a controlling reverence and sense of religious obligation. In studying the character of eminent men like Judge Church we soon see that it was not intellectual superiority alone that gave them their strong influence, but also purity of intention, which imparted tranquillity of soul, composed the passions, and illuminated the mind; so that, following duty, the man knew many things, and was wise in action.

Mr. Sullivan would have been too modest and unconscious of self to have described himself in any such words; and yet those who knew him will recognize in them an outline of his own character, which is as clean-cut as cameo.

Mr. Sullivan was a great lover of children and of young people;

and he never appeared more charming than in his addresses to them upon religious and other subjects.   He saw in the young the hope of the republic and of the Church, and he always took the most ardent interest in every effort to train them up in the love of country and of God.   The young people of that church of which he was a member found in him their natural leader in all their efforts to rouse their own and others' interest in its growth, and he drew to himself their enthusiastic admiration and affection.   He never was too weary after the exhausting professional labors of the day to give an evening to them; and the writer of this article several times has stumbled upon the fact that he had declined many invitations of the most attractive kind in order not to disappoint his young friends, for he was the life and inspiration of all their meetings.   This trait of character in one so absorbed in public life was most refreshing and winning, and it showed the deep sweetness of his nature.   He was as simple-hearted as a child, as gentle as a woman, as chivalrous as a knight.

In the picture of him drawn by affection and memory there is another striking feature, and that was his sunny faith and breezy hopefulness.   No one interested with him in any common enterprise ever went near him without feeling stronger and more courageous.   If with you he believed in any cause, his buoyant faith made you feel that you were bound to win; and it was a great pleasure to have such a spirit as his for a co-worker.   And he showed this trait in the darkest hours.   His courage rose against disaster as a kite would against the wind, and when things looked black he never threw the blame on his associates; but, stiffening his own resolution, he always put failure or disappointment behind him, and turned a brave, bright, trustful face to the front.   Such courage was most contagious, and it was an inspiration to stand with him in any undertaking.

It will be interesting to recall at this point some words of eulogy uttered by Mr. Sullivan at the obsequies of Bayard Taylor, many of which will be seen by his friends to describe his own character with remarkable exactness:

His voice we shall hear no more. His manly form and character-expressing features remain for memory alone. But there are deeper memories with us of his social qualities: his enthusiasm for his work; his ingenuousness in his own estimate of himself; his sensibility to criticism; his modesty, coupled with independence and dignity; his freedom from pretension; his cool reflection; the fixedness of his principles, yet with toleration and liberality abounding; his freedom from discontent, without grudges against fortune; his constancy and warmth in friendship; his good sense; his pleasure in his work; his courage and enterprise; his love of the arts; his hopefulness; his high aims in existence.

His love of peace has already been mentioned. Coupled with this there always went a passionate devotion to justice; and his aim in his professional career was always to make these two ends meet, by endeavoring, if possible, to settle his cases without the help of judge and jury, so avoiding litigation. He once told a fellow-lawyer that where he tried one case he composed thirty or forty out of court. Truly a noble use of his legal attainments, striving always to earn the blessing of that most musical of the beatitudes, "Blessed are the peacemakers"! As this same lawyer expressed it in a public tribute to his memory:

He not only made his profession, with Lord Coke, "the perfection of reason," but, with Howard, the great philanthropist, a road through the higher humanities of life and a "circumnavigation of charity" among his fellow men.

No picture of Mr. Sullivan would be complete without recalling the many-sidedness of the man. He seemed to "stand four-square to every wind that blew" in this great city. Full of public spirit, with a mind that was hospitable to every great "enterprise of pith and moment," he touched the great life of the metropolis at many and most diverse points. Music, literature, art, and the general civic interests claimed his attention. He was a part of the life of the city, filling a place in it which few men of this generation have filled. The waters of the great heaving ocean close over the stateliest and mightiest vessel, and

THE BUST OF
ALGERNON SYDNEY SULLIVAN
IN THE
ALPHA DELTA PHI HOUSE
NEW YORK CITY

(Inscription)

Presented in 1907 by Citizens of New York
to the
Alpha Delta Phi Club
in honor of
ALGERNON SYDNEY SULLIVAN
A brother in the Alpha Delta Phi Fraternity
1826—1887

Able, brilliant accomplished; constantly employing
his great talents; always a leader at the Bar and in
public affairs; high-minded and of great moral courage;
with unusual powers to charm, influence and persuade; he so used his powers in his public, in his
professional and in his private life that he was ever a
help, an encouragement and an inspiration to his
fellow men.

It is well for men to mark their admiration for
greatness of soul and beauty of character, and to
express their grateful appreciation of service to mankind in private life, by public commendation of some
such man as this as an illustrious example.

Drawing by W. E. Mears

not a ripple is left on the surface to show where it once rode in proud majesty; the confession that "the place thereof shall know us no more forever" (a confession so humbling to the pride of man) must be made even of the kingliest spirits of our race; but the men of New York will not soon forget him whose name stands at the head of this article. For he gave of his strength to the community in such a way that he seemed to belong to it more than many other men who were born here. He was associated intimately with all of its progressive life; and when he died the leading representatives of legal, political, commercial, art, social, and philanthropic circles, and of numerous other departments of interest and effort in this full-lifed city, gathered around his bier to do him reverence, filling the church to overflowing. There was a universal sense of loss; the whole community mourned for one of its first citizens.

Most of that remarkable gathering of the choice spirits of New York knew Mr. Sullivan, as the distinguished lawyer; the public-spirited citizen; the potent adviser in the inner councils of his political party; the persuasive and versatile popular orator; the charming after-dinner speaker; the delightful raconteur; the social leader; the graceful, genial gentleman, treasured by his friends as faultless in all the courtesies of life; a very Mæcenas in his enthusiastic and intelligent patronage of music, of letters, and the arts,—a remarkably many-sided man, *tres atque rotundus*. And yet all these gifts were but the engaging, winning externals of his life; and these representatives of metropolitan activity, who had gathered around his bier in that church which he loved with passionate devotion, were come to the place, which, as we who stood near knew full well, was the outward and stately symbol of that which was the true source and the dearest possession of his life. His springs were in God. His religion was not merely one of many real interests; his loving fear of God, his faith in Jesus Christ (which was of a child-like and ardent type), and his large-hearted love for man—*was his life*. He was always a regular and reverent attendant upon the public worship of God; he joined with contagious heartiness in the hymns of praise and gave the

preacher his earnest, sympathetic attention, knowing "the helpfulness of hearing." He was rarely absent from his place in the
Sunday-school, and his class of young boys idolized him as
the model of a Christian gentleman. His work for and with the
young people of his church has already been alluded to. It was
also his practice for many years to visit one of our hospitals every
Sunday afternoon, to give the patients words of Christian exhortation and cheer. Beyond this he was not permitted by his
full life in the world to take much active part in the ordinary
modes of Christian activity. What he did in this way was so
quiet and local that many of his friends and admirers, who only
knew the other sides of his life, were surprised to learn of the
light in which the people of his church regarded him. But none
the less was his religion the controlling and formative element
in his life and career. In the frequent conferences which I was
privileged to hold with him in behalf of that venerable church
which we both wished to serve, he gave me many unexpected
glimpses of his nature in his descriptions of his ideals of helpful
preaching, and in the plans for the enlargement of our field of
usefulness with which his fertile brain was teeming. I was often
struck with his deep, sweet, strong, manly spirituality and his
simplicity of faith, and I was always made to feel, as we were
considering these interests of Christ's Kingdom in our midst,
that we were circling about what was the deep throbbing center
of all his many-sided activities.

Without intruding upon the dear sanctities of his household, I
may be permitted to tell a little incident (it was almost a daily
one) of his home-life. Perhaps his favorite hymn was one of
those sung at his funeral: "Art thou weary, art thou languid?"
Note by note, with almost boyish persistence, he had picked it
out upon the piano; and for many years hardly a day passed
without his singing it to himself with his own accompaniment.
Often it was the signal to the household that he had come up-
town from his work. It was a simple thing; and yet in truth the
little habit betrayed the secret of the man's life. The plaintive
notes of the familiar hymn at once spoke the yearnings of his own

heart, and recalled it to its divine home—the love and care of
the great Redeemer. From the strife of courts, from the turmoil
of public affairs, from the whirl of social pleasures he always
came back, like a tired child, to what after all and under all was
the true center and spring of his life.

Upon the back of a picture of Mr. Sullivan which I treasure
among my choicest possessions, a loving hand has written some
lines which are so beautifully and accurately descriptive of our
friend, that they must have been suggested to the pious Keble
by some loving spirit like his:

> Men there are in this loud stunning tide
>   Of human care and crime,
> With whom the melodies abide
>   Of the everlasting chime;
> Who carry music in their heart
> Through dusky lane and wrangling mart,
> Plying their daily task with busier feet,
> Because their secret souls a holy strain repeat.

Such a man was Mr. Sullivan. The music of true joy and
peace sounded in his heart—because his life was thus "hid with
Christ in God."

I cannot close this modest sketch without recalling one feature
of the funeral exercises which made a profound and lasting
impression upon those who were present. I refer to the hymn
with which the simple obsequies concluded. I quote it here,
because it is one of those noble modern Anglican lyrics which has
only found its way into our more recently compiled hymnals, and
many of the readers of *The Evangelist* may not know it:

> For all thy saints, who from their labors rest,
> Who thee by faith before the world confessed,
> Thy name, O Jesus, be forever blessed.
> > Hallelujah!

> Thou wast their Rock, their Fortress, and their Might;
> Thou, Lord, their Captain in the well-fought fight;
> Thou, in the darkness drear, their Light of light.
> > Hallelujah!

O may thy soldiers, faithful, true, and bold,
Fight as the saints who nobly fought of old,
And win, with them, the victor's crown of gold.
            Hallelujah!

O blest communion, fellowship divine!
We feebly struggle, they in glory shine;
Yet all are one in thee, for all are thine.
            Hallelujah!

And when the strife is fierce, the warfare long,
Steals on the ear the distant triumph-song,
And hearts are brave again, and arms are strong.
            Hallelujah!

The golden evening brightens in the west;
Soon, soon to faithful warriors comes the rest;
Sweet is the calm of Paradise the blest.
            Hallelujah!

But, lo, there breaks a yet more glorious day:
The saints triumphant rise in bright array;
The King of glory passes on his way.
            Hallelujah!

From earth's wide bounds, from ocean's farthest coast,
Through gates of pearl streams in the countless host,
Singing to Father, Son, and Holy Ghost,
            Hallelujah!

The funeral exercises began and to some extent of necessity ended in a sad minor strain; for the departure of such a man left a painful vacancy in many lives and enterprises. And yet with this hymn the service seemed to close upon a glad triumphant major key. At first that sorrow-stricken crowd did not have much heart to sing a song of thanksgiving. But we gathered strength and hope and courage with every line of that martial hymn, and its closing verses came from over a thousand throats and hearts, and rolled through the vaulted gothic arches like a very pæan of victory. It was sublime and uplifting, and the service at this point reached the true ideal of a Christian's funeral.   I think all present realized very keenly the elements of gladness and triumph in the death of a faithful disciple; and, as with blinding tears of sorrow we looked into the golden sunset of the life of our friend and hero, joy and thanksgiving made them flow the faster; for we thought that what to us was a going down of the sun was for them upon the other side and for him a rising into a larger and more glorious life.   The *heimgang* (as the Germans beautifully name death) of a man of God is not a defeat, but a complete triumph; "thanks be unto God who giveth us the victory through our Lord Jesus Christ."   Therefore we chanted no mournful dirge as about the body of a slain warrior; but we sang a song of victory, which was but the faint far-off earthly echo to that "Singing to the Father, Son, and Holy Ghost" which bursts from the lips of "the countless host" of those who have triumphed through "the power of His resurrection."   For "the redeemed of the Lord shall return and come with singing unto Zion; and everlasting joy shall be upon their head; they shall obtain gladness and joy; and sorrow and mourning shall flee away."   The ear of faith caught the echo of these heavenly strains, and so, with a song of thanksgiving and of expectation, we bade our friend *auf wiedersehn*.

Such men never die.   They live on in lives made better and braver and brighter for their presence.   For he went through life doing good and, what was more, *being* good; for that is the taproot of true doing.   When I think of our friend, I often recall that beautiful exhortation of the great Apostle, to which he gave heed as earnestly as any man I ever met:

> Finally, brethren, whatsoever things are true, whatsoever things are honest, whatsoever things are just, whatsoever things are pure, whatsoever things are lovely, whatsoever things are of good report; and if there be any virtue, and if there be any praise, think on these things.

The serenity of genuine goodness shone like a star in his face. He rarely touched his fellow-men, except to help them and cheer them on to high thinking and noble doing; and this, I would earnestly insist, is the best form of "Christian work." "May his tribe increase."

The contemplation of a character like this may inspire a man to sing as an aspiration of his life that noble hymn of the poet of Agnosticism, only it is with a fullness of meaning into what, alas, she never seemed to enter; because we set it to the music of the resurrection and so gave efficient motive power to the noble desire for an immortality of influence, by adding to it the sure and blessed hope of a personal individual immortality in the fellowship of the Christ of God:

> O may I join the choir invisible
> Of those immortal dead who live again
> In lives made better by their presence. So
> To live is heaven. . . .
>   . . . This is life to come,
> Which martyred men have made more glorious
> For us who strive to follow. May I reach
> That purest heaven, and be to other souls
> That cup of strength in some great agony,
> Enkindle generous ardor, feed pure love,
> Beget the smiles that have no cruelty,
> Be the sweet presence of a good diffused,
> And in diffusion ever more intense;
> So shall I join that choir invisible
> Whose music is the gladness of the world.

First Presbyterian Church,
  New York, November 22, 1888.

MEMORIAL RESOLUTIONS AND ADDRESSES

COURT OF COMMON PLEAS—PART I

Proceedings on motion to adjourn out of respect to the memory of Algernon S. Sullivan.

NEW YORK, December 5, 1887.

Present: Hon. Henry Wilder Allen, J.

Mr. William J. Curtis, Mr. W. W. Niles, and Mr. Blair spoke in support of the motion.

In ordering the adjournment, Judge Allen said:

The motion which has just been made is very appropriate, and will be granted.   Mr. Sullivan was conspicuous for his learning and great charms of character.   The tributes which have been paid to his memory by the members of the bar who have just spoken are well deserved.   The Court will stand adjourned until to-morrow morning at eleven o'clock.

G. W. COTTERILL:

On Motion to adjourn the Court of Common Pleas, December 5, 1887.

Mr. Sullivan's life, both professional and private, was an exemplar.   His excellent qualities of mind and heart were so fittingly blended that he became a lawyer instinctively, whose paramount consideration was the right and justice of the cause that he was called upon to espouse.

Professional ambition, vanity, or emolument were powerless to obscure his vision in this regard.   As an advocate he was gifted with a fluency and clearness of expression, which, combined with a vivid imagination, took the form of eloquence when he addressed himself to audience or jury.   But facility of expression never betrayed him into weakness of logic.   It was impossible to come in contact with him without being impressed by the candor and fairness of his character.   As an associate in professional life his conduct was marked by such an extreme unselfishness towards his brother lawyer that the utmost harmony prevailed, and the latter felt that he had gained a disinterested friend.   In meeting him as an adversary one could not but be impressed by his urbanity, his fairness; and even defeat at his hands was deprived of its sting.   As a citizen he was universally esteemed, and was regarded as the type of the true American gentleman.

I therefore suggest that the minutes of this Court bear witness to the respect for the memory of one whom we so delight to honor, and that the Court do now adjourn in token of our bereavement.

WILLIAM J. CURTIS:

On Motion to adjourn the Court of Common Pleas, December 5, 1887.

May it please your Honor, the public press of this morning has brought to our notice the sad and very sudden news of the death of a gentleman who has been for upwards of twenty years a very prominent member of the New York Bar.   It would be perhaps more fitting that the fact should be called to the attention of the Court by some gentleman of more mature years or longer practice at the Bar than myself; but an intimate and very close association in the office of Mr. Sullivan upwards of seven years seemed to make it fitting that I should say a word here at this time in commemoration of him.

I knew him as a man, as a father, as a citizen, and as a lawyer. As a father he was tender and loving, considerate and true.   As a man he was always unostentatious; he was always considerate of the feelings of others; he was warm in his greeting, and democratic in his ideas.   His greetings to the messenger boy in his office were as courteous and thoughtful and as considerate as to the most distinguished citizen of our city.   For seven years of his life, although I saw him almost daily during that time, I never heard a harsh, unkind or inconsiderate or intemperate word pass his lips regarding any person or any thing.   He was an ideal Christian gentleman.   He was tolerant in his ideas, gentle and liberal in his views although of the Evangelical faith, and treated the feelings and convictions of others with respect.   As a public citizen he always desired to do his duty in every respect. He was governed by the highest ideals. As a lawyer he was perhaps best known by his forensic ability; but it was not in that line that I most admired him. Knowing him as I did in the confidence of his office I admired him most because of his wise and judicious counsel; because of his sympathy for those in adversity; because of the confidence and trust reposed in him by his clients. There was that existing between him and his client which was almost an ideal relation. Their cause was his cause and their successes were his successes; he made them his own, and he therefore entered into his work with the most serious convictions and feelings. As a lawyer he perhaps was not looked upon as combative or litigious; but still he had a very strong will and a very strong character under that unassuming and unostentatious presence, and a moral courage which was possessed to a greater degree by no one, so far as I know, at the Bar. I very well remember of his telling me in the lull of business one afternoon of his experience a great many years ago, when the souls of men were so tried during the war, when he was made conspicuous by his arrest when he was called upon to defend the owners of a rebel blockade-runner that was under the control of the Confederate government. He was called upon by the Attorney-General of the Confederate government to defend them in this matter. His motives were misunderstood, and he was arrested and cast into prison without trial and without examination. He was afterwards released and attended court to defend his clients. He was called upon by many members of the Bar, some distinguished and learned men; he was told: "Sullivan, you must not stand here and defend these gentlemen; your life is in danger; you cannot reach your home in safety if you do." His simple, true, and ingenuous reply was, "But I am retained as their attorney." "That doesn't make any difference; you must not sacrifice your life, or injure your life in their interest." He said, "That is a consideration which I as a lawyer cannot entertain; if my clients do not desire to avail themselves of my services they can excuse me and employ some one else; but if they insist upon my representing them, I as a man and as a lawyer must stand and do my duty." And he did his duty at the request of his clients even in the face of danger. That is, I say, an indication of his moral courage. His was a beautiful character; I know of none more lovely.

It is not the proper time or place to expand upon his virtues which crowd upon me, but I knew him so many years that I am very glad to stand here and pay this simple tribute to his memory. Well it might be said in the language of Bacon, "He moved in charity, rested in Providence, and turned upon the poles of truth." I now desire to make the appropriate motion that this court stand adjourned until to-morrow morning in memory of Mr. Sullivan.

W. W. NILES:

On Motion to adjourn the Court of Common Pleas, December 5, 1887.

The progress of this world and the course of the Divine Providence seem to me that the best respect we can pay to the memory of an active and diligent man when he has passed out of his environments here, is that we should go right on and complete the work that he has left for us. But the course of habit and the sense of the people through all time has been that when one passes off from this stage of existence they should toll the bell, which I understand to mean that we should go slow; that we should stop and think a moment; and it seems to have become rooted in the practice of the bar and the courts that the appropriate way to pay respect to the memory of one who has been prominent and active, who has done something to help on the progress of the human race, and especially who has done it in a kindly and gentle spirit—the best way to pay respect to his memory is to stop the whirl and swirl of business and think of it. If that is the true way, there is no more appropriate occasion for doing that than this. I had the honor of knowing Mr. Sullivan for a good while; at the bar he was diligent, intelligent, and faithful. In society by his gentle and happy temper he secured the respect of people, and by his thorough kindness he secured the love of his friends in the smaller circles. When although, as a rule, the dropping out of any one man from this world amounts to nothing, it is like a drop of water in the ocean, yet for the encouragement of his fellows, and particularly for the encouragement of the young men who are following on in his footsteps, it is well that it should be seen that people take notice of the passage of such a man. I therefore, without attempting to enlarge upon his virtues or occupy the time on this occasion, second the motion that we do now adjourn.

B. F. BLAIR:

On Motion to adjourn the Court of Common Pleas, December 5, 1887.

This is the first time that I have had the privilege of speaking upon the occasion of the announcement of the death of a fellow-member of the bar. I shall not occupy much time; I only desire the opportunity to lay here a slight token to his memory, and to say that in all my experience at the bar I have never met any man whom it seemed to me I could more safely point out to all the younger members of the profession as a model; whom I could more fully commend as such, than this one, our brother who has gone. I had the privilege for many years of knowing him intimately. My acquaintance with him began during his occupancy of positions of trust in the District Attorney's office, and it has continued ever since I came to know him; and the feeling has become one almost akin to brotherhood. I knew him at the Bar, and recognized in him so many qualities that go to make up a lovely character; and I am doing but scant justice to my feelings as a member of this Bar in seconding the motion.

COURT OF COMMON PLEAS—PART II

Proceedings on motion to adjourn out of respect to the memory of Algernon S. Sullivan.

NEW YORK, December 5, 1887.

Present: Hon. Richard S. Larremore, C. J.

At the opening of this Court, Mr. Henry P. Townsend made the following motion:

Out of respect to the memory of Algernon S. Sullivan, a gentleman well known to all the members of the profession, his character and eminent position at the bar, all of which are elegantly noticed in the newspapers, I respectfully move that the Court do now adjourn.

Mr. N. Quackenbos: I second the motion.

The Court: It is unnecessary on this occasion to attempt anything but a recognition of the propriety of the application just made. A long acquaintance, personal and professional, with Mr. Sullivan has taught us his worth and value to the profession of which he was an honored member. We hope that a suitable opportunity will be afforded when his merits will be presented in a more detailed form which will serve as a lasting record of his past career.

The clerk is directed to enter upon his minutes the motion just made, and the Court will now adjourn.

COURT OF COMMON PLEAS—EQUITY

Proceedings on motion to adjourn out of respect to the memory of Algernon S. Sullivan.

NEW YORK, December 5, 1887.

Present: Hon. Henry W. Bookstaver, J.

Mr. George W. Cotterill moved that the Court adjourn out of respect to the memory of Mr. Algernon S. Sullivan.

Mr. John Clinton Gray seconded the motion.

In ordering the adjournment, Judge Bookstaver said:

Of commanding appearance, kind and frank, he was always welcomed by the Court in any case in which he appeared, because it was felt that his learning, ability, and absolute truthfulness would assist the Court in the trial of any question of law and fact with which it had to deal. He was of great equipoise and absolutely master of himself, so that his life was free from petty bickering or unrest.

YOUNG MEN'S DEMOCRATIC CLUB

F. R. COUDERT, President.

NEW YORK, December 19, 1887.

Resolved, that in the death of the late Algernon S. Sullivan this city has lost one of its most patriotic, public spirited, and useful citizens; the Bar and the law a most upright, eloquent, and able counselor; the club a most conscientious, disinterested, wise, and earnest supporter and member; the Christian community one in whose life is singularly exemplified the truth that the constant consciousness of direct responsibility to God, the creator, is the only adequate and reliable guide and incentive for human conduct.

Resolved, that the community has cause for profound gratitude for such a life as that completed in the death of Mr. Sullivan. Born of most pure and patriotic Christian parentage; educated in the midst of the young, resolute, and inspiring life of the growing West; fitted by natural endowment and by early and thorough study of our Constitution and government for the broadest and most useful activities in his profession, and as a citizen, his whole career was marked by a love of country which excluded sectionalism and embraced every part of the republic, while his efforts were directed ever to promote and secure the great end of our government, the dignity, independence, and sovereignty of the citizen through local self-government.

Resolved, that the life and career of this eminent citizen and pure patriot furnish an example to the young men of the country which will be held in grateful remembrance and is worthy of all imitation.

O. B. POTTER:

Few men whom I have known in this city during the last twenty-five years have been as willing to forego their private interests and convenience in order to contribute counsel, effort, and means to advance the public good as he. His example remains to us, and well will it be for our country, State, and city, if those who shall follow him in the ranks of this great profession shall be equally constant in anxiety and effort for the public good. Henceforth, those who stand for and labor in this cause against all comers in this great city, at the sacrifice of private interest, and if need be partisan affiliation, will miss from their active number one of the most constant and able, Algernon S. Sullivan. May this loss be in some measure compensated by such devotion to the public interest in the younger members of the Bar as his example cannot fail to inspire.

OHIO SOCIETY OF NEW YORK

Special Meeting in Memoriam Algernon S. Sullivan

December 6, 1887.

The Committee reports the following resolutions:

Among those who have cherished with us here the ties of birthplace or of early association, there has been no sweeter or braver spirit than Algernon S. Sullivan, one of our Vice-Presidents, now removed from us by death. His distinguished eminence, arising from his value to the community at large in his public, professional, and individual relations, and his excellence in all these, have made his active interest from the first in this Society a source of strength to it; while his engaging qualities have made him to us individually the object of affectionate regard. The memory of such a man is precious; and these resolutions shall be entered upon our records in commemoration of his worth.

A copy of them shall also be sent to Mrs. Sullivan in token of our sympathy with her in her affliction.

J. C. Zachos.
Wager Swayne.
James Q. Howard.
F. C. Loveland.
George B. Hibbard.

[Seal.]

(Attest): Homer Lee, *Secretary.*

Address of General Thomas Ewing

He was one of the brightest and best of our Society.   A better man is not to be found in this splendid metropolis.

On last Wednesday night, one week ago, I dined with him in a party of twenty gentlemen at Delmonico's.   He never was more full of life or in higher spirits.   He made a thoughtful speech, and towards the end of the evening sang a song with improvisations between the verses, charmingly hitting off traits of the other guests.   It was as genial and often as witty a bit of fun as Goldsmith's *Retaliation*.

One short week ago; and now he lies dead!   But, gentlemen, he was ready to go.   And after all it matters little when we die, though it matters much how we live and what example we leave behind us.

How can any of us hope to do better than he?   How few of us can expect to do as well!

As I think of him now, I know not which most to admire, his genial temper, his generous heart, his brilliant intellect, his simple and sterling character, or his Christian life and example.

He came to New York from Cincinnati in his early prime, ambitious for wealth and fame.   He came where wealth and reputation are added to those who bring both, but are rarely won by the honest effort of strangers who enter the stern struggle with neither.

He had no adventitious help, no powerful friends, but worked his way up by patient and self-reliant industry and frugality, growing each year in public respect and confidence until he stood in the front rank at the Bar and in all the walks of life.

He was cut off without warning in mid-career.   What better could he have done had he been given time to get ready?   Nothing.   He lived his life as he went along—from day to day.   And now, looking back over it, all who knew him unite in words of love and admiration.   There are none to damn with faint praise,

or to keep a discreet silence, or to intimate faults in his character
or conduct. All know him to have been uncorrupted and in-
corruptible, a Christian gentleman, whose brilliant and beautiful
life is a happy memory to his friends, and a priceless heritage to
his wife and child.

Address of General H. L. Burnett

It was my good fortune to know Mr. Sullivan well for many
years. Our lives touched socially and professionally at many
points. His personal character inspired me with warm regard
and attachment and his intellectual qualities with sincere admiration. Few men whom I have ever known in our profession
of the law or in any other possessed such roundness or completeness of culture, or such equal and well-adjusted intellectual
powers. In his work there was such readiness, versatility,
smoothness, and ease, so little apparent effort or labor that one
hardly realized the strength and force of the man, like a perfect
machine, whose parts are so well adjusted and adapted that it
works and wields its great force without noise or wearing friction,
and without always adequately impressing the beholder. On
the platform he was peculiarly attractive and effective. He was
tall, well proportioned in form, handsome of face, graceful in
movement and gesture, and of a most winning manner and
presence. His voice was full, penetrating, and musical, and had
in it that sympathetic and magnetic quality without which no
man can be truly eloquent, and which has that mysterious
power of carrying the feeling and meaning in the heart of the
speaker to the hearts of his hearers almost without words.

Both as a writer and speaker he had a most pure style, was a
master of good English, and his words had in them those qualities
possessed only by cultured minds and pure, strong natures—
directness, simplicity, and vivid reality.

Of his place and achievements at the Bar it is not my purpose
here and now to speak. It is sufficient to say that, coming here
from a Western State nearly a quarter of a century ago, he very

soon made his place in the front rank of the profession, and was quickly recognized as among the ablest of the great lawyers of the State. That place he maintained, his fame as a great advocate and lawyer growing brighter and stronger until he passed from us and death made for him another life.

There is another phase of his character, however, which it seems fitting and proper we should recall. It is not too much to say, I think, that there was no man in this great city who did more for the poor than Algernon S. Sullivan. Of him how pertinent and true are the words of Horace Mann:

> The soul of the truly benevolent man does not seem to reside much in its own body. Its life to a great extent is a mere reflex of the lives of others. It migrates into their bodies and identifies its existence with their existence, finds its own happiness in increasing and prolonging their pleasures, in extinguishing or solacing their pains.

There was no organized movement in this great city for the alleviation of suffering, for help and succor to earth's unfortunates, which did not receive his warm, strong sympathy and his efficient aid. It was known of all the good men and good women how ready he was to do all in his power to help forward any good work, and so it came about that when an effort was to be made to organize some charitable movement, to enlist and arouse the people in behalf of some good cause, to relieve suffering, to drive out vice, to lift up the fallen, Mr. Sullivan was expected and was there, always found leading, giving expression and direction to the effort.

In appealing to the people in such a cause, how eloquent, how pathetic he was, what sympathetic, what pleading, what tender tones in that musical voice as he told of the long hours of toil, the dark days of sickness, the endless misfortunes and voiceless sufferings of the poor and the unfortunate! He kept himself poor by his giving, and he wore his life away in this striving to help his fellow-man. His great powers of mind and heart were ever at their best in this work. Of him, how true it was, "God uses us to help each other, so lending our minds out."

In the death of Algernon S. Sullivan a great mind richly stored, a knightly soul aiming ever at highest achievement, a warm, strong, sympathetic human heart passed from among us, and we bow our heads in mourning.

NEW YORK PRODUCE EXCHANGE
December 6, 1887.

At a meeting of the members of the New York Produce Exchange held December 6, 1887, relative to the death of Algernon S. Sullivan, the following preamble and resolutions were unanimously adopted:

Whereas, the members of the New York Produce Exchange have heard with sincere regret the melancholy announcement of the death of Algernon S. Sullivan, a public-spirited citizen, a distinguished lawyer, a man of sterling, robust honesty, and

Whereas, the memory of Mr. Sullivan has particular claim to our grateful remembrance, because of the willingness with which he always responded to any demands made upon his talents and time by the officers of this body, and especially in recognition of the dignified, scholarly, and eloquent address delivered by him on the occasion of the laying of the corner stone of the Exchange; therefore

Resolved, that in the death of Mr. Sullivan we deplore the loss of a gifted scholar, an upright citizen, a good man, and to his stricken family we offer our deepest sympathy in unstinted measure.

Resolved, that a committee of twenty-five members be appointed to attend the funeral of our deceased friend, and that this preamble and these resolutions be spread upon the minutes of the Exchange, and a copy thereof suitably engrossed be presented to the family of the deceased.

A. E. ORR, *President.*

[Seal.]   THOMAS P. WHITE, *Secretary.*

ALPHA DELTA PHI FRATERNITY

Whereas, our Heavenly Father has removed by death our honored and beloved brother Algernon S. Sullivan, one of the members of this council, who by his devotion to A Δ Φ during the years of his connection therewith, and by his warm-hearted attachment to the members of that Fraternity with whom he has been personally associated, has in a marked manner won our affection; who as an associate with us in the deliberations of this council has been a wise director of the Fraternity, who by his legal attainments and his marked ability as an advocate has honored the Fraternity he so sincerely loved, and who by his affable manners, his constant urbanity, and his high moral tone has left to us the memory of a man occupying a most enviable position in the community as citizen, lawyer, and friend;

Therefore it is by the Executive Council of the Fraternity

Resolved, that by the death of our brother Algernon S. Sullivan this council and the Fraternity of A Δ Φ have suffered an irreparable loss.

Resolved, that this council do extend to the family of our deceased brother in their bereavement the sympathy of the council.

Resolved, that the community has lost an upright citizen.

Resolved, that these resolutions be spread upon the minutes of the council, and that a copy thereof be transmitted to the family of the deceased, and that the resolutions be reported by this council to the next annual convention of the A Δ Φ Fraternity.

WILLIAM TALCOTT.
W. B. RANKIN.
B. W. FRANKLIN.

YOUNG PEOPLE'S ASSOCIATION, PRESBYTERIAN CHURCH

The members of the Young People's Association of the First Presbyterian Church, reverently acknowledging their dependence upon their Heavenly Father, who rules all that is done for human good, desiring to express the emotions with which they have been filled by the sudden death of their beloved President, Mr. Algernon S. Sullivan, unanimously adopt the following minute:

In the march of his busy life Mr. Sullivan found time to devote himself to the interest of this honored church, to study its welfare and to advance its usefulness, giving fully of his substance and counsels for its benefit. His active, unfailing interest in the Young People's Association was evidenced by the service which he generously gave as its President, and his familiar presence at our meetings; indeed, to his wisdom, ability, counsel, and material assistance we attribute our success as an organization. In his life the members of this association have an example of a devoted, consistent, exalted Christian character, which will abide with them always as a cheering and guiding light, unobscured and inextinguishable. In his death we sorrowfully part with one whom we have been accustomed to esteem not only for the simplicity and nobility of his mind and abounding sympathy of his nature, but as the embodiment of the qualities of a sincere follower of Christ. His death comes to us all with the shock of a personal affliction, and we shall never cease to mourn his loss.

Our secretary is directed to transmit this expression of the sense of our great bereavement, suitably engrossed, to the family of Mr. Sullivan, and to convey to them the tenderest assurances of our profound sympathy in their affection.

> THOMAS E. SATTERTHWAITE, *Vice-President.*
> HARRY C. PERLEY, *Secretary.*
> E. M. BOGERT, *Treasurer.*
> LADISLOS KARGE,
> CHARLES M. BERGSTRASSER,   } *Committee.*
> WILLIAM F. HAEMER.

NEW YORK MERCANTILE EXCHANGE
Corner Hudson and Harrison Streets

NEW YORK, December 26, 1887.

At a public meeting held upon the floor of the Exchange, December 26, 1887, the following resolutions were adopted:

The New York Mercantile Exchange, learning with sincere

regret of the death of their friend Algernon S. Sullivan, desire to express their appreciation of him and their sense of the loss which they in common with the community have sustained in his removal. In Mr. Sullivan's character they recognize the honest man, the gentleman. Sensitive and honorable, he was unselfish and generous in his intercourse with his fellows. The sterling citizen, he was courteous to his opponents, faithful to his associates, superior to partisanship, and uncompromising in adherence to truth and duty. Gifted with powers of oratory to sway his listeners, he used them for no mercenary purpose, but only to refine, to elevate society.

The Exchange feels that they owe to Mr. Sullivan a debt of gratitude for distinguished services which he gave them without expectation of reward, and which they can now repay only by honoring and revering his memory, and by placing in their archives this, their memorial tribute to his many virtues.

BENJAMIN WINER, *Chairman.*

M. FOLSOM,
JOHN A. SMITH,
GEORGE B. DOUGLAS,
W. L. TEMPLE.
} *Committee.*

NEW YORK COLLEGE OF MUSIC

Whereas, the Trustees of the New-York College of Music have learned with sorrow of the death of their President, colleague, and friend, Mr. Algernon S. Sullivan:

Resolved, that in the death of Mr. Sullivan the College of Music loses a man who has befriended it in countless ways from its beginning; whose feelings, strength, and time were always effectually enlisted in its service.

Resolved, that the efforts of Mr. Sullivan contributed greatly to the progress and well-being of this institution.

Resolved, that our relations with the deceased were always marked by a spirit of generous and open-hearted courtesy on his part, and that we deeply mourn his loss.

Resolved, that the Secretary enter these resolutions upon our minutes and send a copy thereof to the family of Mr. Sullivan.

Resolved, that the New-York College of Music be closed during the funeral of Mr. Sullivan, and that the faculty and students be invited to attend the same.

ALEX. LAMBERT,
Director.

LATHAM G. REED,
Secretary.

HARLEM DEMOCRATIC CLUB
13, 15 and 17 East 125th Street

NEW YORK, December 21, 1887.

At a meeting of the Harlem Democratic Club, held Wednesday evening, December 7, the following resolution was offered by the Hon. Chas. W. Dayton, and unanimously carried:

The Harlem Democratic Club has heard with profound sorrow that Algernon S. Sullivan is dead.

His name is associated with the early history of our organization at a time when his wisdom and eloquence lent their great force to the public announcement of our plans and purposes, a service generously given by him and warmly welcomed by us.

An upright life, a high position at the bar, a courtly manner, a singular charm of person, a nature where amiability and strength of character were perfectly combined, all served to make him one of the most attractive and influential orators of our time.

His devotion to the principles of true Democracy was pronounced and recognized, and his unselfish endeavors for the good of this country gave added force to his labors and brilliant utterances as a patriot with whom politics was a duty.

His example should be emulated and his fame dearly cherished.

Resolved, that a copy of the foregoing be duly attested and transmitted with our condolences to Mr. Sullivan's family.

JOSEPH J. CASEY, *Secretary.*

J. R. MCNALTY, *President.*

AMERICAN SAVINGS BANK

501 Fifth Avenue

NEW YORK, January 9, 1888.

Dear Madam:

With deep sympathy in your recent affliction we beg, at the request of all the Trustees of the American Savings Bank, to send you the following copy of a preamble and resolution adopted at their last meeting, namely:

Whereas, it has pleased the Almighty to remove by death from among us one of our associates, the late Hon. Algernon S. Sullivan.

Resolved, that we, the Trustees of the American Savings Bank, desire to record the great loss we feel in being deprived of his wise counsel and willing assistance in the management of this institution, and to express the high estimation in which we held him on account of his sound judgment and sterling integrity, which were always combined with the kindly and courteous manners of the true gentleman.

With great respect, we remain, madam,

Your obedient servants,

DANIEL T. HOAG, *President*.

GRANVILLE B. SMITH, *Treasurer*.

WILLIAM IRWIN, *Secretary and Counsel*.

To MRS. ALGERNON S. SULLIVAN.

JEWELERS' SECURITY ALLIANCE

At a special meeting of the Executive Committee of the Jewelers' Security Alliance, held December 7, 1887, the following preamble and resolutions were read and unanimously adopted:

Whereas, in the providence of God Algernon S. Sullivan, late counsel of this Alliance, having been suddenly removed by death, and

Whereas, his faithful services as legal counselor of the Alliance and his devoted interest to its affairs from the date of its organization to the present time should have befitting acknowledgment, now therefore be it

Resolved, that by the decease of its late counsel, Hon. Algernon S. Sullivan, the Jewelers' Security Alliance has lost a most able, earnest, and faithful administrator of its affairs, who was endeared to the associate officers by many ties of friendship growing out of long acquaintance, and a just appreciation of his sterling integrity and noble qualities.

Resolved, that this Board attend the funeral services in a body, and that a copy of the proceedings of this meeting be prepared by the secretary and forwarded to the family of the deceased.

NEW YORK JEWELERS' BOARD OF TRADE

MRS. ALGERNON S. SULLIVAN AND FAMILY.

At a meeting of the board of directors of the New-York Jewelers' Board of Trade, held on Tuesday, Dec. 13, 1887, the following resolutions were unanimously adopted:

Whereas, the Almighty has in his infinite wisdom seen fit to remove from our midst our late respected counselor and friend, the Hon. Algernon S. Sullivan, we deem this a proper time to express our feelings of sorrow and regret at the untimely ending of a useful and honorable life; therefore be it

Resolved, that we hereby tender to his bereaved family our sincere sympathy and condolence in this their hour of affliction.

Resolved, that a copy of these resolutions be transmitted to the family of the deceased, and the same entered upon the minutes of this Board.

F. H. RICHARDSON, *President.*

(Attest): H. M. CONDIT, *Secretary.*

VETERANS OF THE SEVENTY-FIRST REGIMENT, N. G. S. N. Y.

HEADQUARTERS 71ST REGIMENT ARMORY,
NEW YORK, December 21, 1887.

My Dear Madam.

At the meeting of the Association when the moment came to take action upon the death of our honorary member, the formal resolutions which it is customary to pass seemed to us one and all to give no expression to the general feeling, and one of our members arose and said, "Commander, I feel that no resolutions we could pass would give voice to the deep feeling Mr. Sullivan's death has stirred among us. One of our comrades has gone, one who has always given us his cheerful aid and countenance in all our doings. He gave us aid and counsel in anything proposed for the general welfare and pleasure. He helped us care for our sick, bury our dead, and succor the widow and orphans. He was our friend and comrade, one of us, and I beg you, Sir, to write in kind words our sympathy and sorrow which no formal resolutions can tell."

Sincerely yours,

CHARLES F. HOMER,
Col. 71st Regt. Veterans.

LETTER FROM WILLIAM NELSON CROMWELL

To MRS. A. S. SULLIVAN.

There has been and is such a deep sense of personal loss by the Bar as well as by the general community that ordinary forms of expression seem too commonplace for such a rare and peculiar example. The bench adjourned with record of its regard, the Bar attended his obsequies, and everywhere, on the street and in the court, now speak of his loss as that of a personal friend; the press of all political shades lavished its space, and for the first time within my knowledge were in accord on a common subject. The great exchanges and societies tried to tell their sorrow in fitting resolutions, and met at his funeral through their most distinguished representatives. Business men everywhere praised his virtues, and his intimates and clients were not ashamed to weep. The city lowered its flags, and its most honored citizens were the bearers of his dear remains.

We loved, idolized him so much, that it seems to us but natural to find in him something to admire and esteem, but it is not, after all, remarkable that from all classes and all parts of the country, even from persons who were but slightly acquainted with him, there should come the expression of such grief as is generally evoked by the loss of kin only?

Although one of the greatest he was one of the simplest of men, with no vulgar aims, and with an unswerving faith in God and human kind. He was the purest, sweetest, wisest man of his time. For nearly fifteen years I have been looking daily into his heart, and during all those years and under the thousand temptations of a busy life, professional, social, political, I never found there even remotest approach to sin. Not an unkind or harsh word to any human being, not a falsehood, not a bitter thing, not a profane or indelicate thought ever passed those lips. Always gracious and altogether lovely; putting aside, not putting forward, his own great personality; reaching out both hands in constant helpfulness to men.

This is not the tribute of affection, nor its exaggeration; I mean my thoughts to be literally and exactly taken.

Of whom else, man or woman, in all this world could this be honestly witnessed? Unlike most great men, he grew greater the nearer we approached him. These qualities were stamped by God on his noble face and were shown in every act of his daily life, so that all men who met him went away somehow refreshed and ennobled. Such a life cannot be phrased, it can only be loved; such a life cannot die; such an influence is more potent than man himself.

WILLIAM NELSON CROMWELL.
January 1, 1888

❖

EXTRACTS FROM NEWSPAPERS

NEW YORK TIMES

December 5, 1887.

The announcement that Algernon S. Sullivan is dead will prove a great shock and a cause of honest regret not only to his friends and acquaintances, who are many, but to the public at large, for he was looked upon as a man of great ability, of a kindness of heart that could not be measured, of a never-ending desire to promote such projects as were for the benefit of the people, and more than all, he was considered a politician who was absolutely pure.

NEW YORK TRIBUNE

December 5, 1887.

Mr. Algernon S. Sullivan was an active man and prominent in all phases of social life. He was the President of the Southern Society, a Vice-President of the Ohio Society, a member of the Lawyers' Down Town Club and the Manhattan Club; he was the honorary President of the New York College of Music, a Director of the Presbyterian Hospital, and a Trustee of the First Presbyterian Church at Fifth Avenue and 11th Street. He was a teacher in the first Presbyterian Sunday School, and active in many branches of the Church's work.

His pleasant, kindly ways were known to all with whom he came in contact.

NEW YORK HERALD

December 5, 1887.

Mr. Algernon S. Sullivan was for many years one of the best known figures in New York. A leader at the Bar, a leader in politics, a leader in society, he was known far and wide as a gifted orator, and his tall, spare figure was familiar to most New Yorkers. His strong, clear-cut features, his gleaming dark eyes, his short, snow-white mustache, his large head fringed with closely cropped white hair, and his scrupulous neatness of attire were known to nearly everybody in this city. His manner was ordinarily mild and affable and his words slow, precise, and very distinct.

NEW YORK SUN

December 5, 1887.

Mr. Algernon S. Sullivan's death removed a gracious and unique figure from metropolitan life. He was a lawyer by profession, but by taste was more devoted to music, art, and society than to the dry path of a legal career. In the latter he was painstaking, thorough, and above all, courteous and eloquent. His voice was musical and melodious like his name. Tall, slender, and graceful in figure, with silvery hair, closely trimmed mustache, he attracted attention wherever he appeared in public; in court or on the public platform, where he was heard as well as seen, he held this attention by the felicity of his language and his earnestness and apparent candor and frankness.

NEW YORK MORNING JOURNAL

December 5, 1887.

The news of the death of the prominent lawyer spread over the city in an incredibly short space and everywhere men looked sad as they listened, for few men were so well known and so well beloved.

Mr. Sullivan was to have delivered an address before the Sabbath Commissioners, one of whom he was, but his illness prevented. He was a thoroughly religious man, and with the Rev. Dr. Crosby, and others, strenuously advocated the enforcing of the Sunday laws.

NEW YORK GRAPHIC

December 5, 1887.

The death of Algernon S. Sullivan removes from New York society one of the most amiable and lovable characters that embellished public life for many years.

Manful in all his ways and methods, clear headed, big brained, and widely read in all the realms of literature, he was as tender-hearted as a child and as gentle as a woman.

His law practice at an early age of his career in this city was in the criminal courts, but he soon withdrew from that uncongenial field and devoted himself to the lines of civil procedure.

As a public speaker he had few superiors in this city, and as a whole-souled friend to struggling genius in all ranks of life, there was no man who did more with his means than the white-haired, stalwart lawyer, who died at his home in West 11th Street last night. . . .

In the Court of General Sessions this afternoon, on motion of Mr. Delancey Nicoll, the Court ordered a minute entered expressive of the regret felt at Mr. Sullivan's death.

In the Court of Common Pleas eulogistic remarks were made by Chief Justice Larremore and Judges Bookstaver and Allen. Appropriate minutes were made upon motions by H. B. Townsend, N. Quackenboss, George W. Cottrell, and John Clinton Gray.

Mr. Sullivan's death was a great shock to the profession, many of whom had seen him only a few days since.

New York Evening Post

TRIBUTES IN COURT TO THE MEMORY OF ALGERNON S. SULLIVAN
December 5, 1887.

In Part Second of the Court of General Sessions this morning, Assistant District Attorney Nicoll addressed Judge Cowing, who was presiding, and said he had a motion to make which may be deemed appropriate. Continuing, Mr. Nicoll said: "We were all greatly surprised this morning at the announcement of the death of a well-known member of the Bar and an officer of this Court, one who enjoyed the confidence and respect and love of the entire community. I need scarcely say I refer to Mr. Algernon S. Sullivan, who came to this city many years ago, bringing with him an enviable reputation as an orator and as a lawyer.

"He was the trusted Assistant District Attorney of Garvin, and afterwards filled the office of Public Administrator. He was a man whose character shed luster on his profession, and his death is a calamity to this community.

"I therefore move that an appropriate minute be made upon the records of this Court in recognition of his services and as a mark of respect for his character."

"Judge Cowing: The motion made by Mr. Nicoll is one that is eminently proper. I knew Mr. Sullivan well. He was an able lawyer and a kind-hearted gentleman, who was beloved by the whole community. He passed away very suddenly. It seems but as yesterday that I met him on Broadway and shook him by the hand; that was only a few days ago, and he seemed in the best of health.

"An appropriate minute will be entered on the records of this Court in recognition of his services both as a member of the bar and an officer of the court."

All the branches of the Court of Common Pleas were adjourned to-day on account of the death of Algernon S. Sullivan. Motions were made for the adjournment by H. P. Townsend, Edward N. Quackenboss, George W. Cottrell, and John Clinton Gray. In granting the motions, Chief Justice Larremore and Judges Bookstaver and Allen made appropriate remarks. Judge Larremore testified to a strong personal friendship with Mr. Sullivan, and Judge Bookstaver feelingly referred to the eulogy on Aaron J. Vanderpool delivered a few weeks ago before him by Mr. Sullivan, who was then in excellent health.

New York Mail and Express

December 5, 1887.

The news of the death of Mr. Algernon S. Sullivan comes as a sad surprise to those who knew him best, for it was but a few days since he was one of the conspicuous figures at the annual Chamber of Commerce dinner, and looked as though he might last for twenty years more of high and noble activities.

Mr. Sullivan will be greatly missed in many large circles, professional, social, artistic, and religious. He was always ready to lend the aid of his quick and tender Christian sensibilities and sympathies, and he was a cheerful and enthusiastic helpful power in many different quarters.

Mr. Sullivan was very earnest, decided, and outspoken in his convictions, whether political, religious, or otherwise, but his invariable courtesy and carefulness of statement, his clear appreciation of the rights of other men to opinions opposed to his own, and his genial manner captured the confidence and won the good will of his bitterest political and professional opponents.

New York Commercial Advertiser

December 5, 1887.

Mr. Sullivan stood in the front rank of his profession in this city. He was at one time Public Administrator. As a public speaker with a felicitous diction and graceful presence he had few peers at the bar; but his popularity was even greater than his shining abilities. Although he was in no sense a politician, he was a public-spirited man and took the keenest interest in the economic questions of the day.

In the earlier part of the summer he spoke at the opening of the Consolidated Exchange, warning his hearers against the growing power of Trust combinations.

Mr. Sullivan was a gentleman with manners of the old school, but at the same time was one of the most democratic of men.

New York News

December 5, 1887.

The news of Mr. Sullivan's death, the well-known lawyer, was received with expressions of sorrow throughout the city. Few men were better known or more highly respected than he. At no time during his busy life did he consider that he could not devote a portion of his time to charitable objects.

The remains were to-day placed in the front parlor of his residence No. 16 West 11th Street, and only a few of the most intimate friends of the family were permitted to look at him.

All day long carriages rolled up to the residence bearing relatives and friends who called to tender their sympathy, and many simply sent in their cards or brief notes of condolence, and a large number of dispatches were received from out-of-town friends.

A large number of lawyers and friends have called during the day to express their sympathy.

BOSTON GLOBE

December 5, 1887.

Algernon S. Sullivan, one of New York's best-known lawyers, is dead. The announcement will prove a great shock not only to his friends, who are many, but to the public at large, for he was looked upon as a man of great ability, of a kindness of heart that could not be measured, of a never-ending desire to promote such projects as were for the benefit of the people, and more than all, he was considered a politician who was absolutely pure.

BOSTON JOURNAL

December 5, 1887.

Mr. Algernon S. Sullivan, age 60, died suddenly at his home in New York last evening. He was a prominent Democrat and one of the best-known men in that city.

NEW YORK TRIBUNE

December 6, 1887.

The death of Algernon S. Sullivan will be very sincerely regretted by all who knew that honorable and upright citizen. Always genial and courteous in his demeanor, an effective orator, whether pleading at the bar or entertaining a social gathering, a true and sympathizing friend, he was well fitted to be a universal favorite. Everybody liked him, and his loss will be felt in his profession and in the many circles in which he moved.

Mr. Sullivan was a man of large benevolence, and many who were the recipients of his favor will especially deplore his unexpected demise. His death is indeed a public loss.

THE ORIGINAL PLAQUE
ISSUED BY THE
ALGERNON SYDNEY SULLIVAN
MEMORIAL COMMITTEE

1909

IN 1909 the Algernon Sydney Sullivan Memorial Committee issued a plaque cast from a design of J. Scott Hartley. Its purpose is best explained in the words of the Committee:

"Though dead for more than twenty years, Algernon Sydney Sullivan is remembered with esteem and affection for his devotion to and interest in all affairs which contribute to the welfare of this community, both philanthropic and civic.

"The lapse of time has naturally removed from the hearts of the Committee that peculiar sense of the loss of a beloved friend which is apt to warp the judgment and magnify the virtues of that departed friend.

"The Committee, therefore, is not actuated by a desire to pay a tribute, now belated and useless, to Algernon Sullivan, but the Committee believes in the educational value of public commendation of good citizenship as an effective counterpart to public condemnation of bad citizenship. The latter method of influencing mankind is, unfortunately, perhaps necessarily, in far more frequent use than the former.

With this in mind, the Committee wishes to make use of Mr. Sullivan's remarkable character, noble nature and philanthropic life as a method of publicly commending in all men those general excellencies of character and conduct which in fact he, as an individual, so well exemplified; and it especially hopes that the method taken by it will be an evidence to other men of aspiring and generous natures, that the life of a good man is not forgotten by his fellow men.

In fine, in issuing this plaque the Committee is using the life of Algernon Sydney Sullivan as an illustration of its underlying purpose which is to commend noble, moral and altruistic conduct wherever found— for its own sake."

Plaques were placed in the Brick Presbyterian Church, Grace Church, University Place Church, the East Side Settlement House, the Educational Alliance, St. George's Evening Trade School, New York Trade School, Horace Mann School, Barnard School for Boys, The Browning School, Collegiate School, Columbia Grammar School, Charlton School, Columbia University Law School, New York University Law School, College of Pharmacy of Columbia University, Cooper Union, Lambs Club, City Club, Lawyers' Club, Manhattan Club, New York County Lawyers' Association, the New York Produce Exchange, the Consolidated Exchange, the Mercantile Exchange.

New York World

December 6, 1887.

There is a universal feeling of sadness prevailing in this city over the death of Algernon S. Sullivan, and telegrams of condolence have been received by the bereaved family from all parts of the country. . . . Down town the feeling of sorrow was widespread. . . . A waiter in the Astor House paid him a tribute, saying, "He was a great enough man to be able to treat those below him with respect."

New York Herald

THE BENCH AND THE BAR ARE LOUD IN THEIR PRAISES OF THE LATE ALGERNON S. SULLIVAN

December 6, 1887.

The announcement yesterday of the sudden death of Mr. Sullivan, the well-known lawyer, was a great shock to the members of the New York Bar.

Mr. Sullivan's brilliant talents, the fairness he always evinced toward his legal opponents, and the charm of his manners had gained for him a popularity both on the bench and at the bar, which has rarely been equaled in the city. Of uncommon appearance, kind and frank, he was always welcomed by the Court in any case in which he appeared, because it was felt that his learning, ability, and absolute truthfulness would assist the Court in the trial of any question of law and fact with which it had to deal.

He was of great equipoise and absolutely master of himself, so that his life was free from petty bickering or unrest.

New York Star

MOURNING IN THE CITY FOR ALGERNON S. SULLIVAN

December 6, 1887.

The announcement of the death of Algernon S. Sullivan, the well-known lawyer, was received with expressions of profound sorrow, not alone in legal circles, but by the entire business and social community. He was prominently identified with many charitable and humane enterprises, and few men were better known or more highly respected than he. His social life was as brilliant as his legal career, and his taste for art, music, and the drama afforded enjoyable relaxation from the dry details of law and politics.

Mr. Sullivan's tall, slender, graceful figure, his white hair and silvery mustache attracted attention wherever he went. In the parlor, on the rostrum, his eloquence, candor, and frankness commanded attention. His sweet, musical voice and the felicity of his language were a matter of common remark, and early in his residence here he became known as the "silvery-voiced orator from Ohio."

New York Press

December 6, 1887.

In the death of the late Algernon S. Sullivan, the Bar of New York has lost one of its most eloquent orators and the country one of its most distinguished and loyal citizens. The great respect in which Mr. Sullivan was held was plainly shown by the sympathy that has been extended on all sides. All day long the offices of Sullivan & Cromwell were filled with prominent lawyers and leading citizens, who had called to express their condolence with the members of the firm. At Mr. Sullivan's late home in West 11th Street many friends called. The majority of the Courts took formal notice by adjournment or motions that the death be recorded on the Court minutes.

Scores of telegrams and letters were received, both at the house and at the office of the firm, from all parts of the country and all classes of men.

New York Telegram

December 6, 1887.

The late Algernon S. Sullivan was one of the kindest hearted men I ever knew, said one of his law partners to a *Telegram* reporter yesterday. If he had not been so liberal with his money

he would have died a millionaire. He was continually beset by
pensioners upon his bounty and time, and again I have known
him to give away or lend all the ready cash he had in his pockets,
and then when he wanted to use some money for himself he
would have to borrow of me or draw from his bank. Although
he had a large number of wealthy clients, he had many poor ones
also, and it was no uncommon thing for him to spend his time
talking to a poor laborer about some petty legal point and keep
clients who had big cases waiting for an audience. He was one
of the old-fashioned lawyers who thought a great deal more of his
profession than he did of dollars and cents.

New York Herald

49 Avenue de l'Opera, Paris

December 6, 1887.

Mr. Algernon S. Sullivan, one of the best-known figures in
New York circles of law, politics, and society, died last night
after a brief illness. He was sixty years of age.

New York Sun

December 7, 1887.

There is a particularly kind reminiscence of the late Mr.
Algernon S. Sullivan on the Produce Exchange. On May 6,
1884, when the new building was to be opened with great ceremony, Senator Evarts was to have been the orator. At eleven
o'clock on that day the Senator sent word that he had an illness
which would prevent his carrying out his part of the programme.
The committee was agitated and flew after Mr. Sullivan and
asked him to take the Senator's place. The ceremonies were to
begin at two o'clock. Mr. Sullivan got excused from other
duties, and at two o'clock he appeared on the platform to deliver
the oration. In appreciation of Mr. Sullivan's kindness the
managers voted him the privilege of the floor for his lifetime, and
when he died the flag was run up at half-mast.

New York Times

December 7, 1887.

The funeral of Algernon S. Sullivan will take place to-morrow morning at ten o'clock from the First Presbyterian Church, Fifth Avenue and 11th Street. The Rev. Richard D. Harlan will conduct the services. The pall-bearers will be the Hon. Abram S. Hewitt, Judge John R. Brady, Judge Edward Patterson, Surrogate Daniel G. Rollins, James C. Carter, Joseph H. Choate, William Moir, John H. Flagler, Andrew G. Dickinson, and John A. Hardenburg.

The Southern Society will furnish a guard of honor, and deputations will be present from the Archæological and Numismatic Society, the Bar, the Produce Exchange, the Faculty of the College of Pharmacy, the New York College of Music, and the Ohio Society.

New York Tribune

December 7, 1887.

At a special meeting of the Ohio Society at its rooms, No. 236 Fifth Avenue, last evening, Gen. Thomas Ewing, the President, announced the death of Algernon S. Sullivan, one of the Vice-Presidents, and pronounced a touching eulogy upon his life and character. Gen. Wager Swayne also paid a glowing tribute to the memory of Mr. Sullivan. Judge Warren Higby, C. C. Shayne, and Col. C. W. Moulton bore testimony to the dead man's remarkable talents and qualities in well-chosen words, after which the resolution was adopted unanimously.

The following members were appointed a committee to attend the funeral: President Thomas Ewing; Vice-Presidents Whitelaw Reid, L. Strong, and Gen. Wager Swayne; Secretary Homer Lee; Recording Secretary John Q. Mitchell; Treasurer William Perry Fogg; Governing Committee, H. L. Burnett, A. J. C. Foye, George Follett, Joseph Poole, John Dickson, William H. Eckert, C. W. Moulton, A. D. Juilliard, Warren Higby, Jerome D. Gellett, Calvin S. Brice, Carson Lake, Charles Sprague, A. W.

Green, H. H. Brockway, P. B. Armstrong, L. H. Crall, C. C. Shayne, and H. A. Glassford.

The committee will meet at the Society's rooms at 9:30 A. M. to-morrow and march to the church.

NEW YORK WORLD
December 6, 1887.

At a meeting of the Southern Society, of which Mr. Algernon S. Sullivan was President, the officers, executive committee, and the following special committee were named to represent the Society at the funeral services: John R. Abney, H. Bristow, George W. Bee, Hugh L. Cole, the Rev. C. F. Deems, A. J. Dickinson, Chandos Fulton, Hugh R. Gardin, Douglas Green, Pickney F. Green, John H. Inman, J. Fairfax McLoughlin, John C. Graham, Dr. J. H. Parker, Dr. William M. Polk, Octavus J. Norris, Theodore H. Price, R. T. Wilson, Anson Maltby, Frank R. Chambers, James Swan, Percy S. Mallett, Gen. John Newton, William W. Sharp, and J. McKenzie Semple.

NEW YORK EVENING SUN
December 8, 1887.

The death of Algernon S. Sullivan, said one of the prominent members of the Bar to an *Evening Sun* reporter, is a great loss to the Bar, but a greater loss to the community. No more just estimate than this could be given of the man whose kindness of heart made him revered by the poor and beloved by the rich. After a life spent in relieving the poor and conciliating the angry, it was meet that after his work was done, death should overtake him as it did. He passed away while quietly sleeping.

NEW HAVEN JOURNAL AND COURIER
NEW HAVEN, December 8, 1887.

To the Editor of the Journal and Courier:

The announcement of the death and burial of Algernon S. Sullivan of New York City has sent through the hearts of many, even here, a chill such as only sudden death can inflict.

This gentleman in life was the friend of every one who was

right-minded and honest without regard to race, nationality, or creed. It was his pride and pleasure as a lawyer to defend the right, and he could not be retained to defend the wrong; though he might make an effort to palliate mistakes and accord to the law its demands discounted by mercy to one who had without knowing it trespassed upon its requirements. We have known Mr. Sullivan to refuse large retainers when offered to defend purposely wrongdoers, and to serve innocent wrongdoers without charge. We have known him to answer his political friends no, when he thought the use of his name would lead confiding friends to act directly contrary to public interest. In short he stood upon his own pedestal of right and justice regardless of the rule of the legal bar to take retainers and throw the great power of his moral character and the influence of his professional prestige into cases where it would become necessary to strive to make the court swerve from its ermine purity or to so bemuddle a jury as to close their eyes to the light of truth. . . . As Public Administrator of the city of New York Mr. Sullivan filled the place and performed its duties for years, and left the office of choice rather than embark in the thralldom of political methods of advancing party interests and securing wealth to themselves.

No man was more gentle, nor more firm, and no lawyer was more believed in and beloved, even by his opponents. Respect and self-respect went hand in hand with his elegant person wherever he went, and they will meet a common grave when the earth shall open to receive its treasure.

Though living in another State it was our good fortune to be a friend of his and client as well, whereby we became acquainted with one whose character shone in dark days, and who never evaded a duty which conscience and a kind heart prompted him to perform.

GOUVERNEUR.

CHICAGO INTER-OCEAN

December 9, 1887.

The late Algernon S. Sullivan of New York, distinguished lawyer, just man, and good citizen, was beloved in life and honored in death. He was addicted to helping meritorious young men—a precious proclivity.

NEW YORK PRESS

REMINISCENCES OF A LAWYER'S CAREER BY A FRIEND

December 11, 1887.

No better evidence of the life and esteem almost amounting to veneration, in which the late Algernon S. Sullivan was held, could be found than in the fact of the presence at his funeral last Thursday of citizens and persons in all stations of life, from the highest city dignitary to the most humble laborer, not to take into consideration the pretty little school children who attended with tearful eyes the ceremony that finished the great patriot and able lawyer's earthly career. Like all true philanthropists he never wanted credit for his noble deeds, but was satisfied with the reward of his own virtue, the knowledge that he had done good to a fellow-being. And now that he has gone from us forever, it is but fitting that his noble-mindedness and philanthropic generosity should be known to the world. . . . As a lawyer he was one of the finest in the world—distinguished for his forensic ability. His presence and character as a man gave force to anything he said. He carried with him conviction that he was on the right side. But to people who knew him, his greatest charm was his beautiful loveliness of character. He was the same lovable person to a poor one in need as to the greatest of the many great men with whom he came in contact, and no one ever presented himself to him for help without having his request granted. While apparently and actually as gentle as a dove in his feelings, at the same time he was a man of very firm will when occasion demanded that he should assert himself. He was not combative in spirit, but when forced into a controversy he was always equal to the occasion, and one of his striking qualities was his great moral courage.

He had the honor of making the motion to admit the first colored member to the New York Bar, which he seemed to take special pride in doing as a Democrat. He was always a friend to the colored people of this city and was well known among them. He seemed to charm everybody who came in contact with him, and while being as gentle as a lamb, was as bold as a lion and firm as a rock when in the right.

Indianapolis Sentinel

When the telegraph lately announced the death of Algernon S. Sullivan, the public only thought of him as the eminent orator and lawyer of New York City.   Very few knew that he was almost equally prominent in Indiana forty years ago in a most exciting epoch of that State's history and before he had reached his majority, and that he was then affectionately known as the "boy orator" and similar titles of the kind current in the somewhat effusive West.

Though Mr. Sullivan ranked high as a lawyer and orator, he never attained to anything like the national fame which his early friends in Ohio very confidently predicted for him.   Perhaps the reasons may be found in the remarkable political changes.   When he stumped Indiana in 1846 and 1847, the Democratic party was in the full tide of its aggressive energy, and he was advocating the most progressive measures Indiana ever adopted.   When he settled in the city in full maturity of his powers, the Democratic party was entering upon its long period of exclusion from office as an opposition party.   Through all the years of greatest political excitement he was unfaltering in his political faith; but opposition was not in the line of his abilities.

St. Louis Republican

December 11, 1887.

It is nothing new to hear of an Eastern man coming West and growing up with the country, but the number of Western men who have turned eastward and caught up with the country could be easily enumerated.

Perhaps no Western emigrant in New York ever succeeded in making such a pleasing impression on the natives as the late Algernon S. Sullivan, whose death was announced a few days ago.

New York Observer

December 15, 1887.

Mr. Algernon S. Sullivan's funeral, Thursday last, in the First Presbyterian Church of this city, was largely attended by leading citizens and devoted friends. His abilities, character, and attractive qualities made him prominent and influential in public and social life. His bereaved household have the sympathy of a wide circle that includes many who are far and near.

Charlestown Free Press

Charlestown, W. Va., December, 1887.

For twelve years the writer of this slight reminiscence of the life of a very remarkable man saw and conversed with Mr. Sullivan almost every day, and saw and felt some new amenity in his character whenever that character was called into play. His home life was as beautiful as all the rest, but God and fire-side are sacred subjects from the profane gaze, and as his noble widowed spouse and son, carrying out the wishes of the dear one gone, are said to have desired no eulogies to be spoken at the bier of him with whose praises the whole city is ringing, so let me pause at the portals of domesticity and cast a spray of flowers on the lintels to express how responsively the great heart of the city is beating with the hearts of those within.

J. F. McL.

New York, December 8, 1887.

New Orleans Picayune

ALGERNON S. SULLIVAN AND HIS SHINING LIFE

December 9, 1887.

A leading lawyer, a leading Democrat, a leading club man, a leader in society—all these and more was Mr. Sullivan. He was one of the silver tongued of his generation. No public occasion was considered complete unless heightened by his eloquence. His was a universal and cosmopolitan genius. In every department of life he seemed to have interest and insight. He was emphatically one of those New Yorkers like to point out as representative citizens. There is none to fill the vacancy he left in the ranks.

❖

AN INTERVIEW RELATING TO THE LATE ALGERNON SYDNEY SULLIVAN

Given by Mr. J. Fairfax McLaughlin in 1888 to a reporter of the New York World

The second annual dinner of the New York Southern Society which took place at the Hotel Brunswick, on the evening of the 22nd, proved one of the most enjoyable social events of the winter. The Society has had remarkable success, and has a membership of nearly five hundred. It has already become one of the foremost societies of New York, and owes its prosperity in a very large degree to its founder and first President, the late Mr. Algernon S. Sullivan.

The members and visiting guests of the Society made feeling allusion to Mr. Sullivan at the second anniversary meeting and showed in manner and word what a deep hold he had possessed on their affections. A fine painting of Mr. Sullivan surmounted the wall behind the President's chair.

A reporter of the *World* called on Mr. J. Fairfax McLaughlin, Clerk of the Surrogate's Court, and one of the members of the Southern Society selected to speak at the Sullivan Memorial meeting last December, upon the life and character of the deceased President, and learned from Mr. McLaughlin some interesting facts connected with Mr. Sullivan's career.

I first became personally acquainted with Mr. Sullivan, said Mr. McLaughlin, about fifteen years ago, but knew of him very well for years before that time, through mutual friends.

It is unnecessary to repeat the biographical account, as that was done fully by the press at the time of his death. If I could give you an inner view of Mr. Sullivan as he was known to me and depict impressions made by those thousand and one little things in the life of a man which are not translatable into words, but which denote character so unerringly, I am sure our readers would be interested. Sound, movement, color and form, all are arts of the individual, but I know of no transmitting process by which they can be reproduced. We can hear, and feel and see them, but cannot make others do so. Every one must see the original for himself in order to catch the life currents.

When Mr. Sullivan first came to this city, he had not a single acquaintance here. He was a young man without means and without friends. He had some letters of introduction from friends in the West, but nothing came of them. Yes, there was one exception. The late Mr. Daniel Lord, to whom he had brought a letter, recognized in the young man one worthy of his regard. A friendship followed, and Mr. Sullivan cherished a tender recollection through life of his meeting with Mr. Lord. People are too heedless in this matter of writing and receiving letters of introduction. If no man would write such a letter except for one fit to be presented to his friend, and only put in it the exact truth instead of idle compliments, such letters would come to be regarded more seriously, and many a worthy person, like young Sullivan who was deserving of all that was said about him, would be spared the mortification of going through an empty and un-availing formality.

Mr. Sullivan's first years in New York were attended with trials and difficulties of no ordinary character. His untiring energy and strong faith in himself carried him safely through them all. His faculty of making friends was truly remarkable, and every case which he tried increased the circle of his ad-mirers. Had he been a mere money maker he could easily have amassed a large fortune, but his generosity and charity were so great that he never acquired the habit of accumulating money for itself. He would encourage young lawyers by a story in relation to the first windfall he received from one of the courts.

One of the judges sent him a reference, and when he got his fifty
or sixty dollars fee he felt himself quite rich. "It was a starter,"
he used to say, with a merry laugh, "and from that time I began
to jog along the professional road at a more lively pace." The
way Mr. Sullivan happened to tell me of this incident was also
characteristic. "Let us go and lunch together, I have something I want to talk to you about," he said to me one day, four
or five years ago. We went. "Now," said he, "you are acquainted with Judge ———. He is poor and I want to try and
help him. Can't you and I see some of the judges, of the courts
and persuade them to do something for the Judge, to send him
a reference now and then, and the like?" I said I would gladly
coöperate. "But," continued Mr. Sullivan, "the judges have
a great many matters to look after and may have their hands
full. It would be still better if we could get some of our political
friends to take an interest in the old Judge and secure him a
place of some sort. He is a most competent man and deserves
anything they may give him." He then went on to tell me how
much interest he felt in the matter, and related the incident in
his own early days of struggle when that Judge was a power in
this city and sent him the reference already mentioned and one
or two other little court favors.

I recall another incident of the same kind. There was an old
gentleman in New York, a Mr. Winder who, in former years, had
been very wealthy, but was then in reduced circumstances.
He was a man of education and refinement. Mr. Sullivan took a
warm interest in this old gentleman and, as in the other case I
have just mentioned, he called to talk with me about him. I
entered into his plans, and together we saw the mayor and others
in the old man's behalf: but while he had succeeded in the other
case and had the satisfaction of seeing the ex-Judge well provided for, in this second endeavor his other old friend got nothing
but evasive promises and disappointments. I well remember
how earnestly Mr. Sullivan took up the old gentleman's cause.
I have yet, somewhere, a letter he wrote me on the subject.
In a short time the office of Public Administrator became vacant,

and Mr. Whitney, the present Secretary of the Navy, who was then Corporation Counsel, tendered the position to Mr. Sullivan, and the late Mr. John Kelly, who was at that time Comptroller, urged him to accept it. Mr. Sullivan, whom I saw nearly every day, told me of this offer to him, and said, "You are aware that my practice has become so large that I cannot, without some sacrifices, accept the office of Public Administrator, and yet," he added with feeling, "I have decided to accept it, and make the sacrifice in order to provide a place for my friend Mr. Winder, who is a most competent and worthy man." Mr. Sullivan became Public Administrator and was an admirable one, and old Mr. Winder was appointed to a clerkship in the office. Few persons, if any, knew of the unselfish motive which prompted Mr. Sullivan, then in the full tide of an immense law practice, to accept that office.

There was not a particle of false pride in him. He would speak of his early trials in the frankest, off-hand manner, and no one who heard him ever detected either affected humility or obtrusive egotism in his anecdotes of those days.

While he was relating an incident to me one day, of this sort, I asked him whether any adventitious aids ever came along at that period, to lighten the burden, or whether his ultimate triumph was solely due "to the law of development, that is to say, to yourself?" "Well," he said, "I had to work very hard, but I do recall a matter I was interested in which was the means, perhaps, of first securing for me what I deemed from my education and family connections to be my rightful position in this community. That was the removal of the remains of ex-President Monroe, from New York to Richmond, Virginia. My father, who was a Virginian, and a great admirer of Monroe, with whom he was well acquainted, had taught me also to admire him. I had not lived here very long when I happened to read, in a magazine or newspaper, a sketch of Monroe. The writer dwelt upon the comparative poverty in which the old patriot had died in this city, and the suggestion occurred to me, or perhaps the article contained the suggestion, that it was a pity his body should not have been carried back to old Virginia, his native State, for burial. 'This ought to be done yet,' I said to myself. The idea took hold of me completely. I spoke of it to others, but no one but old Dr. Jones seemed to be impressed with the subject as much as myself. The Doctor and I talked the matter over frequently. Finally, I wrote to some friends in Virginia, Dr. Jones wrote to Governor Wise, the Virginia Legislature took up the proposition, and a formal application was finally made by the Virginia State authorities to the authorities of this city for leave to remove to his native State the remains of ex-President Monroe. But before the affair reached this promising stage, committees were organized here in New York, the proposition was submitted and the agitation begun. Now I can say to you, without any undue vanity at all, that on my shoulders the whole burden of these preliminary measures, and meetings, and resolutions devolved. People would come and make fine speeches and then at the next meeting, when something practical was to be done, only three or four persons would be present: adjournment after adjournment would occur, and what was everybody's business as usual became nobody's business. My heart was in the movement, and I never got tired of the good work. Finally, after almost incredible pains, the movement assumed solid business shape, the State authorities of Virginia took action, those of New York responded, the Federal Government participated, and the remains of Mr. Monroe, fifth President of the United States, were removed from the cemetery in Second Street to Virginia, and the whole American people were profoundly interested, and a great National pageant followed, almost as solemn and impressive as that of the removal of the remains of President Lincoln from Washington to Illinois.

"I was the proudest man you ever saw, for I assure you that I originated that pious public act, and it was because of my father's love for Mr. Monroe, which I had inherited, that I was induced to take the part I did. When I saw the great procession moving down Broadway under command of General Winfield

Scott, Lieutenant General of the United States Army, tears coursed down my cheeks, for I felt that I had at last done something worthy of my own honored father, and of the great and good old President James Monroe."

I looked upon Algernon S. Sullivan as the best organizer of any public movement of general utility or charity, whether to honor the dead or living, that I ever met in my life. He was a very earnest and constant member of the Presbyterian Church, attending the Sunday School and church meetings regularly, and giving the church authorities aid and counsel on all occasions. But he was no bigot. He was equally a favorite with Catholics, Protestants and Jews, and with white and black. He delivered lectures for his own co-religionist, for the Nun of Kenmare, for the Hebrew Orphan Asylum, and for the religious societies of the colored people of New York, among all of whom he was greatly respected and admired.

Some seven or eight years ago at a church fair for St. Lawrence's Catholic Church in East 84th Street, a handsome cane was raffled off for presentation to the most popular man in the State. The three principal contestants, all since dead, were Secretary Folger, John Kelly, and Algernon S. Sullivan. The cane was awarded to Mr. Sullivan. Judge John R. Brady presented it to him in a happy and humorous little address, and Mr. Sullivan in accepting it made an interesting speech, concluding with a graphic and touching account of the martyrdom of St. Lawrence, the patron Saint of the Church.

In politics Mr. Sullivan was a Democrat and a strict constructionist of Codes and Constitutions. In practice he was a conservative and was never radical or intolerant of opposition in anything or from anybody.

I remember, during some of the hot faction fights in this city ten or fifteen years ago, what a peacemaker he was. Here is an extract from a letter he wrote to me when the Democrats were divided, and angry feeling was running very high among the leaders: "I think I could contribute somewhat to the party weal. We need above all other things the spirit of peace, for in the passionate politics of the hour the Democrotic cause is suffering grave injury."

That expression "passionate politics" is characteristic. He was essentially a man of peace, a Democrat of the Horatio Seymour stamp, courageous as any of the bravest, but delighting to bring about reconciliation rather than to revel in strife.

In private life Mr. Sullivan was the centre of a very great and astonishing variety of agreeable societies. He was a strikingly handsome man, polished in his manners, courtly in deportment and agreeable in his conversation. He came as near filling the Chesterfield maxim of the true gentleman as any one I ever knew: "the true gentleman is he who rarely unintentionally and never intentionally wounds the feelings of another." And he was above all a charitable man. The poor never knocked at his gates in vain. To be such a benefactor to the poor, as Algernon S. Sullivan was, is the best way, in my opinion, to win a celestial crown.

❖

AN APPRECIATION OF MR. ALGERNON SYDNEY SULLIVAN

By Mr. Alfred Jaretzki, 1888

In the five years that I was a clerk and junior to the late Mr. Sullivan, I had an excellent opportunity to note the manner of his work as a lawyer; in some respects, indeed, my relation to him enabled me to form a more accurate and just opinion of his merits and methods as a lawyer than was possible for any one who was not as intimately associated with him in his work. It is for this reason alone that I have presumed to add a word to what has been already said, and so well, by others—the tender, loving words and feeling tributes of friendship, the fond recollections of the life of a noble man.

Mr. Sullivan was a lawyer of the old school—a student of principles rather than of cases. In his younger days he must have been an indefatigable and yet discriminating reader; such familiarity, as he possessed, with legal and equitable principles, such unerring judgment and nicety in their application; such accuracy and confidence in the statement of the law (a statement often made by Mr. Sullivan without referring to case or text book) could be the result only of wide and intelligent reading. But how wide and how intelligent that reading was and how persistent that study must have been, only those who have made the law their life study can fully appreciate.

Add to this mastery of legal principles an eloquence that never failed him, a commanding presence, a handsome and winning face, a noble head, and a most engaging manner—and there are all the elements of a powerful and successful advocate. And yet there was one other quality that was peculiarly Mr. Sullivan's, that distinguished him from the other great leaders of the Bar. It was his recognized fairness. Not that the others were not fair men, but Mr. Sullivan was fairer. This quality was recognized everywhere and stood him in good stead. In matters of arbitration and compromise it enabled him to accomplish what to others would have been impossible; for all classes of society, without any exception whatever (the capitalist and the workingman, the rich and the poor, the worthy and the outcast), trusted implicitly in his fairness.

A curious instance of this implicit faith in him by all classes was seen when some years ago in a negotiation that was pending between a bank and a burglar who was living abroad, for the return of some stolen securities, the burglar expressed a willingness to deposit the securities with Mr. Sullivan. His only acquaintance with Mr. Sullivan was in the latter's capacity as a public prosecutor!

In the courtroom his fairness won him the respect and attention of the Court, and it extorted from his opponent an attempt to be equally fair. It thus rid the argument of a difficulty to the Court that ought never to exist, the difficulty of acquiring a true understanding of the facts of a case when there should be no question about them, and it enabled the Court and the attorneys to devote their entire attention and argument to the legal questions involved—an example which, if everywhere followed, would free the legal profession of much of its reputation for pettifogging and aid much in the speedy administration of justice.

Even in the cross-examination of witnesses—where more than anywhere else a lawyer has an opportunity for originality in the manner of his work and where so many fail and even the most skilful are often baffled—Mr. Sullivan was eminently successful in a large measure because of his fairness. Almost all witnesses desire to speak the truth. Prejudice or interest may distort their views and color their statements, but witnesses are seldom guilty of deliberate perjury.

Now Mr. Sullivan believed that the love of truth was as deeply implanted in the breast of his fellow man as it was in him, and he acted upon this belief in conducting his cross-examination of his adversary's witnesses. He never attempted to brow-beat or confuse a witness; he never distorted the statement of a witness. He sought to bring out the truth, as he knew it, and he usually succeeded. And yet no one was more successful in exposing a rogue on cross-examination or more scathing in his rebuke of the wrongdoer, and his invariable courtesy and kindly tone only made the rebuke the more severe and telling when he found it necessary to administer it.

It was before a jury, however, that Mr. Sullivan achieved his greatest successes. Juries recognize and are very ready to reward fairness, and the fair and manly way in which Mr. Sullivan tried his case could not fail to redound to the advantage of his cause. In almost every case that Mr. Sullivan has tried when I was present, I have spoken to the jurymen after their verdict was announced, and in every instance jurymen have gone out of their way to express their admiration for Mr. Sullivan and for his fair and manly way of trying the case. They not merely praised the advocate but they spoke in terms of sincere admiration for

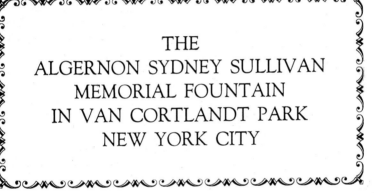

THE
ALGERNON SYDNEY SULLIVAN
MEMORIAL FOUNTAIN
IN VAN CORTLANDT PARK
NEW YORK CITY

THE Sullivan Memorial Fountain in Van Cortlandt Park, New York City, stands on Mosholu Parkway Road near the lake. It bears this inscription:

In Honor of
ALGERNON SYDNEY SULLIVAN
Jurist, Statesman, Orator
Born 1826—Died 1887

He reached out both hands in
constant helpfulness
to his fellowmen

An immaculate life devoted
with never failing fidelity
to public and private
trusts

Erected by the Citizens of New York
1906

During his address at the presentation ceremonies, Mr. Walter McCorkle, Secretary of the Committee said:

"As we observe the dates upon this fountain, which show that it was erected nineteen years after the death of Mr. Sullivan, I ask what better evidence could there be to others that the uplifting of a noble life does not end with death? . . . An editorial in the *Boston Herald* upon the erection of this fountain, in speaking of the inscriptions used the following words:

"'Surely these are noble epitaphs, wholly human in their quality and their suggestion to every soul who may come near to them. There is none so great or so humble who may not imitate this manner of usefulness to the world.'"

HONOR I.E
ALGERNON SYDNEY SVLLIVAN
JURIST - STATESMAN - ORATOR
BORN 1826   DIED 1887
HE REACHED OVT
BOTH HANDS
IN CONSTANT HELPFVLNESS
TO HIS
FELLOW MEN

ERECTED BY
CITIZENS
OF
NEW YORK
1906
FRANK E. RUSSELL
ARCHITECT

Drawing by W. E. Mears

the man.   There seemed to be something in Mr. Sullivan that drew toward him at once the love of every honest man he met. I call this quality his humanity.   It was a reciprocal feeling; Mr. Sullivan dearly loved his fellowmen and was dearly loved by them in return.

How far reaching was Mr. Sullivan's sense of fairness and how sincere his feeling of love for his fellowmen, were illustrated every day in his office work—often, as it seemed to us, to his own great personal pecuniary disadvantage.

' No person however low in society's scale or however poor was ever refused an audience by him, at any time; and he would listen with attention to some poor wretch's tale of woe, for which probably his own charity was the only means of alleviation, while bankers and capitalists, attending to consult him with large retainers and the prospect of still larger fees, were obliged to wait.

I have only spoken of one phase of Mr. Sullivan's character and life, because that was best known to me.   I need hardly add that everyone who was associated with him loved and admired him, for he was a good man as well as a great man.

ALFRED JARETZKI.

❖

PROCEEDINGS UPON THE OCCASION OF THE PRESENTATION OF A DRINKING FOUNTAIN IN HONOR OF ALGERNON SYDNEY SULLIVAN

To the City of New York, by a committee of its citizens, on Saturday October 27, 1906.

The fountain is erected in Van Cortlandt Park, near the lake and on the Mosholu Parkway road.   It bears the following inscriptions:

IN HONOR OF
ALGERNON SYDNEY SULLIVAN
JURIST, STATESMAN, ORATOR
BORN 1826, DIED 1887
HE REACHED OUT BOTH HANDS IN CONSTANT
HELPFULNESS TO HIS FELLOWMEN
AN IMMACULATE LIFE, DEVOTED WITH NEVER
FAILING FIDELITY TO PUBLIC AND PRIVATE
TRUSTS
Erected by Citizens of New York
1906

Mr. McCorkle, the secretary of the committee, in addressing the friends assembled at the dedication, spoke as follows:

Ladies and Gentlemen: Upon behalf of the Algernon Sydney Sullivan Memorial Committee, it is my pleasant duty to welcome you here upon this occasion and to state that several years after the death of Mr. Sullivan a committee of citizens of New York was formed for the purpose of testifying in some manner their appreciation of the life and character of one who had been so useful in this community.

As a result, we are today upon this spot to dedicate this fountain in honor of Mr. Sullivan, but although his name is thus permanently preserved in honor the fountain is not erected in order to discharge a debt of friendship to him, nor to add lustre to his name, nor to prolong among his friends, for a brief period, the memory of his clear-cut and winning presence, or the memory of his unusual talents, his eminence at the Bar, or of his leadership and precious influence in the public affairs of this great metropolis and in national politics.

Their purpose is to make use of the nobility of his life as a rare public opportunity for illustration of the human and civic virtues and the qualities which bind man to man.

They hope that by the very act itself of thus recording this man's character they will stir and encourage the nobler emotions lying in other generous natures, even if they be not accompanied by similarly lofty gifts which bring them into the same prominent and gratifying recognition.

It is further their purpose to remind the young and aspiring of coming generations that if a man will conduct his daily affairs with strict integrity and with loving and generous interest in the welfare and rights of others, he will be regarded by them as a benefactor of his race, superior to those men who have the distinction of high office or the purchasing power of great wealth, only. When men of that kind die, they vanish and others take their places—but what man, today, fills the place Mr. Sullivan occupied in the heart of his community?

It was our regret that there had been delay in the beginning as well as the completion of this movement, but now as we observe the dates upon this fountain, which show that it was erected nineteen years after the death of Mr. Sullivan, I ask what better evidence could there be to others that the uplifting influence of a noble life does not end with death? It makes the struggle doubly worth while.

Yesterday I observed in the *Boston Herald* an editorial upon the erection of this fountain. In speaking of the inscriptions the following language is used:

"Surely these are noble epitaphs, wholly human in their quality and their suggestion to every soul who may come near to them. There is none so great or so humble who may not imitate this manner of usefulness to the world."

I now take great pleasure in introducing to you Mr. Paul Fuller of this city, who will make the address of presentation to the city.

ADDRESS OF MR. FULLER

What manner of man was this to whom the freedom of the Imperial City is thus extended for all time, that every wayfarer passing through this public pleasure ground may look upon his finely moulded features and draw a lesson from the loving and lasting tribute here erected in his honor?

Of Irish ancestry, of Virginia parentage, of Western birth and training, and of New York fruition, this man united in himself all the elements of the best Americanism. His young manhood made such an impression upon his fellow citizens of Cincinnati that at the early age of twenty-five, he was chosen their delegate and spokesman and sent to New York to speak their sympathy and welcome to the exiled Hungarian orator and patriot, Louis Kossuth.

This glimpse of the great city and of its gigantic opportunities doubtless impressed itself upon his discerning mind, and a few years later he made it the permanent home of his adoption, coming to it without extraneous aids or promise of patronage, confident in his purpose and in his patient strength. He chose wisely; he was fitted for the struggle, and from the outset his thorough legal training, his strength and purity of purpose, his fearlessness and his devotion to the tasks set before him earned him a secure foothold in the arena already crowded with strong competitors, until he became a notable part of the public, professional and social life of our city,—a part which increased in magnitude until his death. He was a goodly knight whose lance was always in rest, and to works of benevolence, of social aid and regeneration, of public good and civic advancement, he was constantly called and constantly responded, and throughout all conflicts his inspiring courage rose at every obstacle, dissipated every cloud, and kept always before him the vision of the sunlight.

But it was not by these powerful elements of successful effort that he made his way into the hearts of men. It is not so much the unusual things done upon extraordinary occasions that mark character and achievement in the moral sphere,—that serve for example and lesson and encouragement to the generation among which a man moves,—it is the daily life, the common experience, the ever recurring episodes that best illustrate the man, determine his influence and the type to which he belongs,— what Wordsworth, with poetic simplicity has pictured as:

> That best portion of a good man's life,
> His little, nameless, unremembered acts
> Of kindness and of love.

It was in these that Algernon Sullivan illustrated the beauty of his character, and gave us a type for universal emulation. It was this constant following of the heart's guidance that impressed his personality upon all sorts and conditions of men, so that a multitude, of the most diverse pursuits and habits of thought, united in admiration of this ideal.

The ambition and the struggle for wealth, or fame, or power,— the inspiration to highest achievement, which were properly his, conscious as he was of his gifts, never clouded his insight nor dulled his sympathy. His was never "the strife for Triumph more than Truth." He was never too much pressed to tarry for a kindly act, never so eager for the prize as not to see and spurn the wrong that so often brings it within reach.

However high his goal he realized that men live from day to day, and that from day to day we tread the path and do the things that lead to ultimate victory or defeat in that life long tournament where the prize is awarded but once. The hopes and desires of to-morrow never interfered with the task of to-day, so that each day saw him turn aside from the lures of the future to minister to the needs of the present. To the lowliest call from the roadside for personal aid and sympathy, as readily as to higher summons of public spirit, he gave the same prompt answer, ever postponing the pursuit of personal advantage.

He realized and exemplified the inspiring tenet of Wendell Phillips that "Power, ability, influence, character, virtue are only trusts with which to serve the time."

Contemplating such a character, we may not stop to grieve at the loss, but rather to be thankful for the blessing that such men have lived and that the world was the gainer by their living,—and thankful that this generous nature, unaided by the power and attraction of high public station so impressed itself upon the community as to deserve and call forth the grateful and appropriate expression of esteem typified in this fountain, from which will flow for generations to come refreshing waters for man and beast, freely given and without stint. From this public testimonial all who will may draw the comforting assurance that a generous life such as Mr. Sullivan's, devoted always to the right, regardless of personal consequences, meets its recognition; and that the self-denying, not the self-seeking elements, are those which most endure, and which bring out in turn the most enduring esteem and the warmest affection. Self-effacing, or rather without thought as to his individual claims for recognition or reward, his strong personality was asserted with towering strength, unflinching courage and indomitable perseverance in aid of every cause that appealed to his sense of right, and this it was that made him a natural leader.

His was the type that kindles in other men the spark of latent good lying buried in the worst of us, and helps to smother the smouldering evil from which none of us is free. Living to ripeness of years, he died young, for to the end he never knew the

> Hardening of the heart
> That brings irreverence for the dreams of youth.

and to the end therefore he was in touch with all the conflict and struggle which is the portion of those who seek for better things, —he was at one with all the noble ambitions, with all the high aspirations, with all the love and charity for his fellows which are at once the guerdon and the solace and support of high natures.

Throughout his whole career, in times of ill-requited labor, as well as in the days of universal and ample recognition, it was his distinguishing trait that,—in the words of one of those who knew him best, he always stretched out both hands to aid his fellow men.

These are the gifts, this is the ideal, which appealed silently and strongly to all who knew him, and it is the lesson of that life which this memorial must continue to teach to young and old who look upon it through the coming years, recalling to them the encouraging thought that modesty, kindliness, self-forgetfulness, and an intuitive and unfailing devotion to the needs of others, are seeds that blossom and bear fruit even in the barren soil of selfish endeavor that in this day covers so large a portion of the land.

(The water was then turned on and flowed from the fountain.)

The Honorable Joseph I. Berry, Park Commissioner of the Bronx, representing the Mayor, then accepted the fountain in behalf of the city. In doing so, he spoke, in part, as follows:

I first heard of Algernon Sydney Sullivan from my school teacher, who told the pupils how Mr. Sullivan had, during the Civil War, upheld the dignity of the law and the rights of persons in distress to engage legal counsel by agreeing to defend the sailors of the Confederate privateer *Savannah* when they were being tried for their lives as pirates. Feeling ran so high that Mr. Sullivan was arrested by the Federal Government and imprisoned for three months awaiting its decision. After this time, without trial, without explanation and without knowledge of his accusation, he was released, and immediately thereafter appeared in court and proceeded with the trial.

This deeply impressed me and all of the other young scholars.

Later on, when I became a member of the Bar, and met older men who were nearer contemporaries of Mr. Sullivan, time and time again I heard them speak of the aid and open support he had so often given to men struggling against corruption in the administration of the government of this city, even though, in at least one great struggle of historic interest, about 1870, it was apparent to them and to him that he was taking the chance of sacrificing all probability of political advancement and influence.

He never did obtain high political advancement in office, but his influence with the leaders of his party, with the officers of the City Government and with the public at large, continued to increase until his death. Since his death, I have, with great frequency, heard his name mentioned, and always with admiration and reverence.

I knew him but slightly, and yet I feel that I knew him well.

It is said that he had the rare faculty of impressing himself immediately upon the depths of one's nature—upon that enduring part of one's nature from which springs the greatest and best of our emotions. I think that that is the reason he remains so long in our memories.

I agree, however, with Mr. McCorkle that the great value of such memorials as these is the unquestionable evidence they give that the general public are not unobservant of or uninfluenced by lives full of patriotism, and that such evidence always tends to encourage others to continue in similar endeavors and for these reasons, I personally, and as representative of the City of New York, welcome and accept this fountain.

Two interesting incidents occurred during the ceremony:

A teacher, with her class of twenty children, came walking by the fountain, and she stopped with them and read to them the inscription. "Children," she said, "those are noble sentiments, they should encourage one to help others. You must remember them."

After the water was turned on, and during Commissioner Berry's address, a little boy came running down the road. Seeing the water flowing from the fountain, he turned aside and drank, and then ran on, oblivious to the speaker and his audience.

Thus, during the opening ceremonies, the fountain entered upon its double line of usefulness—service and influence.

Editorial in the *Boston Herald*, Friday, October 26, 1906:

An Impressive Memorial

A somewhat unique public memorial has been erected to a New York lawyer, the late Algernon S. Sullivan. It is in the form of a drinking fountain for humans and animals in Van Cortlandt Park. Mr. Sullivan has been dead several years, and the committee which undertook the task was not promptly constituted, all of which tends to show that a good man's memory is not always soon forgotten.

The memorial is constructed of granite, and on opposite sides are profile portraits of Mr. Sullivan and inscriptions. What is noticeable is that there is not a word relating to his professional distinction, which was superior.   On one side this is said of him: "He reached out with both hands in constant helpfulness of his fellowmen."   On the other side the legend is: "An immaculate life devoted with never-failing fidelity to public and private trusts."

Surely these are noble epitaphs, wholly human in their quality and their suggestion to every soul who may come near to read them.   There is none so great or so humble who may not imitate this manner of usefulness to the world.

❖

Extracts from the proceedings at the presentation of a Bust of Algernon Sydney Sullivan by the Memorial Committee to the Alpha Delta Phi Club, New York, October 23, 1907

Presentation Address by Mr. W. M. K. Olcott:

Gentlemen of the Alpha Delta Phi Fraternity:

Algernon S. Sullivan was a man whose memory is a synonym of the helpfulness of living.

"I am a man and a stranger to nothing human" has been quoted in biography of him, but I feel that it falls short of satis- fying our affectionate remembrance.   For, at least to those of us who were young men when he died, to those of us who had felt the encouragement of his hand-clasp just as we were commencing our efforts to scale the heights which he had climbed, his person- ality seemed more than human; and there were many human things to which his great heart was a stranger.

It would have been human for this man to be impatient with the erring; but he was always sympathetic.

It would have been human for him to have reckoned his own qualities high; but he was of all men most modest.

Greatness of gift and of acquirement generally goes hand in

hand with a self-centered reserve, but Mr. Sullivan was as generous in exhibiting as he was in holding his intellectual riches.

How then shall we place our tribute so well as here where contemplation of that calm face will cheer the aged and help the young—in this temple dedicated to the fraternal spirit which he knew so well and had so perfectly?

Alpha Delta Phi has as its corner stone the rock of helpfulness; its strength is found in fellowship and the cohesive force of intelligent love. Mr. Sullivan's life was a constant exemplar of these things.

If he were here today his voice would be heard in eloquent tribute to the fellowship of man. Let his countenance, full of benign dignity, express to *our* hearts the language of *his*.

From the Address of acceptance by Mr. William Ives Washburn:

I would that it had fallen to the lot of someone more gifted with eloquence than myself to render tribute at this time to the memory of one whom we delight to honor. Yet, I do not understand that we are here today to mourn the loss of that brother who has gone on before to "the undiscovered country from whose bourn no traveller returns," but rather to rejoice that he passed along our way, and that in that passage we enjoyed the privilege of coming in touch with his noble character and of benefitting by its element of loving friendship.

Of all the men in Alpha Delta Phi—and we might name the greatest of them, the orators, the clergymen, the lawyers, the statesmen—I do not know of one star in that brilliant constellation now shining in the sky, embraced within the horns of the ever-growing crescent, that glows with a more serene and perfect and pure light than that of Algernon Sydney Sullivan.

We all remember the lines of Hunt where he speaks of Abou Ben Adhem, who, waking one night from a deep dream of peace and seeing an angel writing in a book of gold, asked "What writest thou?" The angel said, "The names of those who love the Lord." "And is mine one?" he asked. "Nay, not so," replied the angel, but with humility Ben Adhem said, "I pray thee, then, write me as one that loves his fellow-men." The angel wrote and vanished and the next night came again and unfolding the scroll, "Lo! Ben Adhem's name led all the rest." Such was our brother! He was a lover of his kind and because love follows love, his kind loved him.

Pardon a word of personal reminiscence! Many years ago, only two or three years before his death, I met Mr. Sullivan during a short visit at one of the lakes of New Hampshire, and in some way he discovered that I was a member of this Fraternity. In his usual charming and gracious manner he made himself known to me, and we had several days of delightful companionship. I take this opportunity to say, as a tribute on my own behalf, that in all of my intercourse with men of high and low degree, no man has ever made a more lasting impression upon my own life than did Mr. Sullivan, even in that brief period. Oftentimes I wish that more opportunities had been afforded for fellowship with that noble spirit, and many, many times has the longing taken possession of me that I myself might be such a man, such a citizen and such a lawyer as Algernon Sydney Sullivan.

But, as I said in the beginning, we are not here to mourn for him after the lapse of twenty years. While his departure left a void never to be filled in the hearts of those who loved him and were near and dear to him, time has softened that acute pain felt when he was parted from us, and we are here now simply to rejoice that such a man lived, that such a man it was given to us to know, and that one of our chapters, Miami, gave him to this Fraternity.

What was the great secret of Mr. Sullivan's force, and when I say force I mean the power to impress others with that grand personality which he so strongly possessed? The answer is character.

* * * * *

And so, Gentlemen of the Memorial Committee, we accept this gift with the hope and with the object of honoring one whom we love to honor, and of perpetuating in our building the name of

one whom we can never forget, that we who knew him ourselves
may extend the knowledge of his sterling qualities of mind and
heart to those who shall come after us, to inspire them to lives
of the highest patriotism, for he was a patriot; of scholarship,
for he was a profound scholar; of brotherly kindness, of which
he was a shining example; of exalted ideals, for these were always
maintained by Algernon Sydney Sullivan.

❖

ALGERNON SYDNEY SULLIVAN—AN APPRECIATION
By William J. Curtis, January 16, 1925

Algernon S. Sullivan was the founder of the law firm of Sullivan & Cromwell, which has retained his name at the head of the
firm although he died forty years ago.   It was Mr. Sullivan who
laid the foundation of the phenomenal success which the firm
has enjoyed for forty-five years.

Mr. Sullivan was in his prime one of the most popular and
distinguished citizens of the city.   He was identified with almost
every public activity of importance.   As a public speaker he
was in constant demand.   In this respect he was highly gifted.
Physically a man of dignified and fine presence, possessed of fine
imagination and an attractive voice, he was a natural orator, and
while he one day told me that when he began his career as a
public speaker he was afflicted with stage fright to such an extent that his knees shook as he arose to speak, this diffidence
was soon overcome.   Throughout his life he was always ready
to respond as a speaker on all important public occasions.   He
had so much charm and graciousness that he was constantly
sought after to attend public dinners, which he graced by
his presence and entertained with his delightful and brilliant
speeches.

His popularity was due, not only to the qualities above referred to, but to his extreme simplicity and democracy. I have never known a finer democrat, using that word in its broadest meaning and significance. He was never condescending or patronizing in manner, but always gracious, approachable and cordial to the least as well as to the greatest. He could lead the march of the Sullivans in a Democratic parade without loss of dignity; at the same time be chosen to represent the city of Cincinnati on great public occasions, such as the greeting of the Polish patriot, Kossuth.

Politically, he was a Democrat, but not a slave to party. Public virtue and courage received prompt approval and recognition from him. I well recall the occasion during Mr. Cleveland's first term of office of the serious contest that arose over the appointment of a postmaster of the city of New York. The incumbent was a Republican whose term was about to expire. Naturally the Democratic politicians desired to have one of their own number and political party appointed to the office. President Cleveland refused to make any change and reappointed the incumbent, having sole regard to the public welfare and the recognition of the principle of civil service reform. On this occasion Mr. Sullivan wrote to the President a most enthusiastic letter of approval of his independent course, and in telling me about it he was so pleased with the President's courage and independence that he used in substance the following expression: "I don't care what the President may do hereafter. He can drive a coach and four through the White House. This act stamps him as a brave man."

In private life Mr. Sullivan was a sincere and devout Christian in the broadest and most catholic sense. I know nothing of his particular theological views, but I do know that he stood for and represented the best Christian ideals. Speaking of the duty of young men to attend some church, he said that if on no other ground it was desirable because the church was a great body of citizens working for the right, and the association with and ideals of such persons must prove beneficial to young men.

In his personal and professional relations he was not only a man of sterling probity and character and of unbending integrity, but of the very highest ethical ideals and principles. He was not perhaps ranked among the most profound lawyers of his day from the point of view of case learning or book knowledge, but no lawyer was held in higher general esteem by the public as well as by the Bar. He had such an innate and intuitive sense of justice that his judgment was sought and relied upon by a large class of important clients. He respected the well-known principle that a lawyer should not permit his personal opinions and prejudices to influence his duty to his client, who is always entitled to be fully represented in the presentation of the merits of his case, whatever they might be, regardless of the personal opinion of lawyers.

I once had a talk with him about the much debated question which frequently arises as to the duty of the lawyer to his client in criminal cases. He maintained that it was his duty to present the client's case in the most favorable light which the facts and the law of the case would permit, leaving the decision of the case to the judge and jury, saying that oftentimes the personal opinion of the lawyer in the case might be prejudicial and actually unjust to his client, and cited a number of historical illustrations to prove this contention. But it was inevitable in the trial of cases that jurors, many of whom knew him by sight as well as personally, and all of whom probably knew him by reputation, should feel the force of his fine personality and character. This was true to such an extent that he was almost invincible in jury cases.

As a lawyer he on one occasion at least displayed moral courage which is worthy of historical recognition. He was retained by the Confederate Government to represent the officers and crew of the blockade runner *Savannah*, who were being tried in the Federal Court in New York for violation of the laws of war. In accepting the retainer in the heated state of the public mind during the war, he naturally took a great risk, for there was no appreciation in the public mind of his duty as a lawyer in such cases. It was his acceptance of this retainer which

THE
ALGERNON SYDNEY SULLIVAN
AWARD MEDALLION
ISSUED BY THE
NEW YORK SOUTHERN SOCIETY

THE Medallion which is part of the permanent Algernon Sydney Sullivan Award for character was established in 1926 by the New York Southern Society in fifteen universities and colleges.

The design, reproduced in copper, is the work of the artist, J. E. Roiné and carries appropriate inscriptions:

THE ALGERNON SYDNEY SULLIVAN MEDALLION
Established by the New York Southern Society in 1926

"As one lamp lights another nor grows less
So nobleness enkindleth nobleness."—*Lowell.*

"He reached out both hands in constant helpfulness to his fellow men."—*Sullivan Memorial Fountain.*

"And never yet was anything seen so beautiful or artistic as a beautiful life."—*A. S. Sullivan.*

"I must not consider how much they love me but rather how much I love them."—*A. S. Sullivan.*

The Award is in use in the Universities of Virginia, North Carolina, South Carolina, Alabama, Kentucky; Mercer University, Washington and Lee University, George Peabody College for Teachers, the College of William and Mary, Antioch, Hampden-Sidney, Davidson, Rollins, St. Johns', and Judson.

THE ALGERNON SYDNEY SULLIVAN MEDALLION
ESTABLISHED BY THE NEW YORK SOUTHERN SOCIETY 1925
"AS ONE LAMP LIGHTS ANOTHER NOR GROWS LESS
SO NOBLENESS ENKINDLETH NOBLENESS"   LOWELL
"HE REACHED OUT BOTH HANDS IN CONSTANT HELPFULNESS TO
HIS FELLOW MEN"   SULLIVAN MEMORIAL FOUNTAIN N.Y.
"AND NEVER YET WAS ANYTHING SEEN SO BEAUTIFUL OR SO
ARTISTIC AS A BEAUTIFUL LIFE"   A.S. SULLIVAN
"I MUST NOT CONSIDER HOW MUCH THEY LOVE ME BUT
RATHER HOW MUCH I LOVE THEM"   A.S. SULLIVAN

AWARDED

caused his arbitrary arrest by the Federal Government and his incarceration in one of the forts of the harbor without warrant and without authority. The facts were no sooner known than there was a loud expression of public dissent and criticism for this arbitrary act. Mr. George Jones, who was then the proprietor and editor of the *New York Times*, took a leading part in protesting against the injustice to Mr. Sullivan, and in association with other citizens secured his release. When, after his release, the case was about to be tried he was approached by several of the leaders of the Bar, including Mr. Daniel Lord, one of the most celebrated lawyers of his day, who advised him against continuing to act in the case on the ground that his personal safety was involved, as public feeling was running very high. This advice was rejected by Mr. Sullivan in a very brief and modest statement in which he said, in substance, that as he had accepted a retainer from the Confederate Government to represent the defendants in this case, it was his duty to continue in that service and to perform his duty as best he could, unless his continued appearance as counsel in the case might prove prejudicial to the defendants. It was for his client, the Confederate Government, to suggest that and not for him. Suggestions as to his own personal safety would not influence him, and unless his client dismissed him he would continue to represent the defendants in the case. This he did with so much success and dignity that Justice Nelson, who presided at the trial, called him to the Bench and publicly congratulated him upon his ability, fearlessness and fairness in the conduct of the case.

While this is an exhibition of rare courage, it required no effort on Mr. Sullivan's part to accept the responsibility that he did, for he was a lawyer and a man of indomitable courage and fearlessness. I can imagine no situation in which he could have been placed as a citizen or a lawyer in which he would have hesitated to perform his full duty, whatever the cost to himself. I am inclined to think this was in part an inherited quality, because I recall his telling me of a very interesting incident in his childhood when his father, who was a distinguished citizen of Indiana, and at one time judge of its highest court, was threatened during some political contest with physical violence in case he attempted to vote. This threat did not deter the father from fearlessly doing his duty. He took his little son by the hand, marched to the polls, surrounded as it was by these ruffians who had threatened him, and cast his vote, overawing them by his dignity and courage. This undoubtedly left an impress upon the child which was never effaced in after life.

I recall an interesting illustration of Mr. Sullivan's natural dignity and fearlessness in the trial of a case. I was associated with him in the trial before Judge Truax, who, although very able, was somewhat captious and irritable, and quite prone to make sharp and impatient comments in the course of the trial of a case. I was examining a witness and asked a question to which an objection was made. Mr. Sullivan, who was acting as counsel in the case, opposed the objection and urged the propriety of the question. After a brief argument Judge Truax, addressing him in a snarling and irritating voice, said: "Mr. Sullivan, don't you know that in a certain case in Jones & Spencer (citing it) this Court has decided against your view of the materiality of this question?" Mr. Sullivan arose and, with a dignity of manner that was deeply impressive, said: "May it please your Honor, I have practiced long enough at this Bar to have the courage to admit that there are cases in Jones & Spencer's Reports which I haven't even read." The effect upon the Judge was very interesting. He changed his tone and became more courteous in manner, although he sustained the objection.

It will be recalled by those who knew Mr. Sullivan that he was at one time Assistant District Attorney of the City of New York. A few years ago I happened to notice in a catalogue of a book sale in Boston a book written by Henry L. Clinton, who in his day was a noted lawyer of this city and the attorney in many very important criminal and quasi-criminal cases. This was an account of a number of these cases, one of which was of the greatest public interest in which Clinton defended the criminal. Mr. Sullivan was the prosecuting attorney. I found the book filled with side notes written by someone whom I was unable to identify, but who was evidently a lawyer thoroughly familiar with the history of the Bar of those days. In this particular case to which I refer, Clinton made some allusion to Mr. Sullivan. Upon the margin of the page opposite Mr. Sullivan's name was this note by the former owner of the book: "Who was recognized by everyone as one of the fairest and ablest prosecutors that New York City ever had."

On one occasion while I was associated with Mr. Sullivan he incidentally remarked to me that he had that day signed an application for the pardon of a criminal whom he had prosecuted and convicted. He said it was the only case that he ever tried as a prosecuting officer wherein he felt he had in his zeal exceeded the bounds of his professional duty as a public prosecutor, and that he was only too glad to atone in some way for what he considered his excessive zeal by applying for the man's pardon. This is an interesting illustration of that fine sense of duty and high ethical quality which always controlled Mr. Sullivan in his public and private life.

Mr. Sullivan's ethical qualities were illustrated also in his dealings with a number of poor people who had bought shares of stock in a company of which he was made president by his clients. At the time the company was founded it was thought that it would be a successful and safe commercial undertaking, but after a brief existence it was found that the officers were mistaken in their view of the success of the business, and it was compelled to discontinue, resulting in an almost total loss to all who had purchased the shares of stock. The fact that Mr. Sullivan was president of the company had induced a number of poor people, some of them servants, to purchase the stock, relying wholly upon his name. On several occasions after the cessation of the business these poor people called upon him to inquire concerning the business. Without any explanations concerning it he asked them if they were stockholders and had their shares with them, and upon learning how much they had paid for their stock, he immediately drew his own personal check and repaid them in full for their investment. I do not know how many cases of this character occurred, but I do know there were a number. There was no legal obligation requiring him to do this, but he was prompted by a desire to protect these poor people against loss.

Mr. Sullivan was not a preacher or poseur in the assertion of his moral standards and ethics, but he always lived and practiced the highest ethical principles. In speaking with me on one occasion concerning a subject that was under discussion he told me of the rule of conduct which always governed his actions, and that was if there was any room for doubt as to the propriety of his conduct he never hesitated to decide for the right, even against his own interests. In other words he never allowed himself seriously to debate between the right and wrong course.

The qualities I have above referred to were those which enabled the firm at the outset to command the confidence of many influential clients. It would be easy to show the direct influence of his character and standards as a man and lawyer upon the business of the firm today, which of course has grown and expanded very largely since his death owing to the ability of these who have succeeded to the business. But some of their most important and remunerative clients can be directly traced to his influence and the relations established with the firm during his brief connection with it.

There is scarcely any limit to the influence of such a life and character as his, as is seen by the continuing and very successful business conducted by the firm which he founded and as can be illustrated by the love and esteem in which his memory is held by the diminishing number of those who knew him and who are living.

WILLIAM J. CURTIS.

New York, January 16, 1925.

❖

LETTER FROM FRANCIS T. A. JUNKIN

At Baden-Baden, September 6, 1926.

To Mr. George Hammond Sullivan,
   16 West 11th Street,
      New York City, N. Y.

My dear George:

I have your letter of August 24th, and I am responding in rather lame fashion, I fear, to your request. It is true that in speaking to the Bar Association of Virginia in August, 1925, I dwelt at considerable length and a good deal in detail on my memory of your revered father as "The Ideal Lawyer." But a spontaneous and enthusiastic deliverance from one's heart and mind under the inspiration of his subject and his discriminating and understanding hearers—for all the leading and high-minded judges and lawyers of Virginia attend—is impossible to reproduce at the cold point of a pen a year or more later. Besides, if I attempted to tell all I said in the way of comparative analysis with Choate and Carter and others, and their seeming ideals and your father's, you would not have room for it. During several days after the meeting many of the leading men of the Association came to me to express their interest and to hear more of your father's career. And I was requested formally to reproduce the speech for publication in their annual report, but I could not do it, for it would not have done justice to your father or to my presentation of him.

The address was only a response to a toast at the banquet of the annual meeting of the Virginia Bar Association, held always at Hot Springs, Virginia. With no notice I was called upon to respond to the toast to "Lawyers of Other States." I took as my text, instantly, "Impressions of a Young Virginian on Going to Practice Law in Wall Street." I spoke longer than I intended because they seemed to want more on account of my contemporary observations of so many distinguished men who were in the category of comparison at that time. But I know that the comparison of all—and I had opportunity to observe—

placed your father on the pinnacle of my own ideals.   Of course I cannot give you what I said in comparative value of the men under the inspiration of the occasion, but I have put on the enclosed paper a brief and inadequate relation of it.

Your mother and your father were to me the very ideals of high womanhood and manhood, and I have always thought of them as being the complement of each other, each necessary to complete the circle of high endeavor to make happiness and fineness of the world more worthy and more beautiful.

Will you please present to your mother my loving remembrances and say to her that I have a great sense of obligation to her and to her noble husband for inspiring effort in my social and in my professional life.   Your father's career and example have been an inspiration to many men of our profession, and to many others.

Always with true friendship,

Yours,

(Signed)   FRANCIS T. A. JUNKIN.

❖

Extract from remarks of Francis T. A. Junkin, LL.D., before the Virginia Bar Association at its Annual Meeting at Hot Springs, Virginia, August, 1925

Some of the towering figures at the Bar of New York at that period were: William M. Evarts, Ashbal Green, John H. Parsons, James C. Carter, Elihu Root, Francis Lynde Stetson, Robert G. Ingersoll, John L. Cadwallader and others I could name. Most of them were founders of great legal firms whose offices have been nurseries of achieving and successful lawyers for our whole country for a number of generations.   Among these truly great jurists stood Algernon Sydney Sullivan, in dignified physique and splendid intellectuality, the equal of the best of them in the forum; the superior of almost all of them in legal acumen and debate and in oratorical brilliance; but approached by few, and surpassed by none in those beautiful qualities of character that adorn and dignify the noble man in all his relations in life; that are the foundation of the ethics of our profession; that relate not only to the law in its loftiest aid and guidance of humanity in distress, but to the love of and the uplifting of all that came within the radius of his wide influence. With his Christian courtesy and sympathy for all his fellow men, his gracious and genial personality, his helpful kindness and consideration for young practitioners, his profound knowledge of the law, his devotion to the ethics of his profession and his convincing power of oratory, Algernon Sullivan was preëminently to the mind and the heart of the youthful Virginia lawyer who had come to Wall Street with absorbent and inquiring observation, the loftiest ideal upon which to pattern his own career.

INDEX

INDEX

Abbey, Henry E., 207
Abolitionists, 38
Abou Ben Adhem, 254, 332
Act of 1784, 213
"Act of the States", 100
Adams, Charles Francis, 162
Admiralty Court, 98
Aeschylus, 117
Ahlborn, Mrs. Leah, 205
Alabama, 96; Mr. Charles Deshon of, vii
Alexander of Macedon, 193
Alexandria, 174
Algernon Sydney Sullivan Memorial Fund, 84
Allen, Judge Henry Wilder, 279, 301
Alpha Delta Phi Fraternity, 17; Miami University branch of, 221; bronze bust of Algernon Sydney Sullivan presented to, 84, 331-4; address delivered by Algernon Sydney Sullivan at the Semi-Centennial Convention of, 184-5; address delivered by Algernon Sydney Sullivan at the Semi-Centennial Celebration of the Amherst Chapter of, 221-6; Memorial Resolutions of, 290-1
Altruism, 55
America 92, 211, 225, 318. See also United States
American Bar Association, Resolutions of Regret, 83, 261-2
American Numismatic and Archaeological Society of New York, 172, 204, 308; Algernon Sydney Sullivan a life member of, 68; Memorial Fund established in, 84; address by Algernon Sydney Sullivan before, 191-4
American Pantheon, 206
American Poets' Corner, 175, 206, 208
American Revolution, see Revolution
American Savings Bank, 295
Anderson, Charles, 22
Anderson, Mary, 207
Annapolis, 228, 229

Anthon, Charles E., 192
Aspen Hill, 30
Apollo, 175
Aqueduct, Croton, 215
Arcadian Club, address by Algernon Sydney Sullivan, 110; Algernon Sydney Sullivan vice-president of, 71
Archaeological and Numismatic Society, see American Numismatic and Archaeological Society of New York
Archaeological Institute of America, 193
Archaeology, 191, 192, 193, 194
Arnold, Dr., 181
Art, 172, 197, 258, 262, 272, 273, 306
Arctic Circle, 71, 178
Asia, 130
Assis, 193
Association of the Bar of the City of New York, see Bar
Astor House, 305
Atheism, 133
Athens, 93-4, 148
Atlantic Monthly, 66
Augusta County, Virginia, 4
Augustus, 174
Austria, 110
Award, ix, x, 84, 85

Babcock, 167
Bache, Theophylact, 182
Bacon, 270
Baker, Governor, 12
Baker, Thomas H., 43, 94, 96, 110
Baltimore, Maryland, 42
Bangs, Francis N., address delivered by Algernon Sydney Sullivan in memory of, 231-3
Banking, 31, 32
Bankrupt Law, 236
Bar, Algernon Sydney Sullivan and the, 65, 249, 256, 261, 263, 280, 281, 283, 284, 285, 286, 287, 288, 290, 294, 297, 299, 301, 303, 305, 306, 307, 308, 309, 310, 311, 321, 322, 324, 336, 342
Bar, New York, 33; Algernon Sydney Sullivan admitted to, 36; address